© 2018 by the Education Law Association
Cleveland, Ohio 44115-2214
Phone: 216-523-7377 / Fax: 216-687-5284
www.educationlaw.org

Administrators' Guide to Employment Law and
Personnel Management in Schools
No. 99 in the ELA K-12 Series

Printed in the United States of America
ISBN-10: 1-56534-186-4
ISBN-13: 978-1-56534-186-9

Education Law Association Publications

Founded in 1954, the Education Law Association is a nonprofit, nonadvocacy member association that seeks to improve education by promoting interest in and understanding of the legal framework of education and the rights of students, parents, school boards, and school employees.

Both authors and editors who collaborate on ELA publications include many of the best-known experts in their fields: deans, professors of education or law, school administrators, and attorneys specializing in education law.

Whether you're doing research as an educational administrator, attorney, or student—or you are a professor selecting high-quality and affordable textbooks—help yourself succeed by choosing education law publications from ELA's bookstore on our website, www.educationlaw.org.

I0131785

Editors

Mark A. Paige (Coeditor) is currently an associate professor in public policy. His research focuses on education law matters, including teacher evaluation, and special education. As a former school law attorney, he represented school districts in special education and employment matters before state and federal agencies and courts, including the New Hampshire Supreme Court. He started his career in education as a fifth-grade teacher in Austin, Texas.

Adam Ross Nelson (Coeditor) is currently a policy advisor. His research focuses on student behavior, campus crime, and the transition(s) students experience after secondary education. Nelson teaches courses on the legal aspects of education. He also consults for students who are facing school disciplinary proceedings in all grades and at college. His career in education began as a teacher of English in Budapest, Hungary.

Authors

M. David Alexander, Ed.D.: Professor, Leadership, Counseling & Research, Virginia Tech, Blacksburg, VA

Justin M. Bathon, J.D., Ph.D.: Associate Professor, Educational Leadership Studies, University of Kentucky, Lexington, KY

Tina Chang, J.D., Ph.D.: Executive Director, PNW Institute Special Education and Law, Los Angeles, CA

Suzanne E. Eckes, J.D., Ph.D.: Professor, Educational Leadership & Policy Studies Dept., Indiana University, Bloomington, IN

Kelly Frels, J.D.: Of Counsel, Bracewell LLP, Houston, TX

Jesulon Gibbs-Brown, J.D., Ph.D.: Superintendent, Orangeburg Consolidated School District 3, Holly Hill, SC

Janet Horton, J.D.: Partner, Thompson & Horton LLP, Houston, TX

Richard E. LaFosse, J.D., M.Ed.: Doctoral Student, Education Policy, Indiana University, Bloomington, IN

Kenneth E. Lane, Ed.D.: Professor Emeritus, Educational Leadership & Technology, Southeastern Louisiana University, Hammond, LA

Sean E. Maguire, M.A.: Graduate Student, Educational Leadership Department, University of Nevada-Reno, Reno, NV

Lisa R. McBride, J.D.: Partner, Thompson & Horton LLP, Houston, TX

Evan G. Mense, E.M., EdD.: Associate Professor, Educational Leadership & Technology Dept., Southeastern Louisiana University, Hammond, LA

Adam Ross Nelson, J.D, Ph.D.: Senior Divisional Policy Advisor, University of Wisconsin, Madison, WI

Gretchen Oltman, J.D., Ph.D.: Assistant Professor of Interdisciplinary Studies, Creighton University, Omaha, NE

Allan G. Osborne, Jr., Ed.D.: Principal (Retired), Snug Harbor Community School, Quincy, MA

Mark A. Paige, J.D., Ph.D.: Associate Professor, Department of Public Policy, University of Massachusetts-Dartmouth, N. Dartmouth, MA

Nathan M. Roberts, J.D., Ph.D.: Dean, College of Education, Mr. & Mrs. E.P. "Pat" Nalley/BORSF Professor in Education, University of Louisiana at Lafayette, Lafayette, LA

John E. Rumel, J.D.: Associate Professor, University of Idaho College of Law, Boise, ID

Charles J. Russo, J.D., Ed.D.: Joseph Panzer Chair of Education and Director of Ph.D. Program in Educational Leadership in School of Education & Health Sciences; Research Professor of Law, University of Dayton, Dayton, OH

Lynn Rossi Scott, J.D.: Attorney/Shareholder, Brackett & Ellis P.C., Fort Worth, TX

Ralph Sharp, Ed.D.: Professor Emeritus, Education Department, East Central University, Ada, OK

William E. Sparkman, Ph.D.: Professor, Educational Leadership, University of Nevada, Reno, NV

Jennifer A. Sughrue, Ph.D.: Professor, Dept. of Educational Leadership, Technology, and Research, Florida Gulf Coast University, Ft. Myers, FL

Table of Contents

Chapter 5 – Federal Antidiscrimination Law
John E. Rumel

Section III – State and Local Laws

Chapter 6 – Evaluations
Lynn Rossi Scott

Chapter 7 – Documentation
Kelly Frels, Janet L. Horton, and Lisa R. McBride

Chapter 8 – Teacher Dismissal
Evan G. Mense, Nathan M. Roberts, and Kenneth E. Lane

Chapter 9 – Collective Bargaining in Public Schools
Justin M. Bathon and Richard E. LaFosse

Chapter 10 – Teacher Certification
Tina Chang, Sean E. Maguire, and William E. Sparkman

Chapter 11 – Student Injury
Suzanne E. Eckes and Jesulon Gibbs-Brown

Section IV – Applying the Law to Practice

Sample Cases for Class Exercises

Mark A. Paige and Adam Ross Nelson

x

Section I – Chapter 1

Introduction

Mark A. Paige and Adam Ross Nelson

School administrators, like superintendents and principals, are in the "people business." First and foremost, of course, they care for and educate children. School leaders and educators are generally well-prepared for this responsibility by the time they take an administrative role. They have had years of experience in this regard as students, teachers, or parents. Their skills and knowledge are honed through graduate school programs that address topics of curriculum design, effective use of data, leadership, and best practices for instruction. The most well-prepared will also have worked and studied under the tutelage of advisors and mentors.

But school administrators are also in the people business as employers. Importantly, the law—in the form of constitutions, statutes, regulations, and cases—affects how administrators manage human capital in this role. Representative examples of legal authorities impacting schools are as follows: the Americans with Disabilities Act (ADA), Section 504 of the Rehabilitation Act (Section 504), the Age Discrimination in Employment Act (the ADEA), the Family Medical Leave Act (FMLA), Title VII of the Civil Rights Act, and the U.S. Constitution. We could generate another list based on state laws or regulations. The list grows further when we consider the implication of collective bargaining agreements. The role of law in the domain of public school human resources is significant, to say the least.

The complexity of employment law and human resources in managing schools can be daunting for administrators who are not trained as lawyers. Yet, understanding the law as it relates to managing personnel is critical, especially given the close connections between teacher quality and student outcomes. Unfortunately, this is also an area where many leaders may have received inadequate training. Teacher training programs, where most school administrators start their careers, frequently overlook the relationship between the law and public education. For teachers, educational programs that do include instruction in the law may be likely to exclude legal issues related to faculty or staff supervision in favor of other provisions most essential to teaching and instruction. Teachers and administrators have clearly stated that they *want* more and robust training concerning the legal aspects of their job.[1] Yet, demand for this training has outstripped supply, creating a legal knowledge gap.

School law attorneys also need resources that assist them in developing productive attorney-client relationships.[2] School law attorneys may frequently engage in conversations with clients that are loaded with legal jargon. While sometimes necessary, legalese can cloud administrator understanding. While attorneys recite "courtroom talk," administrators often converse in "chalk talk," vernacular linked to the education profession. Not unlike legal jargon, the specific language of schools and classrooms can also be difficult to penetrate for those not accustomed to or immersed in its daily use, like attorneys. There is sometimes a chasm between legal professionals and their educational clients. In worst-case scenarios, legal professionals and educational clients speak over or past each other. Of course, the most effective attorneys find ways to develop collaborative and productive relationships that support client goals.

Professors of school law are well positioned to help assist in creating more legally literate administrators, but more resources are needed, especially as they relate to understanding employment matters. Several instructional texts exist that deal with school law in general, but those dealing with more discrete topics, are few and far between.[3] This book provides a thorough and comprehensive compilation of all the major legal areas that impact school districts as employers. Importantly, this book aims to provide a comprehensive compilation in a neutral, readable terms so that it can be a resource that supports effective attorney-client relationships, and enhances the training school administrators receive. The goal is to assist professors, educators, administrators, and attorneys in closing the gaps mentioned above.

Connecting Dots: Law, Personnel Management, & Levers of Opportunity

School administrators such as superintendents and, certainly, school human resource officials, recognize the amount of time and knowledge required to effectively navigate the various rules of employment in public education. Every day there are myriad employment and personnel issues that require some level of legal knowledge and insight. This could range from the law and regulations governing a teacher's request for leave under the Family Medical Leave Act, or a school board proposal to change the start time of the school day, which might require bargaining with a union. When mishandled, this can invite lawsuits. Of course, few ever seek to litigate. Lawsuits are risky, expensive, incur personal costs, and often produce poor results for all participants. They are high-cost, zero-sum-game pursuits.

Preventing lawsuits or legal problems is a particularly noble goal in public education. For public schools, reducing risk translates into money and time devoted to primary education tasks, like teaching and learning. These resources are better spent on opportunities to improve instruction, facilities, or other factors known to improve student and community outcomes. And, as many school superintendents will appreciate, preventing a mistake reduces unflattering press and publicity.[4] Overall, schools are best served when their resources are spent on children, not on lawyers.

We also assert that improving the quality of legal knowledge and raising professional legal literacy improves building or district culture. Employees want to know that they are being treated fairly in the workplace and that, at a minimum, their employer knows and follows applicable laws governing employee-employer relationships. Developing a working understanding of employment and labor law—and being able to effectively apply the law in human resource management—may contribute to employees' sense of fair treatment, thus improving overall culture in schools and districts.

For educators, a deeper understanding of the law discussed in the book may help reverse common perceptions that the law is an obstacle to education objectives or "reform." For legal professionals, a more thorough understanding of the school and classroom context may also assist in mitigating unflattering perceptions of the educator workforce. Instead of generating confusion, anxiety, and animosity, an FMLA request may be better understood for what it is—an employee's sacrifice in the form of unpaid leave designed to care for their loved one, instead of an overly burdensome federal bureaucratic obligation. Instead of appearing as an added hurdle associated with adjusting the school schedule, bargaining with a union may be better understood as something else, such as an opportunity to ensure that educators may provide adequate input in a decision likely to influence the students with whom they work so closely.[5] Aspirationally, this book may provoke fruitful conversations about leveraging law for educational objectives. At the least, this book will assist in recasting a view of the law as a lever of opportunity rather than a hurdle to reform.

Who Can Use this Book

The book contains material that is significant for multiple constituencies, including current and aspiring school administrators, school law attorneys, and professors of education law. To help ensure this book speaks to all constituencies, the authors of these chapters are some of the best school law professors, attorneys, and school administrators from across the country. Some authors have served in multiple roles through the course of their careers. In sum, these pages represent a wealth of knowledge. The book draws heavily from prior chapters in the Education Law Association's popular *The Principal's Legal Handbook*, but goes several steps further. Indeed, this text includes a comprehensive review of federal antidiscrimination laws, as well as several teaching hypotheticals intended to serve as learning platforms to apply legal concepts.

Illustrative, but not exhaustive, suggestions regarding potential use for each stakeholder group are discussed next.

Educational Administrators

Superintendents and Human Resource Officers

Topics in the book are those that human resource officers and school superintendents must deal with on a daily basis. Because those holding these positions handle the great majority of employment and personnel issues, this book may serve as a foundation for improving their own knowledge of the law and as a "desk reference" or "quick reference," when specific issues arise.

School Principals and Assistant Principals

School principals, too, can—and should—use this book to develop their understanding of this area of law. Indeed, principals often are the "first line" in many issues that arise related to employment matters and have been referred to as "legal leaders."[6] For example, principals who evaluate teachers must know the legal issues around this important topic, which we discuss in chapter 6. Our discussions also touch on the work of many other aspects of the principal's role (e.g., obligations to make reasonable accommodations for employees under applicable disability law, such as the Americans with Disabilities Act).

School Attorneys

Legal representatives of school districts can benefit from this book. To begin with, the book is well researched and represents the most recent developments in the law, which can translate into sound advice for clients. Presenting this information (such as issues concerning FMLA and the mechanics of effective evaluation) in one location is both convenient and an excellent starting point when preparing to advise clients or to plan for additional research related to specific matters.

Many school law attorneys reading this book may have additional recommendations to add based on their experiences and cases. Thus, your experience, combined with the resources from this text, can form a rich trove of advice for your clients.

Education Law Professors

The text can be an excellent core for any course related to employment law and human resource management for professors of education law. The sheer number of employment laws and issues with which a principal or law student must be familiar is quite large. This book covers all the major aspects of those laws. If a professor seeks a deeper dive into a particular area of law, then this text represents an excellent springboard, among its other benefits.

Moreover—and importantly—use of an exclusive text for the purposes of training administrators in employment law relating to school personnel signals the significance of the topic. The law's close relationship with managing school district employee operations cannot be understated. A professor of education law who uses this text underscores this point, sending a clear message to school leaders how important it is to understand this particular facet of education law.

Other Stakeholders

We believe there are others who may also find this book informative and useful, including employees, labor organizers, attorneys for employees, students, parents, attorneys for parents, elected officials, government officials, and policy makers. Despite having been written primarily for educational administrators, school attorneys, and education law professors, the authors have produced a transparent and honest portrayal of the law that is suitable for a broad spectrum of users.

Organization of Book

This text consists of eleven chapters and several illustrative case studies, presented in four sections. The first section provides a general overview of the contents of the volume, with the introduction and an overview of the legal system (chapters 1 and 2). The second section (chapters 3, 4, and 5) presents issues that generally arise under federal law. The third section (chapters 6 through 11) relates to state and local laws. The fourth section consists of "case studies," or "hypotheticals," that can be used as an instructional device. These fictional fact patterns will assist when seeking to apply legal concepts discussed throughout the book. We have provided guidance for using these fact patterns in a classroom or professional development seminar context, but readers should adapt them for their own particular needs or objectives.

Section I: Introduction, the U.S. Legal System and Federal Law

Chapter 1. This chapter outlines the organization of the book, including how it may be useful to education law professors, school administrators, and school law attorneys.

Chapter 2. A readable and informative overview of the U.S. legal system is presented by Charles Russo and Allan Osborne. Through this chapter, readers will gain a better understanding of the various sources of law and how the judicial system operates.

Section II: Federal Law that Impacts School Districts as a Workplace

Chapter 3. Ralph Sharp and Gretchen Oltman address laws governing teacher freedoms and employment, especially those that relate to the First Amendment.

Chapter 4. David Alexander and Jennifer Sughrue discuss sexual harassment in the workplace. This area of law is growing as more cases of workplace harassment are reported and litigated.

Chapter 5. John Rumel provides a comprehensive review of federal antidiscrimination and antiretaliation cases including, but not limited to, the Family Medical Leave Act (FMLA), the Americans with Disabilities Act (ADA) and Section 504 of the Rehabilitation Act (Section 504), and the Age Discrimination in Employment Act (ADEA), among others.

Section III: State Law that Impacts the School Districts as a Workplace

Chapter 6. In this chapter, Lynn Rossi Scott discusses legal issues surrounding evaluation. She notes the close link between adopting and implementing sound evaluation systems and successfully defending adverse employment decisions, like termination.

Chapter 7. The topics of tenure, dismissal, and nonrenewal are addressed by Evan Mense, Nathan Roberts, and Kenneth Lane. This chapter outlines the law in these high-stakes areas.

Chapter 8. Kelly Frels, Janet Horton, and Lisa McBride highlight the importance of documentation in this chapter. It outlines easy-to-follow and practical steps to ensure sufficient documentation of an employee's performance that can help defend an adverse employment action.

Chapter 9. In this chapter, Justin Bathon and Richard LaFosse write about the important link between collective bargaining (also commonly known as the "contract"), employees, and unions.

Chapter 10. Tina Chang, Sean Maguire, and William Sparkman discuss teacher certification and note the various ways certification is closely linked to employment decisions at the local level, with substantial responsibility conferred to principals.

Chapter 11. Professors Suzanne Eckes and Jesulon Gibbs-Brown address the topic of student injury, as it relates particularly to the role of a principal. Principals must understand tort law so they can better train their employees to avoid injury and the lawsuits that may result.

Section IV: Applying the Law to Practice

This section presents four different hypothetical cases, or fact patterns, representing different general areas of law. Suggestions are given on how to use these samples in various settings, from simple issue-spotting to using the cases as part of a writing project or assignment.
• Case 1: Williams v. Janesville (discrimination, adverse employment actions under federal law)
• Case 2: Lewis v. Jamestown City Schools (evaluations, dismissals, tenure)
• Case 3: Small v. Spring (collective bargaining, unfair labor practices)
• Case 4: Sampson v. Miller (breach of contract/nonunion, discrimination, and constructive discharge)

Endnotes

[1] *See* DAVID SCHIMMEL & MATTHEW MILITELLO, *Legal Literacy for Teachers: A Neglected Responsibility*, 77 HARVARD EDUC. REV. 257 (2007)(describing the need for improved legal knowledge for school leaders).

[2] *See* JAY HUEBERT, *The More We Get Together: Improving Collaboration Between Educators and Their Lawyers*, 67 HARVARD EDUC. REV. 531 (1997) (noting the disconnect between lawyers and their school clients and outlining the benefits of improved communication between them).

[3] For an excellent example of one text addressing another specific area of school law, special education, see A GUIDE TO SPECIAL EDUCATION LAW (Elizabeth A. Shaver and Janet R. Decker, eds. 2017).

[4] *See, e.g.*, Jason Schrieber, *Suit claims teacher was fired because of pregnancy*, THE UNION LEADER, (Aug. 3., 2017, 10:07 PM), http://www.unionleader.com/courts/Suit-claims-teacher-was-fired-because-of-pregnancy (reporting on a nontenured teacher alleging she was nonrenewed because of her pregnancy, in violation of the Family Medical Leave Act and other antidiscrimination laws).

[5] *See, e.g.*, Mark A. Paige, *Applying the Paradox Theory: A Law and Policy Analysis of Collective Bargaining Agreements and Recent Changes to Teacher Evaluation Laws*, B.Y.U. J. EDUC. & L. 21 (2013) (noting the ways in which approaches to collective bargaining can assist school and district goals).

[6] *See, e.g.*, SCHIMMEL & MILITELLO, *supra* note 1.

Section I – Chapter 2

The American Legal System

Charles J. Russo and Allan G. Osborne, Jr.

Introduction

Pursuant to the Tenth Amendment of the Federal Constitution, education in the United States is a function of the states.[1] Even so, before any discussion of legal issues arising in the context of public education can take place, it is important to understand the legal framework under which American schools operate, on both the federal and state levels. Accordingly, this introductory chapter examines the sources and types of laws in the American legal system. The chapter also reflects on how these various types of laws interact as they impact the daily operations of public schools.

Sources of Law

Generally

There are four sources of law in the United States: constitutions, statutes, regulations, and judicial decisions. These sources of law exist at both the federal and state levels.

A constitution is the fundamental law of a nation or state.[2] A statute, on the other hand, is an act of a legislative body, or a law enacted by Congress or a state legislature.[3] All statutes must be consistent with the controlling constitutions within their jurisdiction. Many statutes are accompanied by implementing regulations or guidelines written by officials in the agencies responsible for their execution and enforcement. Regulations are usually more specific than the statutes they are designed to implement, because they construe legislative intent as to how laws should work in practice.

The many judicial opinions interpreting constitutions, statutes, and regulations comprise a body of law known as case, judge-made, or common law. Relying heavily on the notion of binding precedent—that a ruling of the highest court in a jurisdiction is binding on lower courts in that jurisdiction—case law provides insight into how judges apply constitutions, statutes, and regulations to different factual situations. Cases from other jurisdictions, known as persuasive precedent, have no binding effect on courts outside their jurisdictions. In other words, decisions of courts in one jurisdiction are not binding on those in other jurisdictions, but may have some influence on

9

how other courts may interpret the law, as judges may look to see how other jurists have dealt with the same or similar issues. As an applied example, this means that decisions of the United States Supreme Court are binding on all American courts, while orders of the Supreme Court of Ohio are binding only in Ohio and are persuasive in all other jurisdictions.

Constitutions

Simply put, the Constitution of the United States is the law of the land. Consequently, all federal statutes and regulations, state constitutions, state laws and regulations, and ordinances of local governmental bodies, including school board policies, are subject to the Constitution as interpreted by the United States Supreme Court and other courts. Only a limited number of sections of the Federal Constitution are implicated in school-related cases. For the most part, the amendments protecting individual rights, such as the First, Fourth, Fifth, and Fourteenth amendments, are the sections of the Constitution impacting the operation of the schools most dramatically.

The Federal Constitution specifies the four duties of the federal and state governments. Article I, Section 8, identifies the first, or enumerated, powers, those exclusively within the purview of the federal government. These include the duty "to provide for the common Defence [sic] and general welfare of the United States ... [t]o regulate Commerce with foreign Nations, and among the several States ... [t]o coin Money, and regulate the value thereof ... [t]o promote Post Offices ..., [and] [t]o constitute Tribunals inferior to the Supreme Court."

The second set of powers are implied, meaning that they are reasonably necessary to carry out the express duties of the federal (or a state) government. For example, in providing for the national defense, the federal government has the implied authority to create the Department of Defense and subordinate offices necessary to carry out its duties, such as draft boards during times of war.

According to the Tenth Amendment, the third set of powers, reserved, are those not delegated to the federal government by the Constitution, or prohibited by it to the States or to the people. For the purposes of practitioners and students of education law, the most important reserved power is education. This is because, despite its coverage of a wide area of powers, duties, and limitations, the Constitution is silent with regard to education, thereby rendering it a responsibility of individual states. An example of the final power, concurrent—meaning that it is shared by both the federal and state governments—is taxation.

Along the same line, state constitutions are the supreme laws in their jurisdictions, with which all state statutes, regulations, and ordinances must conform. State constitutions typically deal with many of the same matters as their federal counterpart, but often provide greater detail when addressing education. In operation, insofar as state constitutions can grant their citizens greater, but not fewer, rights than the Federal Constitution, they are supreme within their boundaries.

Statutes and Regulations

As noted, under the Tenth Amendment to the Constitution, education is reserved to the states.[4] Yet, Congress has the authority to enact laws under the General Welfare Clause of Article I, Section 8, by offering funds for purposes it believes will serve the public good. For example, Congress enacted a series of statutes that forever altered the landscape of public education, starting with the Civil Rights Act of 1964,[5] which subjects public school systems to its anti-discrimination in employment provisions.

Federal statutes often make funds available to state and local governments conditioned on their acceptance of specific requirements for the use of the money. As discussed below, when states accept federal funds, educational officials are bound by whatever conditions Congress has attached to the legislation. If challenged, federal courts must be satisfied that the conditions pass constitutional muster.

In 1987, Congress expanded its authority by defining a "program or activity" as encompassing "all of the operations of [an entity] any part of which is extended Federal financial assistance."[6] This broad general prohibition covers "race, color or national origin,"[7] "sex,"[8] and "otherwise qualified handicapped individuals,"[9] categories that have become increasingly important in school settings. For instance, in order to receive funding for students who receive special education under the Individuals with Disabilities Education Act (IDEA)[10]—originally enacted in 1975 as the Education for All Handicapped Children Act—states, often through their local educational agencies or school boards, must develop detailed procedures to identify and assess children with disabilities before serving them by offering each qualified student a free appropriate public education in the least restrictive environment.

Another key example of federal involvement in education occurred when Congress superseded its most recent reauthorization of the Elementary and Secondary Education Act of 1965, as the controversial No Child Left Behind Act in 2002,[11] by enacting the Every Student Succeeds Act (ESSA) in late 2015.[12] The ESSA keeps many parts of the NCLB, but eliminates some of its more controversial elements, such as adequate yearly progress standards, while returning additional power to states.

Regulations promulgated by the Federal Department of Education and other administrative agencies grant the executive branch the means to implement statutes by carrying out their full effect. In other words, while statutes set broad legislative parameters, regulations allow administrative agencies to provide details to satisfy the requirements of the law. Regulations, which are presumptively valid, generally carry the full force of the law unless courts interpret them as conflicting with the legislation.

Most of the laws impacting public schools are statutes enacted by state legislatures. Although, as indicated, state legislatures are subject to the limitations of federal law and of state constitutions, they are relatively free to establish their own systems of education. The law is well settled that state and local boards of education, administrators, and teachers have the authority to adopt and enforce reasonable rules and regulations to ensure the smooth operation and management of schools. State and local rules and regulations are thus subject to the same constitutional limitations as statutes passed by legislative bodies. Accordingly, if it is unconstitutional for Congress or state legislatures to enact laws violating the free speech rights of students, it is impermissible for teachers to do so by creating rules that apply only in their classrooms. It is also important to note that legislation or rule-making on any level, whether federal or state, cannot conflict with higher authorities such as constitutions.

Common Law

The duty of the courts is to interpret the law. When there is no codified law, or if statutes or regulations are unclear, courts apply common law. Common law is basically judge-made law, meaning that the courts may interpret the law in light of new or changing circumstances. The collective decisions of the courts make up the body of common law. When disputes involve legislation, the duty of the courts is to uncover, as best they can, the intent of the legislative bodies that enacted statutes.

To the degree that judicial decrees establish precedent, judges provide a measure of certainty and predictability because in basing their judgments on the collected wisdom of earlier litigation, they do not have to "start from scratch" whenever new, or seemingly new, legal issues arise. In other words, as noted briefly above, when judges consider a novel point of law, they often look to see how other jurists have addressed the same or similar issues in other jurisdictions, but are not obligated to follow those judgments. In this way, judges have considerable weight in terms of providing guidance on how statutes and regulations are to be applied to everyday situations.

Judicial Systems

The federal court system and most state judicial systems have three levels. The lowest level in the federal system consists of trial courts known as district courts. Each state has at least one federal district court, while larger states, such as California and New York, may have as many as four. Federal district courts are the basic triers of fact in legal disputes; they review evidence and render decisions based on the evidence presented by the parties to disputes. Depending on the situations, trial courts may review the records of administrative hearings that have been conducted, hear additional evidence, and/or hear the testimony of witnesses.

Parties not satisfied with the judgment of a federal trial court case may appeal to the federal circuit court of appeals within which their state is located. For example, a decision handed down by a federal trial court in New York would be appealed to the Second Circuit, which, in addition to New York, includes the states of Connecticut and Vermont. There are thirteen federal judicial circuits in the United States, eleven of which are numbered and two of which are housed in Washington, D.C.

Parties displeased with the orders of circuit courts may seek further review from the United States Supreme Court. Due to the sheer volume of cases appealed each year, the Supreme Court accepts less than one percent of the disputes in which parties seek further review. Cases typically reach the Supreme Court in requests for a writ of *certiorari*, which literally means "to be informed of."

When the Supreme Court agrees to hear an appeal, it grants a writ of *certiorari*. At least four of the nine Justices must vote to grant certiorari in order for a case to be heard.[13] Denying a writ of *certiorari* has the effect of leaving a lower court's decision unchanged,[14] but is of no precedential value beyond the parties to the litigation.

Each of the fifty states and various territories has a similar arrangement to the federal scheme, except that the names of the courts vary. In most states, there are also three levels of courts: trial courts, intermediate appellate courts, and courts of last resort. It is important to take great care with the names of state courts. For instance, the highest court in most states is named the supreme court. Yet, in New York, the trial court is known as the Supreme Court, while the state's highest court is called the Court of Appeals, typically the name of intermediate appellate court in most other jurisdictions.

When courts render their judgments, their opinions are binding precedent only within their jurisdictions and are persuasive elsewhere. It should be kept in mind that the term jurisdiction can refer to either the types of cases that courts can hear—such as appeals generally or in specific areas of the law, such as a family or juvenile matters—or the geographic areas over which they have authority. However, in this situation, reference is made to the geographic area. More specifically, this means that a judgment of the federal district court for Massachusetts is binding only in Massachusetts. The federal district court in Rhode Island might find a decision of the Massachusetts court persuasive, but it is not bound by its order. Nonetheless, a ruling of the First Circuit Court of Appeals is binding on all states within its jurisdiction, and lower courts in those states must rule consistently. A decision by the Supreme Court of the United States is, of course, enforceable as binding precedent in all fifty states and American territories.

As indicated, the complex American judiciary operates at both the federal and state levels. The most common feature of these systems is a three-tiered system with trial courts, intermediate appellate panels, and courts of last resort, most commonly named supreme courts.

Trial courts have general jurisdiction, meaning that there are typically few limits on the types of cases that they may hear. Trial courts rely on the case specifics, apply the law to the circumstances, and are generally presided over by a single judge or justice.

Intermediate state appellate courts, often known as courts of appeal, review cases when one or both parties to disputes are dissatisfied with the judgments of the lower courts. Appellate courts are ordinarily not triers of fact; rather, these judicial panels review the lower courts' applications of the law. In rare cases, appellate panels may reject the factual findings of lower courts if they are convinced that they were clearly erroneous. Appellate courts usually consist of a panel of judges. By way of illustration, at the federal level, appeals are usually heard by panels of three judges. In unusual circumstances, a party in a federal court can petition a circuit court for an en banc appeal—literally, "in the bench"—meaning that all justices in the circuit participate in the oral arguments and decision.

Finally, disputes may be appealed to courts of last resort. At the federal level, this is the Supreme Court. The Supreme Court has discretion to review rulings of lower federal courts and state high courts involving federal constitutional, statutory, or regulatory issues.

Insofar as education is a state function and federal courts exist for federal matters, state courts resolve most educational disputes. Unless there are substantial federal questions, disagreements must be tried in state courts. If substantial federal questions are involved with matters of state law, disputes may be litigated in either state or federal courts. When federal courts examine cases involving both state and federal law, they must follow interpretations of state law made by the state courts within the jurisdictions in which they are seated because there is no such thing as federal common law.

Legal Resources

The written opinions of most courts are generally available in a variety of published formats. The official version of Supreme Court opinions are in the United States Reports, abbreviated U.S. The same opinions, with additional research aids that make it easier to locate specific points of law in the opinions, are published in the Supreme Court Reporter (S. Ct.) and the Lawyer's Edition, now in its second series (L. Ed. 2d).

Opinions of federal circuit courts of appeal are published in the Federal Reporter, now in its third series (F.3d); cases that are not selected for publication in F.3d appear in the Federal Appendix (cited as Fed. Appx. or Fed. App'x), but are of limited precedential value. Federal district court cases are published in the Federal Supplement, now in its third series (F. Supp. 3d).

State court cases are published in a variety of publications, most notably West's National Reporter system, which divides the country up into seven regions: Atlantic, North Eastern, North Western, Pacific, South Eastern, South Western, and Southern. Most education-related cases are also republished in West's Education Law Reporter, a specialized series that ordinarily includes peer-reviewed articles on point.

Before being published in hardbound volumes, most judgments are released in what are known as slip opinions, a variety of looseleaf services, and electronic sources. Many commercial services also publish decisions in specialized areas. For example, special education court cases, as well as the outcomes of due process hearings, are reproduced in a loose-leaf format in the Individuals with Disabilities Education Law Reporter (IDELR), published by LRP Publications.

Statutes and regulations are also accessible in a variety of similar formats. Federal statutes are published in the United States Code (U.S.C.), the official version, or the United States Code Annotated (U.S.C.A.), published by West Publishing Company. Agency regulations of the United States appear in the Code of Federal Regulations (C.F.R.). Copies of education statutes and regulations can be downloaded via links on the U.S. Department of Education's website. Legal materials are also available online from a variety of sources, most notably WestLaw and LexisNexis. State laws and regulations are commonly available online from the websites of their states.

Reading Legal Citations

Legal citations are fairly easy to read. The first number indicates the volume number where the case, statute, or regulation is located, followed by the abbreviation of the book or series in which the material may is published. The second number indicates the page on which a case begins or the section number of a statute or regulation; if a second number is present, it refers to the page on which a quote is published.

Other than the Supreme Court, which specifies just the year, the last parts of citations identify the names of the courts and the years in which the disputes were resolved. For example, *Board of Education of the Hendrick Hudson Central School District v. Rowley,* the Supreme Court's first case interpreting what is now known as the IDEA, was originally decided by the federal trial court for the Southern District of New York, 483 F. Supp. 528 (S.D.N.Y., 1980), affirmed by the Second Circuit, 632 F.2d 945, (2d Cir. 1980), but reversed by the Supreme Court, 458 U.S. 176, 102 S. Ct. 3034, 73 L.Ed.2d 690 [5 Educ. L. Rep. 34] (1982). This means that the official version of the Court's opinion, rendered in 1982, can be found in volume 458 of the United States Report, starting on page 176; the other citations read similarly.

The IDEA, 20 U.S.C. §§ 1400 *et seq.* (2005) can be found in Title 20 of the United States Code beginning with section 1400. The IDEA's regulations, 34 C.F.R. §§ 300.1 can be found at Title 34 of the Code of Federal Regulations, starting with section 300.1.

Endnotes

[1] *San Antonio Indep. Sch. Dist. v. Rodriguez,* 411 U.S. 1, 35, 93 S. Ct. 1278, 36 L.Ed.2d 16 (1975), wherein the Justices refused to intervene in a school finance dispute from Texas, the majority ruled that "[e]ducation, of course, is not among the rights afforded explicit protection under our Federal Constitution. Nor do we find any basis for saying it is implicitly so protected."

[2] B. A. GARNER, BLACK'S LAW DICTIONARY (8th ed.) (2004).

[3] *Id.*

[4] *See* Epperson v. State of Ark., 393 U.S. 97, 104, 89 S. Ct. 266, 21 L.Ed.2d 228 (1968).

[5]   42 U.S.C.A. § 2000e–2a.

[6]   Civil Rights Restoration Act, 20 U.S.C.A. § 1687.

[7]   42 U.S.C.A. § 2000d.

[8]   20 U.S.C.A. § 1681.

[9]   29 U.S.C.A. § 794.

[10]   20 U.S.C.A. §§ 1400 *et seq.*

[11]   20 U.S.C.A. §§ 6301 *et seq.*

[12]   P.L. 114-95, Dec. 10, 2015, 129 Stat. 1814.

[13]   The so-called "Rule of Four" is a long-standing judicial creation despite the fact that Congress may have been mindful of it in enacting the Judiciary Act of 1925. Earlier, Congress created *certiorari*, or discretionary review, in 1890 in 26 Stat. 826, Sections 4–6.

[14]   GARNER, *supra* n. 2.

Key Words

appellate court

binding precedent

certiorari

circuit court of appeals

Civil Rights Act of 1964

common law

constitution

court of last resort

district court

Education for All Handicapped
   Children Act

Elementary and Secondary
   Education Act of 1965

en banc

enumerated powers

Every Student Succeeds Act (ESSA)

federal court system

implied powers

Individuals with Disabilities
   Education Act (IDEA)

judicial decision

legal citations

legal resources

No Child Left Behind Act (NCLB)

persuasive precedent

regulation

source of law

statute

supreme court

Tenth Amendment

trial court

U.S. Department of Education

Section II – Chapter 3

Academic Freedom and Censorship

Ralph Sharp and Gretchen Oltman

Introduction

The concept of academic freedom originated at the university level and is more often associated with the university professor's role than with that of the public school teacher. While initially the term was used to describe the professor's right to decide what should be taught, through the years, the term has taken on broader meanings. Today, even at the university level, different views exist as to its nature and its legal status.[1] Although some legal scholars and many academicians adhere to the position that academic freedom is an "inalienable" right of the professor or teacher to select both content and method of instruction, others deny that academic freedom has any sort of independent existence beyond the First Amendment rights possessed by all citizens. Hosting multiple viewpoints is critical to developing students as critical thinkers and thoughtful, engaged citizens. The Supreme Court noted this in *Sweezy v. New Hampshire* when it stated, "Teachers and students must always remain free to inquire, to study and to evaluate, to gain new maturity and understanding; otherwise our civilization will stagnate and die."[2] Protecting a professor's ability to select content, challenge the establishment of the university, or promote dialogue may not be popular, yet remains an important part of learning nonetheless. However, public school teachers face more restrictions when claiming similar protections of academic freedom for several reasons: their public employee status and contractual duty to carry out a local school board's mandates, the captive nature of the youth in their care, and diminished First Amendment protections for speech while in the public employment setting.

While academic freedom typically encompasses the curricular functions of teachers, censorship issues tend to deal with the larger context of appropriate speech and conduct of someone holding a title "within and on behalf of a public school district"—that is, when does the line between private citizen and school spokesperson occur, and how can we tell when someone is acting outside of his or her official capacity as a school employee? Censorship refers to the suppression of speech or other forms of expression and to any disciplinary action taken by government or governmental agencies, such as public schools. The extensive case law on censorship is applicable to all public employees, including teachers. Although the Supreme Court has rendered a series of landmark decisions on this issue, involving both students and teachers over the past four decades, disputes continue. When the terms *censorship* and *academic freedom* are linked, the primary focus of this chapter is teachers' speech related to the curriculum.

Legal Issues

The United States Supreme Court first recognized academic freedom in the 1950s and 1960s in cases resulting from attempts to rid schools of Communist influences.[3] It was not until 1968, in *Pickering v. Board of Education of Township High School District 205*,[4] that the Court ruled that teachers' speech in the form of a letter to a newspaper was entitled to First Amendment protection. The Court held that a teacher cannot be discharged or otherwise punished for speaking out on issues of "public" concern. The following year, in *Tinker v. Des Moines Independent Community School District*,[5] the Court proclaimed that neither students nor teachers "shed their constitutional rights to freedom of speech or expression at the schoolhouse gate"[6] and declared that interference with those rights could be justified only on the basis of "material and substantial disruption."

In *Mt. Healthy City School District Board of Education v. Doyle*,[7] the Supreme Court expressly recognized that other legitimate reasons can exist for disciplining teachers who are exercising their constitutional rights. This 1977 decision established the required approach for deciding such cases. First, the teacher has the burden of showing that constitutionally protected conduct was a motivating factor in the teacher's discharge or other school disciplinary action. Assuming that the teacher successfully makes that showing, the burden shifts to the school officials to prove that they would have followed the same course of action in the absence of the protected conduct. On the heels of that decision, the Court made it clear that speech of public concern is protected speech, even though it may be expressed privately by an employee to a supervisor.[8] In 1983, the Court reinforced its *Pickering* standard by upholding the employer's right to dismiss an employee whose speech was of a private rather than a public concern.[9] And, in 2006, the Court ruled in *Garcetti v. Ceballos*[10] that the First Amendment does not protect a public employee whose statements are made pursuant to official duties rather than as a private citizen.

Until the 2007 opinion in *Morse v. Frederick*,[11] the Supreme Court had rendered its most recent decisions on free speech in schools in the second half of the 1980s. In its 1986 decision, *Bethel School District No. 403 v. Fraser*,[12] the Court found no First Amendment protection for obscene or vulgar speech. Two years later, the Court upheld the authority of school officials to control the curriculum in *Hazelwood School District v. Kuhlmeier*[13] when it permitted administrators to delete objectionable articles from the school newspaper. Even though these cases pertained to students' speech, they have profoundly affected the subsequent rulings of the lower courts in their rulings on teachers' speech, especially those cases in which the teacher claimed to be protected by academic freedom.

Instructional Choices versus Private Protected Speech

Teachers serve as the main vehicles for curriculum delivery in public schools. The role of teacher is broad—to introduce and demonstrate new knowledge, assess learning in formative and summative manners, manage classroom behavior, uphold school policies, promote student engagement, and much more. As such, teachers are entrusted with a great deal of responsibility, including how curriculum is implemented within the classroom. While local school boards determine which curriculum is available, the classroom teacher is responsible for putting that curriculum into action, yet not without boundaries. Instructional choices in K-12 public schools are always subject to local school board control, a much different standard than that at the college or university level. Public school teachers receive much less protection than university-level professors over how and what they teach. Yet, it cannot be overlooked that public school teachers are citizens and their insights into classroom practices, administrative issues, or school board policies are important voices in democratic conversation. In addition, some teachers participate in political speech outside of work on a regular basis. The line blurs, however, when a teacher seeks academic freedom for classroom practices or speech engaged in during the line of duty and not during their time as a private citizen.

It is important to note that public schools are local institutions, mostly run by local and state entities, with ties to the federal government, mostly through federal funding and aid. Therefore, local school boards maintain much of the decision-making authority in regard to curriculum selection, teacher hiring and firing, and overall policies and protocols. In such, community practices can sometimes influence the decision making within a public school district.

Following the Supreme Court rulings in the 1980s, the lower courts became more supportive of school officials in disputes with teachers stemming from the choice of instructional materials and methods. In fact, three state supreme courts adopted the rationale established in *Hazelwood* three years before the High Court ruled. In 1980, the Washington Supreme Court ruled that two teachers had no right of academic freedom to team-teach a high school history course according to their plan to incorporate small group and individual study, as "course content is manifestly a matter within the board's discretion."[14] Due to changes in enrollment, there were not enough sections to offer the team-taught class, and one of the teachers was reassigned to teach a similar class using a single-instructor model. The teachers challenged the district's placement of the teacher citing academic freedom to no avail, with the school demonstrating changing enrollment trends and a lack of demand for the team-taught class. Five years later, the Alaska Supreme Court upheld the dismissal of a teacher who violated a school policy requiring administrative approval of supplementary materials used in classes.[15] The materials in question included a book on gay rights. The court stated that the First Amendment does not "eliminate the school board's right to control the curriculum."[16] Similarly, the Maine Supreme Court rejected the claims of a teacher who alleged that the school board violated his right to academic freedom under the First Amendment by canceling a symposium he had planned.[17] This program, referred to as "tolerance day," was arranged by the teacher in response to the drowning of a gay student by three high school students. The court stated, "However broad the protections of academic freedom may be, they do not permit a teacher to insist upon a given curriculum for the whole school where he teaches."[18]

Beginning in the late 1980s, federal courts decided a number of First Amendment speech cases involving schools. The Sixth Circuit refused to overturn the dismissal of a teacher who had shown an R-rated movie that she had failed to preview prior to showing to high school students on the last day of school.[19] The court's majority, applying the *Mt. Healthy* approach, held that since the movie, *Pink Floyd – The Wall,* was not "expressive or communicative," it did not qualify as speech protected by the First Amendment. In a concurring opinion, agreeing with the outcome, another judge relied on *Bethel*, pointing out the vulgar content of the tape that was shown to a captive audience justified the teacher's dismissal. Two years later, a federal district court in Illinois found that a teacher was not likely to prevail on her First Amendment claim challenging her nonrenewal for showing an R-rated movie containing vulgar and sexually explicit content.[20]

The Fifth Circuit in *Kirkland v. Northside Independent School District*[21] upheld the nonrenewal of a teacher who substituted, without administrative approval, his own supplemental reading list in a world history class for the school's official list. The appellate court determined that the issue of supplemental reading lists did not present a matter of public concern and was rather "nothing more than an ordinary employment dispute."[22] Other federal courts have similarly supported a local board of education's authority to prohibit the assignment of specific books in elective language arts classes[23] and to restrict the use of supplemental materials having religious content.[24] A year after *Kirkland*, the Third Circuit reviewed a decision in a very complicated case in which a teacher sought an injunction to prevent school officials from banning a teaching methodology involving a sports team-like atmosphere to incentivize student learning. The teacher favored this teaching method (which had been invented and promoted by a fellow teacher in the district) and sought to bar the district from interfering with her use and advocacy of the method.[25] Although the appellate court agreed with the district court's denial of the injunction, it observed that if the teacher were disciplined for the advocacy of the methodology outside the school, her First Amendment rights would be violated.

In 1991, the Tenth Circuit considered an appeal of a teacher who was punished with a four-day suspension and a letter of reprimand for remarks made in class during an informal discussion.[26] The offensive remark repeated a rumor about two students "making out" on the tennis courts. The teacher filed suit charging that the disciplinary action "chilled" his free speech rights and violated his academic freedom. Beginning with the first step of the *Mt.*

Healthy analysis, asking whether the teacher's comments were constitutionally protected, the court looked to the analysis in *Hazelwood*. Relying on *Hazelwood*, the court reasoned that the teacher's comments were "school sponsored expression" in a nonpublic forum;[27] therefore, school officials need only show "a legitimate pedagogical interest" in controlling the teacher's speech. The school officials' burden was met because the school was justified in insisting that a teacher "exhibit professionalism and sound judgment" and not "make statements about students that embarrass those students among their peers."[28] Finally, in rejecting the other claim, the court said: "[T]he case law does not support [his] position that a secondary school teacher has a constitutional right to academic freedom."[29]

Speech Related to Curricular Choices

By the end of the 1990s, the Fourth and Eighth Circuits had ruled in cases that clearly involved disputed authority to control curriculum. In *Boring v. Buncombe County Board of Education*,[30] the court affirmed the transfer of a drama teacher who selected a play that administrators later decided was inappropriate for her students. A divided Fourth Circuit, in considering the issue of "[w]hether a public high school teacher had a right to participate in the makeup of the school curriculum through the selection and production of a play" ruled that she did not. Finding that the board had "legitimate pedagogical reasons" for its actions, the appellate court sustained the district court's judgment for the school district.[31] In *Lacks v. Ferguson Reorganized School District R-2*,[32] the Eighth Circuit permitted the board to dismiss a tenured high school teacher after she allowed students to use vulgar language in plays they wrote and performed as an assignment in her creative writing class. This decision turned on the court's findings that the board had established a legitimate pedagogical concern in prohibiting profanity in the classroom, that the principal had warned her of violations of a board policy on profanity, and that she had been dismissed for violating board policy as provided by state law. The Supreme Court declined to review either of these decisions.

The beginning of the twenty-first century saw courts further affirm district authority over the curriculum. In 2000, a federal district court in Virginia upheld the administrative removal of a banned books pamphlet posted by an English teacher on the outside of his classroom door.[33] The court found that the posted pamphlet, as part of the curriculum, was not protected speech; and if it were considered protected, the posting of the pamphlet could still be censored because it "impedes on the school district's ability to teach the selected curriculum based on community values that previously had been approved by the school board."[34] In another Virginia dispute, the Fourth Circuit ruled in 2007 that a Spanish teacher did not have a right to post religious materials on his classroom bulletin board. Citing *Boring*, the appellate court found that the items were curricular in nature since they were posted on school-owned and controlled bulletin boards and designed to impart knowledge to students; therefore, the conflict was simply an employment dispute.[35]

Other decisions since 2000 have upheld district authority to prohibit controversial or inappropriate language in the classroom. *In re Bernstein*[36] saw New York's highest court rule that a district could punish (fine and reprimand) a previously warned English teacher who used sexually explicit language to describe a theory of literary criticism involving phallic symbolism. In *Erskine v. Board of Education*,[37] a federal district court in Maryland (later affirmed by the Fourth Circuit in an unpublished per curiam opinion) upheld the transfer of a teacher who wrote *negro*, the Spanish word for black, on the board when teaching a lesson on Spanish words for color. The problem stemmed from the fact that students reported the teacher wrote the word "nigger" on the board, while the teacher claimed he wrote the word "negro" for his color lesson. The teacher had been under some scrutiny for making derogatory racist statements to students and this incident's investigation led to his teaching reassignment. The court found that the teacher had no protected First Amendment interest in his speech because it was speech used to carry out the curriculum of the school and was not a matter of public concern. In 2003, the Sixth Circuit, in *Lautermilch v. Findlay City Schools*,[38] held that none of a substitute teacher's alleged speech dealt with a matter of public concern and consequently was not protected by the First Amendment, where the substitute had told inappropriate jokes in an Ohio public school classroom. The Seventh Circuit, in 2007, held that an elementary teacher did not have a First Amendment right to insert her personal opinions on political controversies into classroom current events discussions.[39] The principal had instructed the teacher that she could teach about the U.S. policies toward Iraq and use arguments for the different perspectives, but she had to keep her personal opinions to herself. The court declared: "The Constitution does not entitle teachers to present personal views to captive audiences against the instructions of elected officials."[40] In *Brown v. Chicago Board of Education*,[41] a Chicago teacher was fired for reading aloud a note he intercepted. The note included lyrics to a song including the word "nigger." The teacher engaged in a discussion with his sixth-grade class about the use of the word and its inappropriateness for school. Using any racial epithet was strictly forbidden under school policy, and the teacher failed on his claim to challenge the policy that his speech was protected because, while in clear violation of a policy forbidding him to use the word "in front" of students, he nonetheless was engaged in an educational effort to explain why the language was inappropriate.

Two federal circuit courts rejected the claims of repeatedly insubordinate educators that they were terminated or nonrenewed for protected speech. In *Vukadinovich v. Board of School Trustees of North Newton School Corp.*,[42] an Indiana technology teacher, unhappy about his proposed extra-duty compensation for coaching a basketball team, criticized the superintendent and school board in numerous letters to local newspapers. The Seventh Circuit found that the school district had lawfully terminated the teacher for insubordination and neglect of duty, not for his expression. The teacher refused, failed, or halfheartedly attempted on five occasions to comply with his principal's specific instructions to submit his lesson plan book and identify how it addressed the state technology qualifications that his program failed to meet. An Oklahoma elementary teacher similarly failed to comply with reasonable administrative directions in *Greenshields v. Independent School District I-1016 of Payne County, Oklahoma*.[43] The second-grade teacher repeatedly refused to follow her district's science curriculum that incorporated learning modules because she favored traditional science methods and materials. The Tenth Circuit found in 2006 that she was nonrenewed for willful neglect of duty and other statutory grounds (insubordination is not a statutory ground for dismissal or nonrenewal of tenured teachers in Oklahoma), based upon her refusal to follow district curriculum and policies and to comply with administrative directives, not for criticizing the district's curriculum, generating public controversy, and bringing suit against the district.

An exception to the pattern of decisions in favor of school districts came in 2001 in *Cockrel v. Shelby County School District*.[44] The Sixth Circuit reviewed the termination of a Kentucky fifth-grade teacher who had invited actor Woody Harrelson and several farmers to speak on the environmental benefits of industrial hemp, an illegal substance in the state. In remanding the case for a determination of whether termination would have occurred absent the controversial activity,[45] the appellate court found that selection of speakers for a class presentation constituted speech that touched on a matter of public concern and, in this situation, passed the *Pickering* balancing test, despite evidence of some disruption to the educational environment.

Teacher Speech Related to "Official Responsibilities"

Public school employee speech has more recently been categorized under the *Garcetti v. Ceballos*[46] decision, in which the U.S. Supreme Court ruled a public employee's speech made pursuant to his official duties of public office was not protected under the First Amendment. As such, courts now must first decide whether a teacher's speech falls within his/her duties as a classroom teacher, in which there will be limited First Amendment protections, or fall outside the scope of public employment, for which broader First Amendment protections can be had.

Many federal appellate court rulings applied *Garcetti*'s "pursuant to official responsibilities" test to educators' claims their expression was constitutionally protected. The Second Circuit Court, in *Panse v. Eastwood*,[47] affirmed a lower court decision that a teacher's statements were made as part of his official duties as an art teacher and consequently were not protected by the First Amendment. He had encouraged his students, in order to make them more competitive for scholarships to elite college art programs, to take a for-profit course he considered teaching outside of school that included sketching nude models. In 2010, the Sixth Circuit Court similarly found that the First Amendment did not shield a special education teacher's complaints to her supervisors about her teaching caseload because the comments were directly related to her job, and were not part of her speech as private citizen.[48] An Illinois federal court found a teacher was not protected by the First Amendment after lodging several complaints against administrators in his district—including computer misuse, forgery, and misappropriating funds—because his complaints were made pursuant to his official duties[49] A third federal appellate court reviewed a football coach's claim that school district policy violated his constitutional rights by prohibiting him from silently bowing his head during the team's pre-meal grace and from taking a knee during the team's pre-game locker room prayer. The court did not reference *Garcetti*, but found that the First Amendment did not protect the coach's expression because it did not address a matter of public concern and was not protected by academic freedom.[50] In *Mpoy v. Fenty*,[51] a teacher's academic freedom claim failed because the speech he sought to protect (complaints about administrators and working conditions) was clearly related to his official duties.

Speech that falls outside the framework of "official duties" does receive First Amendment protections, and teachers have had some success litigating against their school district/employers for speech that occurs in their role as "private citizens." A Florida reading teacher successfully won a case alleging retaliation for her public declaration of federal fund mismanagement by her district's administration.[52] The court held that the teacher's concerns could have been construed as part of her official responsibilities and not entitled to First Amendment protections; however, the teacher went so far as to report the same complaints to two outside administrative bodies, clearly beyond the scope of her typical duties and more so through her role as private citizen. Even though the information she obtained was through her role working in the school, she did not lose the ability to speak up about matters of public concern and to receive First Amendment protections for doing so. In *Spencer v. Philamy*,[53] a long-term substitute teacher filed two police reports after reporting a student's sexual harassment and abusive behavior in her classroom. After filing the complaint, the teacher received unsatisfactory performance reviews. The teacher received First Amendment protections and protection from retaliatory employment practices because her complaint focused on criminal behavior in school, clearly a matter of public concern.

Social Media and Academic Freedom

Social media has opened a new set of concerns in regard to academic freedom, censorship, and the role of private versus public speech by public school teachers. In 2013, the Missouri state legislature attempted to prohibit public school teachers from using social media tools through which they could privately converse with students.[54] After much public criticism, the law was enjoined and school districts were left to develop district-level social networking policies. However, concerns remain about the appropriate use of social networking technology for educational purposes and exactly when a teacher leaves his or her role as a public employee and moves into the public citizen arena. Proponents of liberal social networking use suggest that it allows for extending teaching into non-teaching hours, promoting curricular understanding, and communicating with students on school-related issues. Opponents cite the potential for abuse or improper communications between teachers and students. It remains unclear, however, whether teachers' communication with students through social networking sites is protected because they are acting as "private citizens" outside of school time, or they are speaking in their official capacity as teachers and, therefore, unable to receive more liberal First Amendment protections for comments made outside the classroom.

A few cases involving teacher use of social media have emerged in more recent years, usually favoring school districts in the outcome.[55] A Connecticut teacher was fired for creating a MySpace account, inviting students to view the account, and subsequently posting pictures of naked men the account.[56] The teacher argued the school district violated his First Amendment rights, yet the court concluded that the teacher's conduct online was outweighed by the need to protect the school from disruption. A Pennsylvania student teacher was unable to complete her student teaching assignment due to her MySpace posts criticizing her faculty supervisor. In the posts, she referenced some problems with her supervisor, although never using the supervisor's name.[57] The teacher eventually agreed that her posts were of a personal nature and not on a matter of public concern, therefore limiting any First Amendment protections that might have been available. Another Pennsylvania teacher used her personal blog to complain about her students, their classroom performance and behaviors, and general complaints about her teaching job.[58] After her eventual termination, the teacher argued that her posts complaining about school issues were matters of public concern and subject to First Amendment protections. The court disagreed and reasoned that even though some of her complaints were certainly of public concern, her speech was so disruptive to the educational environment that it was not protected under the First Amendment. It remains to be seen where the clear line of delineation will fall when it comes to online teacher speech, including that promoting curricular goals.[59]

Recommendations for Practice

Schools, districts, administrators, and teachers today have the guidance of a line of cases in which the courts, with notable consistency for nearly three decades, have supported the authority of the public schools to control curriculum.[60] Nonetheless, school administrators must realize that censorship of teachers' speech still carries with it the risk of a lawsuit;[61] also, teachers should understand their speech is protected by the force of law, which includes the possibility of damages should the teacher prevail in court. Schools, districts, and administrators should know and respect teachers' rights. They should approach personnel problems with a spirit of fairness and attempt to resolve them by doing what is in the best interest of the students. Finally, they should recognize potential legal implications and act under the guidance of competent legal counsel before—and not wait until after—such problems develop. The lessons of the cases reviewed serve as the basis for additional suggestions that follow:

1. Be aware that outside the classroom, including in online settings, teachers have a First Amendment right to express opinions about matters of public concern, even though those views may be controversial and unpopular. The only justification for interfering or disciplining teachers for such speech is material and substantial disruption of the educational process.

2. Exercise extreme caution when recommending the release of inferior or otherwise undesirable teachers who at the same time may be engaged in protected speech or other constitutional rights, including in an online environment. The evidence documenting the legitimate reasons for the action must convince the courts that those reasons alone would have resulted in the dismissal or other disciplinary action.

3. Do not base a recommendation for dismissal or other disciplinary action on what teachers may have said in a private conference or other nonpublic setting, because if the statements are about matters of public concern, they are protected speech. However, comments made about official responsibilities and duties are not protected.

4. If teachers are to be disciplined for what they say in the classroom or for the subject matter or methods they use, make certain that the school has and can show some legitimate pedagogical justification for the actions.

Public school administrators find broad judicial support for their authority to control the curriculum and to prevent disruption within the school environment. In the near future, there is little indication that this authority will be eroded by elementary and secondary school teachers' claims of academic freedom. However, few would question the desirability of teacher involvement in curricular decisions. Teachers are an integral piece of the instructional process, and their professional expertise and involvement in decision making should be encouraged. Maintaining communication between principal and teacher about what is taught, why it meets curricular goals, and how it is taught, is essential to maintaining academic freedom and the professional discourse necessary to productive school environments.

Endnotes

[1] For an example of current higher education issues involving academic freedom, *see* Urofsky v. Gilmore, 216 F.3d 401 (4th Cir. 2000), *cert. denied,* 531 U.S. 1070 (2001), where the Fourth Circuit in 2000 ruled that public university professors do not have a First Amendment right of academic freedom to access sexually explicit materials on state owned or leased computers. *See also* Loving v. Boren, 133 F.3d 771 (10th Cir. 1998).

[2] 354 U.S. 234 (1957)

[3] *See, e.g.,* Keyishian v. Bd. of Regents of Univ. of State of N.Y., 385 U.S. 589 (1967).

[4] Pickering v. Bd. of Educ. of Tp. High Sch. Dist. 205, 391 U.S. 563 (1968).

[5] Tinker v. Des Moines Indep. Cmty. Sch. Dist., 393 U.S. 503 (1969).

6   *Id.* at 506.
7   Mt. Healthy City Sch. Dist. Bd. of Educ. v. Doyle, 429 U.S. 274 (1977).
8   Givhan v. W. Line Consol. Sch. Dist., 439 U.S. 410 (1979).
9   Connick v. Myers, 461 U.S. 138 (1983).
10 547 U.S. 410 (2006).
11 551 U.S. 393 (2007).
12 Bethel Sch. Dist. No. 403 v. Fraser, 478 U.S. 675 (1986).
13 Hazelwood Sch. Dist. v. Kuhlmeier, 484 U.S. 260 (1988).
14 Millikan v. Bd. of Dirs. of Everett Sch. Dist. No. 2, 611 P.2d 414, 418 (Wash. 1980).
15 Fisher v. Fairbanks N. Star Borough Sch. Dist., 704 P.2d 213 (Alaska 1985).
16 *Id.* at 217.
17 Solmitz v. Me. Sch. Admin. Dist. No. 59, 495 A.2d 812 (Me. 1985).
18 *Id.* at 817.
19 Fowler v. Bd. of Educ. of Lincoln County, Ky., 819 F.2d 657 (6th Cir. 1987).
20 Krizek v. Bd. of Educ. of Cicero-Stickney Twp. High Sch. Dist. No. 201, Cook Cnty., Ill., 713 F.Supp. 1131 (N.D.Ill. 1989).
21 890 F.2d 794 (5th Cir. 1989), *cert. denied*, 496 U.S. 926 (1990).
22 *Id.* at 802.
23 Cary v. Bd. of Educ. of Adams-Arapahoe Sch. Dist. 28-J, Aurora, Colo., 598 F.2d 535 (10th Cir. 1979).
24 Williams v. Vidmar, 367 F. Supp. 2d 1265 (N.D. Cal. 2005).
25 Bradley v. Pittsburgh Bd. of Educ., 910 F.2d 1172 (3d Cir. 1990).
26 Miles v. Denver Pub. Sch., 944 F.2d 773 (10th Cir. 1991).
27 *Id.* at 776.
28 *Id.* at 778.
29 *Id.* at 779.
30 Boring v. Buncombe County Bd. of Educ., 136 F.3d 364 (4th Cir. 1998), *cert. denied*, 525 U.S. 813 (1998).
31 *Id.* at 370.
32 Lacks v. Ferguson Reorg. Sch. Dist. R-2, 147 F.3d 718 (8th Cir. 1998), *cert. denied*, 526 U.S. 1012 (1999).
33 Newton v. Slye, 116 F. Supp. 2d 677 (W.D. Va. 2000) (the court denied an injunction).
34 *Id.* at 685.
35 Lee v. York County Sch. Div., 484 F.3d 687 (4th Cir. 2007).
36 *In re* Bernstein, 726 N.Y.S.2d 474 (N.Y. App.Div. 2001).
37 Erskine v. Bd. of Educ., 207 F. Supp. 2d 407 (D. Md. 2002), *aff'd*, 56 F. App'x 615 (4th Cir. 2003).
38 Lautermilch v. Findlay City Sch., 314 F.3d 271 (6th Cir. 2003) (the substitute had also allegedly commented on the size of a female teacher's breasts and acted inappropriately with young people).
39 Mayer v. Monroe County Cmty. Sch. Corp., 474 F.3d 477 (7th Cir. 2007).
40 *Id.* at 480.
41 Brown v. Chicago Board of Education, 824 F.3d 713 (7th Cir. 2016).
42 Vukadinovich v. Bd. of Sch. Trs. of N. Newton Sch. Corp., 278 F.3d 693 (7th Cir. 2002).
43 Greenshields v. Indep. Sch. Dist. I-1016 of Payne County, Okla., 174 F. App'x 426 (10th Cir. 2006).
44 Cockrel v. Shelby County Sch. Dist., 270 F.3d 1036 (6th Cir. 2001).
45 The district cited Cockrel's alleged failure to teach the school's curriculum, calling the principal names in front of students and staff, and failure to cooperate with faculty members and staff at her elementary school. *Id.* at 1041.
46 Garcetti v. Ceballos, 547 U.S. 410 (2006).
47 303 F. App'x 933 (2d Cir. 2008), *aff'g* 2007 WL 2154192 (S.D.N.Y. 2007).
48 Fox v. Traverse City Area Pub. Schs. Bd. of Educ., 605 F.3d 345 (6th Cir. 2010).
49 Smith v. Illinois Sch. Dist. U-46. 120 F.Supp.3d 757 (N.D. Ill. 2015).

[50] Borden v. Sch. Dist. of Twp. of E. Brunswick, 523 F.3d 153 (3d Cir. 2008).

[51] Mpoy v. Fenty, 901 F.Supp.2d 144 (D.C. 2012).

[52] McShea v. Sch. Bd. of Collier County, 58 F. Supp. 3d 1325 (M.D. Fla. 2014).

[53] Spencer v. Philamy, 540 Fed. Appx. 69 (2013).

[54] *See* Amy Hestir Student Protection Act, 2011 MO. LEGIS. SERV. S.B. 54 (West) (providing that "[n]o teacher shall establish, maintain, or use a nonwork-related internet site which allows exclusive access with a current or former student"); Amended Order Entering Preliminary Injunction, Missouri State Teachers Ass'n v. Missouri, No. 11AC-CC0053, 2011 WL 4425537 (Mo. Cir. Ct. Sept. 23, 2011).

[55] *See* Mark Schroeder, *Keeping the "Free" in Teacher Speech Rights: Protecting Teachers and Their Use of Social Media to Communicate with Students Beyond the Schoolhouse Gates,* 19 RICH. J.L. & TECH. 5 (2013).

[56] Spanierman v. Hughes, 576 F. Supp. 2d 292 (D. Conn. 2008).

[57] Snyder v. Millersville Univ., No. 07-1660, 2008 WL 5093140, at *8 (E.D. Pa. Dec. 3, 2008).

[58] Munroe v. Cent. Bucks Sch. Dist., 805 F.3d 454 (3d Cir. 2015).

[59] *See* Rachel A. Miller, *Teacher Facebook Speech: Protected or Not?*, 2011 BYU EDUC. & L.J. 637 (2011).

[60] Higher education case law involving employees' use of sexually and racially offensive language in the job setting has yielded mixed results in the past decade. While the Sixth Circuit upheld the disciplining of two employees where objectionable language was involved (*see* Bonnell v. Lorenzo, 241 F.3d 800 (6th Cir. 2001) and Dambrot v. Cent. Mich. Univ., 55 F.3d 1177 (6th Cir. 1995)), two other appellate court decisions favored faculty who used, or allowed to be used, offensive and disparaging language in their classrooms (*see* Vanderhurst v. Colo. Mt. Coll. Dist., 208 F.3d 908 (10th Cir. 2000), and Hardy v. Jefferson Cmty. Coll., 260 F.3d 671 (6th Cir. 2001)).

[61] *See, e.g.,* Harris v. Victoria Indep. Sch. Dist., 168 F.3d 216 (5th Cir. 1999), *cert. denied,* 528 U.S. 1022 (1999) (which was initiated by teachers who were transferred to other schools in the district after they criticized the school principal).

Key Words

academic freedom
censorship
communication
complaints
criticism
curricular choices
dismissal
disruptive to educational
   environment/process
expression
First Amendment
freedom of speech
gay
instructional materials/methods
insubordination
matters of public concern
MySpace
nonrenewal

obscene
official responsibilities
online
Pickering balancing test
political speech
private citizen
private versus public speech
protected conduct
protected speech
public employees
public schools
religious materials
retaliation
sexually explicit
social media
termination
vulgar

Section II – Chapter 4

Sexual Harassment in the Workplace

M. David Alexander and Jennifer A. Sughrue

Introduction

This chapter is on employee/supervisor-to-employee sexual harassment. It describes the protections that both Title VII of the Civil Rights Act and Title IX of the Education Amendments of 1972 extend to the workplace, as well as the Equal Protection Clause of the Fourteenth Amendment. It also explains how they differ in application in covering claims of sexual harassment. The concluding section offers recommendations to school leaders on how to construct policies and implement practices that create a workplace climate in which school employees and supervisors know that sexual harassment is not tolerated.

Despite the fact that the law protecting individuals from sex discrimination in the workplace has been in effect for more than fifty years, sexual harassment continues to grab headlines. Roger Ailes, the driving force behind the rise of Fox News for twenty years, departed the news organization in light of numerous allegations of sexual harassment by female employees, including one by a prominent female anchor who claims she was forced out of her employment when she refused to acquiesce to his sexual propositions.[1]

Other recent investigations have uncovered a culture of sexual harassment in public agencies, such as the National Park Service and the Fairfax County Fire and Rescue Department in Virginia.[2] The *Washington Post* reported that the culture at one small national park in Florida "became so toxic that the agency's watchdog has conducted four investigations since 2012."[3] The latest report by the inspector general uncovered a pattern of sexual harassment of female subordinates by the chief law enforcement officer at the park. He is still employed with the Park Service, but is required to work from home and has had his commission to carry a weapon suspended.

The Fairfax County Fire and Rescue Department recently lost a suit in which a former female firefighter won $250,000.[4] The jury concluded that the fire department "knew of and tolerated a male lieutenant's sexual harassment" of the plaintiff. This lawsuit is the first of at least two more the county fire department is facing.[5] These lawsuits came on the heels of the report that a female paramedic committed suicide in response to severe and pervasive sexual cyberbullying by people claiming to be her colleagues.

Men are subject to sexual harassment as well, although less frequently. For instance, the Equal Employment Opportunity Commission (EEOC) sued LensCrafters when the company failed to respond to a male employee's complaints that he was constantly subjected to sexual harassment by a female supervisor.[6] The harassment included unwelcome sexual advances, inappropriate touching, and comments of a sexual nature. Without admitting wrongdoing, the company compensated the male employee $192,500 and agreed to provide training to its employees about sexual harassment against men.[7]

Sexual harassment in the workplace is viewed under the law as a form of sexual discrimination and, therefore, a civil rights violation. Sexual harassment results when (1) someone in a position of power or influence uses his or her status to extort sexual favors from a subordinate (quid pro quo), or (2) when an employee's job performance deteriorates due to extensive or abusive sexual innuendo or behavior in the workplace (hostile work environment).

Starting in the 1970s, litigation and the feminist movement prompted various studies on sexual harassment, including Catherine MacKinnon's book, *Sexual Harassment of Working Women.*[8] Sexual harassment in the workplace was raised to national prominence during the Senate confirmation hearings for U.S. Supreme Court nominee Clarence Thomas when Anita Hill, a law professor from the University of Oklahoma and a former employee under Thomas, testified of alleged acts of sexual harassment by him. As a result, sexual harassment became recognized as a serious problem within the workplace.[9]

Protection against sexual discrimination was originally provided under Title VII of the Civil Rights Act of 1964. However, several U.S. Supreme Court decisions[10] and other perceived weaknesses in the law spurred Congress to pass the Civil Rights Act of 1991. Prior to the Civil Rights Act of 1991, the law limited the damages that victims could collect in sexual harassment cases to equitable relief that included back pay and attorney fees, but it did not allow for punitive damages or for other substantial monetary relief. These limitations were ameliorated with the amended Civil Rights Act in 1991, which extended the rights of sexual discrimination victims to sue for damages. The statute delineated the amount for compensatory damages that could be awarded, an amount that was calculated based on the number of employees.

> [The] sum of the amount of compensatory damages awarded under this section for future pecuniary losses, emotional pain, suffering, inconvenience, mental anguish, loss of enjoyment of life, and other nonpecuniary losses, and the amount of punitive damages awarded under this section, shall not exceed, for each complaining party— (A) in the case of a respondent who has more than 14 and fewer than 101 employees in each of 20 or more calendar weeks in the current or preceding calendar year, $50,000; (B) in the case of a respondent who has more than 100 and fewer than 201 employees in each of 20 or more calendar weeks in the current or preceding calendar year, $100,000; and (C) in the case of a respondent who has more than 200 and fewer

than 501 employees in each of 20 or more calendar weeks in the current or preceding calendar year, $200,000; and (D) in the case of a respondent who has more than 500 employees in each of 20 or more calendar weeks in the current or preceding calendar year, $300,000.[11]

The following sections detail the statutory and constitutional law associated with sexual harassment in the workplace, as well as the tests the court applies when evaluating the merits of a case.

Title VII

Title VII of the Civil Rights Act of 1964 and the Civil Rights Act of 1991 protects employees from sexual harassment in the workplace, whether it is a private or public place of business. Title VII makes it "an unlawful employment practice for an employer . . . to discriminate against any individual with respect to his compensation, terms, conditions or privileges of employment, because of such individual's race, color, religion, sex, or national origin."[12] The amended Civil Rights Act of 1991 provides for damages in cases of intentional employment discrimination.[13]

Sexual harassment was not specifically addressed as a form of sex discrimination in Title VII, but in the 1970s, federal courts began recognizing sexual harassment as such. It was not until the mid-1980s that the Equal Employment Opportunity Commission (EEOC) promulgated regulations prohibiting sexual harassment. These regulations provide that:

> Unwelcome sexual advances, request for sexual favors, and other verbal or physical conduct of a sexual nature constitute harassment when (1) submission to such conduct is made explicitly or implicitly a term or condition of an individual's employment, (2) submission to or rejection of such conduct by an individual is used as a basis for employment decisions affecting such individual, (3) such conduct has the purpose or effect of unreasonably interfering with an individual's work performance or creating a intimidating, hostile, or offensive working environment.[14]

It was the U.S. Supreme Court that established the standard for suits involving "unlawful employment practices" under Title VII. Initially, lower courts believed that sexual harassment did not occur unless the behavior resulted in economic or tangible discrimination. However, the Supreme Court interpreted the Title VII phrase, "'terms, conditions, or privileges of employment' [to] evince a congressional intent 'to strike at the entire spectrum of disparate treatment of men and women' in employment."[15]

The evolution in case law has been in the two primary contexts of sexual harassment: quid pro quo and hostile environment. The following explanation compares and contrasts these two contexts, including employer liability under each.

Quid Pro Quo and Hostile Environment

According to EEOC guidelines, there are two types of sexual harassment, *quid pro quo* and *hostile work environment.* The first type, *quid pro quo*, referred to those situations in which employment opportunity or benefit was dependent upon compliance with or acceptance of sexual advances. The second type of sexual harassment, hostile work environment, referred to abusive conditions in the workplace. These conditions could be the result of the sexual nature of comments, stares, jokes, innuendo, unwelcome physical contact, and other similar occurrences.

> The guidelines provide that sexual conduct constitutes prohibited "sexual harassment," whether or not it is directly linked to the grant or denial of an economic *quid pro quo,* where such conduct has the purpose or effect of unreasonably interfering with an individual's work performance or creating an intimidating, hostile, or offensive working environment.[16]

In *Meritor Savings Bank, FSB v. Vinson,* the Supreme Court determined that an employee's coerced participation in a sexual relation creates a hostile environment and a violation of Title VII was not dependent on the plaintiff showing a loss of employment or other economic effect.[17] Vinson, an employee of the bank, was promoted from teller trainee to assistant branch manager in four years. The advancements were based on merit.

Shortly after Vinson was employed, however, her supervisor, Taylor, made sexual advances toward her. Out of fear of losing her job, Vinson consented to having sexual intercourse with Taylor. They engaged in sexual intercourse approximately forty to fifty times over the course of four years. Distressed by this arrangement, Vinson told Taylor she was taking indefinite sick leave. Two months later, she was discharged for excessive use of leave.

The Supreme Court upheld the EEOC guidelines as they pertained to workplace sexual harassment and emphasized the concept of the hostile environment in the workplace. Vinson's supervisor claimed that Vinson's participation had been voluntary, but the Court ruled that the concept of voluntary participation could not be used as a defense if the sexual advances were unwelcome. The Court ruled that the "correct inquiry was whether the bank employee, by her conduct, indicated that sexual advances were unwelcome, not whether her actual participation in sexual intercourse was voluntary."[18]

Thus, the established legal standard requires the environment to be objectively hostile and abusive, which includes the victim's subjective perspective on the situation. The analysis should not rest on a single effect of the harassment, but rather it should focus on the totality of the circumstances. Such was the conclusion of the Supreme Court in *Harris v. Forklift Systems, Inc.*[19]

In this instance, the company's male president often made insulting remarks to the female plaintiff, such as telling her she was a "dumb ass woman,"[20] and using sexual innuendo to embarrass her in front of customers and other employees, such as "What did you do, promise [the customer] . . .

some [sex] Saturday night?"[21] Both the federal district and appellate courts held that the series of comments and sexual innuendo were not sufficient to have "seriously affected the plaintiff's psychological well-being or led her to suffer injury."[22] The Supreme Court reversed their rulings by cautioning that Title VII did not limit an actionable claim to a showing of psychological injury.

In defining the range between what is actionable and what is not, the Court quoted parts of its ruling in *Meritor*. On one hand:

> Mere utterance of an . . . epithet which engenders offensive feelings in an employee, does not sufficiently affect the conditions of employment to implicate Title VII. Conduct that is not severe or pervasive enough to create an objectively hostile or abusive work environment—an environment that a reasonable person would find hostile or abusive—is beyond Title VII's purview. Likewise, if the victim does not subjectively perceive the environment to be abusive, the conduct has not actually altered the conditions of the victim's employment, and there is no Title VII violation.[23]

On the other hand, however:

> Title VII comes into play before the harassing conduct leads to a nervous breakdown. A discriminatory abusive work environment, even one that does not seriously affect employees' psychological well-being, can and often will detract from employees' job performance, discourage employees from remaining on the job, or keep them from advancing in their careers. Moreover, even without regard to these tangible effects, the very fact that the discriminatory conduct was so severe or pervasive that it created a work environment abusive to employees because of their race, gender, religion, or national origin offends Title VII's broad rule of workplace equality.[24]

In summing up its reaffirmation of the *Meritor* standard in *Harris*, the Court opined that "this standard . . . takes a middle path between making actionable any conduct that is merely offensive and requiring the conduct to cause a tangible psychological injury."[25] If the workplace "is permeated with discriminatory intimidation, ridicule, and insult that [are] sufficiently severe or pervasive to alter the conditions of the victim's employment and create an abusive working environment,"[26] then Title VII has been violated.

The questions that follow a determination of sexual harassment are: What is the employer's liability for the actions of its employees? Is the employer automatically liable, or does it have to have constructive knowledge of the harassment to which it did not respond prior to assuming liability? Under what circumstances may the employer offer an affirmative defense?

Employer Liability

The organization for which the offending supervisor works can be held accountable if no action is taken to discourage sexual harassment, even if the employer has no constructive knowledge of the harassment. In *Burlington Industries, Inc. v. Ellerth*,[27] the Supreme Court determined a single test of employer liability for harassment by supervisors under Title VII, opining that even where the employee suffered no tangible retaliation in employment opportunity or benefit, an employer has vicarious liability for a hostile environment created by the severe or pervasive conduct of a supervisor.

Ellerth was a salesperson for Burlington Industries, but she quit her job after fifteen months. She alleged she had been sexually harassed by one of her supervisors. Ellerth suffered no adverse employment consequences a result of rejecting her supervisor's sexual advances, but she claimed the hostile work environment forced her constructive discharge. The Court ruled that "[a]n employer is subject to vicarious liability to a victimized employee for an actionable hostile environment created by a supervisor with immediate (or successively higher) authority over the employee."[28]

In a companion case to *Burlington Industries,* the Court determined that employers should anticipate the potential for sexual harassment.[29] Beach lifeguard Faragher resigned her position with the City of Boca Raton and brought suit, claiming that her two supervisors "had created a 'sexually hostile atmosphere' at work by repeatedly subjecting Faragher and other female lifeguards to 'uninvited and offensive touching,' by making lewd remarks, and by speaking of women in offensive terms."[30]

A lower court ruled that the city did not have vicarious liability because it did not have actual or constructive knowledge of the supervisors' inappropriate behavior. The Supreme Court disagreed, noting that sexual harassment is "one of the normal risks of doing business" and that an employer "can reasonably anticipate the possibility of sexual harassment occurring in the workplace."[31] However, the Supreme Court went further to offer circumstances under which an employer may assert an affirmative defense to counter charges of vicarious liability, but it may do so only in instances in which there was no adverse employment action.

There are two components to an affirmative defense. It must comprise "a preponderance of evidence . . . that (a) the employer exercised reasonable care to prevent and correct promptly any sexually harassing behavior and (b) that the plaintiff employee unreasonably failed to take advantage of any preventive or corrective opportunities provided by the employer or to avoid harm otherwise."[32]

Burlington Industries had a policy against sexual harassment with guidelines for submitting a complaint, but Ellerth did not avail herself of these procedures. In fact, she admitted she did not inform her immediate supervisor because he would have been obligated to report the incidents. Noting these circumstances in its remand to the lower court, the Supreme Court held that Burlington was subject to vicarious liability for the supervisor's actions, but that it should have the opportunity to offer an affirmative defense to its liability.

The City of Boca Raton also had a sexual harassment policy, yet information provided to the Court indicated that the city did not distribute its policy among the beach employees, it did not provide adequate oversight of its supervisors' conduct, and it did not provide any assurances in its policy that the offending supervisors could be bypassed in registering complaints. The Court held that the city "could not be found to have exercised reasonable care to prevent the supervisors' harassing behavior"[33] and, therefore, questioned the city's ability to offer an affirmative defense. The City of Boca Raton lost the opportunity to establish an affirmative defense partially because "it officially made no attempt to keep track of the conduct of [its] supervisors."[34]

In *Vance v. Ball State University*,[35] the Supreme Court reaffirmed the definition of "supervisor" under Title VII that it had adopted in *Burlington Industries, Inc.* and *Faragher. Vance* was about racial discrimination, but the definition of supervisor is applicable to all forms of discrimination and liability under Title VII. Vance, an African American woman, alleged that her employer, Ball State University, was vicariously liable for the racially hostile work environment created by her coworker. Vance argued that her coworker was her immediate supervisor, although the coworker had no authority to take any employment action against Vance. The Court disagreed, stating that "an employee is a 'supervisor' for purposes of vicarious liability under Title VII if he or she is empowered by the employer to take tangible employment actions against the victim.[36]

The early distinction between quid pro quo and hostile environment harassment was modified by the Supreme Court and by updated EEOC guidelines with regard to employer liability. The modification reflects the Supreme Court's creation of a single test (the existence of severe and pervasive conduct) for an employer's vicarious liability and whether an employer will have an opportunity to raise a defense (when there is no evidence of adverse effect on employment) to an ascribed vicarious liability. It is now more accurate to distinguish between "harassment *that results in a tangible employment action* [emphasis added] and harassment that creates a hostile work environment, since that difference determines whether the employer can raise the affirmative defense to vicarious liability."[37]

The Court has continued to make a point of distinguishing between severe and pervasive conduct and the occasional isolated remark. In *Clark County School District* v. *Breeden,* the Court ruled that a single comment during a review of job applicant profiles did not constitute sexual harassment.[38] The Court further provided guidance to lower courts in weighing the nature and degree of harassment.

> [D]etermine whether an environment is sufficiently hostile or abusive by "looking at all the circumstances," including the "frequency of the discriminatory conduct; its severity; whether it is physically threatening or humiliating, or a mere offensive utterance; and whether it unreasonably interferes with an employee's work performance."[39]

The substantive antidiscrimination clause of Title VII is not the only protection afforded to victims of sexual harassment. They are also protected from retaliation when they attempt to exercise their rights to be free from harassment.

Antiretaliation under Title VII

In 2006 the Supreme Court addressed sexual harassment with regard to the antiretaliation provision of the Civil Rights Act of 1964.[40] The Civil Right Act does not specifically refer to "retaliation" as discrimination, but the Supreme Court has interpreted the statute to include retaliation as a form of discrimination. The statue forbids "'discriminat[ion] against' an employee (or job applicant) because he has 'opposed' a practice that Title VII forbids or has 'made a charge, testified, assisted, or participated in' a Title VII 'investigation, proceeding, or hearing.'"[41] This clause is in addition to the general antidiscrimination language of the Civil Rights Act of 1964, which prohibits employment discrimination based on race, color, religion, sex, or national origin.[42]

To successfully advance a retaliation claim, the plaintiff must establish a prima facie case by showing that "(1) [the plaintiff] engaged in protected opposition to discrimination, (2) a reasonable employee would have found the challenged action to be materially adverse, and (3) a causal connection existed between the protected activity and the challenged action."[43]

To hold an employer vicariously liable for the actions of a harassing employee, the plaintiff must show that she suffered retaliation in the form of a material adverse employment action. In the absence of such a showing, then the employer may offer an affirmative defense. For instance, in a 1999 education case, *Scrivner v. Socorro Independent School District*,[44] the plaintiff, an elementary school teacher, alleged that she was sexually harassed by her principal, Cardenas, and suffered job retaliation. She sued the school district for vicarious liability. The school district conceded that a hostile work environment was created by Cardenas's behavior. However, SISD was allowed to offer an affirmative defense because Scrivner could not substantiate her claim she suffered a tangible adverse effect in her employment.

The facts of the case indicate that SISD received an anonymous letter in 1994 complaining about Cardenas's harassing behavior. In response, the district launched an investigation during which Scrivner was interviewed, along with sixty-three other faculty and staff. Although she later detailed incidents in which Cardenas harassed her, she denied in the interview that his behavior was harassing or vulgar. Based on its investigation, SISD found no tangible evidence of sexual harassment, but it warned Cardenas to refrain from making unprofessional "[j]okes, innuendoes, and pointed comments."[45]

Frustrated that Cardenas's behavior worsened after the investigation, Scrivner filed a formal complaint with the district against Cardenas in 1996, claiming that he had called her a lesbian, among other sexually harassing behaviors. The district again promptly initiated and published the results of an investigation, concluding that the principal's behavior created a hostile environment. Cardenas was removed from his position, and he soon resigned from the district.

In its affirmative defense to vicarious liability, the district was able to demonstrate that it had promulgated an antidiscrimination policy, that it had responded reasonably and vigorously to the two harassment complaints filed against Cardenas, and that Scrivner had "unreasonably failed to take advantage of any preventive or corrective opportunities provided by [SISD] or to avoid harm otherwise."[46] As a result, the Fifth Circuit Court of Appeals upheld the lower court's summary judgment for the defendant district.

In *Burlington Northern & Santa Fe Railway Company v. White*, White, the only female maintenance worker in her department, filed suit after suffering retaliation by the railway company for filing complaints alleging sexual harassment by her immediate supervisor.[47] White was originally hired as a track laborer, which involved "removing and replacing track components, transporting track material, cutting brush, and clearing litter and cargo spillage from the right-of-way."[48] When a position came open, based on her previous experience, she was given the position of forklift operator. However, after filing a complaint of sexual discrimination against her immediate supervisor, she was reassigned to track laborer again. At the time, she was told it was because her male coworkers were complaining that a "'more senior man' should have the 'less arduous and cleaner job' of forklift operator."[49] In another instance, she was charged with insubordination and suspended without pay.[50] White requested a review under the company's internal grievance procedures, during which the company determined that she had not been insubordinate. She was reinstated with back pay for the thirty-seven days she was suspended.

After exhausting administrative remedies, White filed a Title VII complaint, alleging that she had been discriminated against because of her sex and that she had suffered retaliation for exercising her right to pursue relief under Title VII. In terms of her retaliation claim, she successfully argued that the change in jobs and the suspension without pay were materially adverse, "which in this context means it will might have 'dissuaded a reasonable worker from making or supporting a charge of discrimination.'"[51]

In upholding the lower courts' rulings in favor of White, the Supreme Court opined that the antiretaliation clause differed from the general provisions of the antidiscrimination clause in that

The antidiscrimination provision seeks a workplace where individuals are not discriminated against because of their status, while the antiretaliation provision seeks to prevent an employer from interfering with an employee's efforts to secure or advance enforcement of the act's basic guarantees.[52]

In a 2015 education case, *Tugmon v. Independent School District #32 of Mayes County, Oklahoma*,[53] a former female high school math teacher, who also held positions as director of transportation and as a bus driver, filed Title VII action against the school district alleging that the high school principal, Hukill, and the district superintendent, Scholfield, retaliated against her when she reported to a school board member that Hukill had sent inappropriate emails to a female janitor. Tugmon also provided the board member with newspaper articles that suggested Hukill had resigned from other schools under suspicious conditions. Following this, Hukill's wife called and threatened her, which she reported to another school board member, who directed her to talk with the Scholfield. She met with Scholfield and shared with him what had transpired, including the text messages to the janitor. Starting the very next day after her meeting with Schofield, Tugmon started receiving written notices from Scholfield, including an Admonishment and Plan for Improvement, which stated that she could lose her job despite having received "exceeds expectation" on her teacher evaluation that preceded her reporting Hukill to Scholfield. Scholfield never took any action against Hukill for the texts to the janitor.

Tugmon was told that she was given the Admonishment and Plan for Improvement because she failed to communicate with a parent as directed by Hukill. However, she provided substantial evidence of her communications with the parent. She also reported that she was subjected to constant retaliation, including a false accusation of inappropriately touching a student, reprimands for minor problems, and being denied personal leave, even though she had followed policy in requesting the leave and in having her class covered.[54]

Citing the Tenth Circuit,[55] the federal district court in *Tugmon* advised that "the plaintiff's burden at the prima facie stage requires only a 'small amount of proof necessary to create an inference' of retaliation, by a preponderance of the evidence, and the burden is 'not onerous.'"[56] First, the court concluded that Tugmon had engaged in a protected activity, a fact that the school district did not dispute. Second, Tugmon submitted sufficient evidence that she had suffered adverse actions by Hukill. Citing *Burlington*, the court stated that:

> Title VII's retaliation provision "is not limited to discriminatory actions that affect the terms and conditions of employment." Rather, "a plaintiff must show that a reasonable employee would have found the challenged action materially adverse," such that a reasonable worker might have been dissuaded from engaging in protected activity. This is so because the retaliation provision aims to deter victims of discrimination from complaining to the EEOC, the courts, and their employers. The standard is stated "in general terms because the significance of any given act of retaliation will often depend upon the particular circumstances."[57]

Lastly, although the school district presented "legitimate, non-retaliatory reasons" for the supposedly adverse actions, such as the admonishment and improvement plan, the court determined that "there [was] a genuine dispute of material fact as to whether the employer's proffered reason for the challenged action is pretextual—i.e., unworthy of belief."[58]

> Based upon the very short time frame [temporal proximity] between her report to Schofield of Hukill's inappropriate text messages and the commencement of a string of negative consequences for plaintiff, Tugmon has established the prima facie element of causal connection between her report and the fallout that followed.[59]

Inasmuch as Tugmon met the three elements required for a prima facie case, the court denied the defendant school district's motion for summary judgment on the Title VII retaliation claim.

White and Tugmon, in their respective cases, were able to convince the courts that the retaliation they suffered was a result of exercising their rights to pursue relief for prohibited discrimination under Title VII. To accomplish that, the plaintiffs had to demonstrate that they suffered adverse employment actions because they had filed complaints about the offending workplace discrimination. The Supreme Court refers to this as the "but-for" cause for retaliatory actions by the employer.[60] In other words, the employers took prohibited employment action in response to the plaintiffs' claims of workplace discrimination.

Title IX

Title IX of the Education Amendments of 1972 also addresses sex discrimination and sexual harassment. Title IX's sexual harassment prohibition is not as clear as in Title VII. Title IX specifies that "No person in the United States shall on the basis of sex, be excluded from participation in, be denied the benefits of or be subjected to discrimination under any education program or activity receiving federal financial assistance."[61] Since Title IX was patterned after Title VI of the Civil Rights Act of 1964 and covers students in educational institutions, some courts initially ruled that Title IX does not cover school employees. In 1982, however, the Supreme Court stated that "while section 901(a) does not expressly include [or exclude] employees within its scope or exclude them, its broad directive that 'no person' may be discriminated against on the basis of gender . . . includes employees as well as students."[62]

The Office of Civil Rights (OCR) of the United States Department of Education (DOE) is the primary administrative agency charged with enforcing Title IX. The Department of Health and Human Services (HHS) also has some authority over Title IX for those programs under its jurisdiction. Both DOE and HHS have promulgated identical regulations for Title IX. Both offices have Offices of Civil Rights for enforcement.[63]

The debate over whether Title IX covers sexual harassment was settled by the Supreme Court in 1992. In *Franklin v. Gwinnell County Public School*, the Court ruled that a damage remedy is available for a sexual harassment action brought to enforce Title IX.[64] Although this case did not involve a complaint by an employee, the judicial standard is applicable all the same. Enforceability is available through an implied right of action.

In *Franklin,* a female student had been subjected to continual sexual harassment from a high school coach/teacher. School officials, after becoming aware of the harassment, discouraged the student from pressing charges against the teacher. Subsequently, the teacher resigned on the condition that all matters relating to him be dropped. The school agreed and closed the investigation. The district court dismissed the student's complaint, ruling that

Title IX did not provide for damages. The Eleventh Circuit Court of Appeals agreed; however, the Supreme Court did not.

> The assertion that Title IX remedies should . . . be limited to back pay and prospective relief diverges from this court's traditional approach to deciding what remedies are available for violations of a federal right. Both suggested remedies are equitable in nature, and it is axiomatic that a court should determine the adequacy of damages of law before resorting to equitable relief. Moreover, both suggested remedies are clearly inadequate in that they would provide Franklin no relief: back pay because she was a student when the alleged discrimination occurred, and prospective relief because she no longer attends school in respondent system and Hill no longer teaches there.[65]

Institutional liability under Title IX was addressed in an earlier case, *Lipsett v. University of Puerto Rico.*[66] The First Circuit Court of Appeals stated that in a Title IX case an educational institution is absolutely liable for quid pro quo sexual harassment and for discriminatory discharge regardless of whether it knew, should have known, or approved of the actions of the supervisor involved.

The educational institution is liable also for hostile environment sexual harassment unless it can demonstrate that appropriate steps were taken to remedy the hostile environment. Among specific behaviors (unwanted and sexual in nature) that constitute a hostile environment created by sexual harassment are touching, verbal comments, sexual name calling, spreading sexual rumors, gestures, jokes/cartoons/pictures, an overly personal conversation, cornering/blocking movements, pulling at clothes, attempted rape, and rape.[67] School districts must have a sexual harassment policy and grievance procedure, or they are in violation of Title IX.[68]

In 2005, in *Jackson v. Birmingham Board of Education,* the Supreme Court ruled that Title IX also included a right to assert a retaliation claim.[69] A girls' basketball coach at a public high school complained that girls did not receive equal funding or equal access to facilities or equipment. After he filed complaints, he started receiving negative work evaluations and was removed as the girls' coach. Although Title IX does not mention retaliation, it implies a right to assert a retaliation claim. As explained previously, Title VII gives expressed authority to do so.

While the Supreme Court has decided that Title IX protection extends to employees as well as students, litigation for sexual harassment under Title IX has remained primarily the domain for student complaints. There is no substantial body of Title IX claims brought by school employees on which federal courts have ruled.[70] The majority of school employee cases are litigated under Title VII.

Equal Protection

Another legal avenue open to public employees in pursuit of relief from sexual harassment is the Equal Protection Clause of the Fourteenth Amendment. This strategy was first asserted in *Bohen v. City of East Chicago*, which was adjudicated by the Seventh Circuit Court of Appeals.[71] Originally, the plaintiff female employee sued on the basis of Title VII and equal protection claims. She alleged that she was fired in retaliation for filing grievances with the EEOC against male firefighters for sexual harassment. The federal district court ruled that her firing was for just cause and not in retaliation, and therefore her Title VII claim was denied.[72] It also ruled that sexual harassment was not actionable under the equal protection clause.

While agreeing with the lower court on the Title VII ruling, the Seventh Circuit departed from the lower court on the issue of her Fourteenth Amendment claim. It opined that the Equal Protection Clause contains a "'federal constitutional right to be free from gender discrimination' that does not 'serve important governmental objectives' and is not 'substantially related to those objectives.'"[73] It further observed that "forcing women and not men to work in an environment of sexual harassment is no different than forcing women to work in a dirtier or more hazardous environment than men simply because they are women. Such unjustified unequal treatment is exactly the type of behavior prohibited by the equal protection clause."[74]

To be successful in an equal protection claim of sexual harassment, the plaintiff must show that the discrimination was intentional.[75] The plaintiff's claim must demonstrate that the sexual harassment was "inten[ded] to discriminate because of her status as a female and not 'because of' characteristics of her gender which are personal to her."[76] This discrimination may be shown by a single event, but it is unlikely that one event will constitute denial of equal protection.

Overview of the Legal Issues

Despite the clarity of the legal language that prohibits such discrimination, sexual harassment is not easily defined and its incidence is difficult to measure. It may range from verbal innuendo to an overt act, and the definition must be broad enough to encompass a range of behaviors. According to the EEOC,

> Harassment can include "sexual harassment" or unwelcome sexual advances, requests for sexual favors, and other verbal or physical harassment of a sexual nature. Harassment does not have to be of a sexual nature, however, and can include offensive remarks about a person's sex. For example, it is illegal to harass a woman by making offensive comments about women in general. Both victim and the harasser can be either a woman or a man, and the victim and harasser can be the same sex. Although the law doesn't prohibit simple teasing, offhand comments, or isolated

incidents that are not very serious, harassment is illegal when it is so frequent or severe that it creates a hostile or offensive work environment or when it results in an adverse employment decision (such as the victim being fired or demoted). The harasser can be the victim's supervisor, a supervisor in another area, a co-worker, or someone who is not an employee of the employer, such as a client or customer.[77]

Although the overwhelming majority of cases involve female workers being harassed by male colleagues or supervisors, there has been a gradual but steady rise in the number of charges filed by men with the EEOC. In FY 1997, 11.60% of the charges were filed by men; the percent increased to 17.1% by FY 2015.[78] Speculation as to why there is a rise in the percent of males alleging sexual discrimination includes an increase in the number of female supervisors in the workplace, U.S. Supreme Court decisions identifying same-sex sexual harassment as protected under Title VII, and publicized settlements, such as the LensCrafter case.[79]

Same-sex harassment was addressed by the U.S. Supreme Court in *Oncale v. Sundowner Offshore Services, Inc.*, in which the Court ruled that both males and females enjoy protection from sexual discrimination under Title VII, including protection from same-sex harassment.[80] In *Oncale*, the Court identified three examples of actionable same-sex sexual harassment: (1) if the harasser is homosexual; (2) if a "female victim is harassed in such sex-specific and derogatory terms by another woman as to make it clear that the harasser is motivated by general hostility to the presence of women in the workplace";[81] and (3) if the victim compares her or his treatment to that of the opposite sex, "offer[ing] direct comparative evidence about how the alleged harasser treated members of both sexes in a mixed-sex workplace."[82] The Court noted:

> We see no justification in the statutory language or our precedents for a categorical rule excluding same-sex harassment claims from the coverage of Title VII. As some courts have observed, male-on-male sexual harassment in the workplace was assuredly not the principal evil Congress was concerned with when it enacted Title VII. But statutory prohibitions often go beyond the principal evil to cover reasonably comparable evils, and it is ultimately the provisions of our laws rather than the principal concerns of our legislators by which we are governed. Title VII prohibits "discriminat[ion] ... because of ... sex" in the "terms" or "conditions" of employment. Our holding that this includes sexual harassment must extend to sexual harassment of any kind that meets the statutory requirements.[83]

Sexual orientation and gender identity have gained recognition by the EEOC, if not *in toto* by the courts, as bases for sexual discrimination and harassment. The Commission, in its 2012 Strategic Enforcement Plan, identified "coverage of lesbian, gay, bisexual and transgender individuals under Title VII's sex discrimination provisions, as they may apply" as a top priority.[84] Although federal courts have declined to extend coverage to LGBT employees under Title VII,[85] the EEOC has pressed forward and filed several lawsuits. Among those successfully negotiated out of court is *EEOC v. Pallet Companies d/b/a IFCO Systems NA, Inc.*[86] Yolanda Boone alleged that she suffered an adverse employment action when the company fired her for complaining about harassment "because of her sexual orientation and/or her nonconformity with the employer's gender-based expectations, preferences, or stereotypes in violation of Title VII."[87] She notified management and called the company's employee complaint hotline, after which she was terminated. IFCO agreed to pay Boone $182,200 and $20,000 to the Human Rights Campaign Foundation, as well as "to retain an expert on sexual orientation, gender identity, and transgender training to assist in developing a training program for IFOC's staff on LGBT workplace issues."[88]

In another case, Lakeland Eye Clinic, P.A. agreed to settle after the EEOC filed a lawsuit charging the company illegally fired an employee "because she is transgender, because she was transitioning from male to female, and/or because she did not conform to the employer's gender-based expectations, preferences, or stereotypes in violation of Title VII."[89] According to the complaint, "the defendant's employee had performed her duties satisfactorily throughout her employment. However, after she began to present as a woman and informed the clinic she was transgender, Lakeland fired her."[90] The company agreed to a two-year consent decree and $150,000 in damages, among other relief.

One of the recurring themes in LGBT-related cases under Title VII is that of gender stereotyping. Gender stereotyping is when employers or coworkers have behavioral expectations of, or ascribe characteristics to, employees or colleagues that conform to social norms linked to their biological sex. Gender stereotyping has been cited as a factor in creating a hostile work environment, and thereby in establishing a basis for alleged sexual harassment.

The Supreme Court addressed gender stereotyping as unlawful sexual discrimination under Title VII in *Price Waterhouse v. Hopkins.*[91] Hopkins, a female senior manager at Price Waterhouse, argued in court that she was denied promotion to partner because she did not adequately conform to some of the male partners' notions of femininity. She was described as "macho" and was advised "to take a course at charm school."[92] The most condemning evidence came from the man who explained to her why her promotion was on hold for a year and advised her to "walk more femininely, talk more femininely, dress more femininely, wear make-up, have her hair styled, and wear jewelry."[93] Writing for the majority, Justice Brennan astutely noted that it does not "require expertise in psychology to know that, if an employee's flawed 'interpersonal skills' can be corrected by a soft-hued suit or a new shade of lipstick, perhaps it is the employee's sex and not her interpersonal skills that has drawn the criticism."[94] In speaking to the illegality of sex stereotyping, Brennan observed that

> [W]e are beyond the day when an employer could evaluate employees by assuming or insisting that they matched the stereotype associated with their group, for "'[i]n forbidding employers to discriminate against individuals because of their sex, Congress intended to strike at the entire spectrum of disparate treatment of men and women resulting from sex stereotypes."[95]

Price Waterhouse introduced gender stereotyping as an acceptable argument for accusations of sexual discrimination. It rebutted traditional notions of male and female, which were based more on social norms and less on biology.

Gender stereotyping is not limited to male expectations of females. In reinstating a jury award to the plaintiff, the Firth Circuit Court of Appeals ruled in *EEOC v. Boh Brothers Construction Company* that same-sex harassment based on gender stereotyping was a violation of Title VII.[96] In this instance, Woods, an iron worker and structural welder, alleged that he was subjected to ongoing sexual harassment by his supervisor, Wolfe. For instance, Wolfe used various derogatory sexual terms to call attention to Woods, sometimes several times a day. He would also simulate sexual acts whenever Woods was bent over while working. Wolfe also frequently exposed himself to Woods.[97]

When interviewed by EEOC, Wolf indicated that he started teasing Woods when Woods told his coworkers that he used Wet Ones instead of toilet paper. He indicated that is not the sort of detail that you tell "a bunch of rough iron workers."[98] Woods was not Wolfe's idea of a manly man.

The jury had awarded Woods $201,000 in compensatory damages and $250,000 in punitive damages.[99] (The district court reduced the compensatory damages to $50,000 to align with a $300,000 statutory cap on the total monetary.)[100] In deciding that the jury's liability finding was substantiated by the evidence, the Fifth Circuit en banc noted:

> Viewing the record as a whole, a jury could view Wolfe's behavior as an attempt to denigrate Woods because—at least in Wolfe's view—Woods fell outside of Wolfe's manly-man stereotype. Thus, we cannot say that no reasonable juror could have found that Woods suffered harassment because of his sex.
> . . . Wolfe hurled raw sex-based epithets uniquely at Woods two-to-three times a day, almost every day, for months on end.
> . . . Accordingly, we conclude that there was sufficient evidence for a reasonable juror to conclude that Wolfe's harassment of Woods was severe or pervasive.[101]

However, the court did not sustain the jury's punitive damage award, noting that the evidence did not support a finding that the Boh Brothers acted "with malice or with reckless indifference to the federally protected rights of an aggrieved individual."[102] The Fifth Circuit also noted that overturning the punitive award would have an effect on the compensatory award that the district court had reduced to $50,000 because of the statutory limit.[103] The court remanded to the district court to further consider whether the evidence was sufficient to support the full compensatory damages award of $201,000.[104]

The Fifth Circuit did uphold the jury's award of the injunction that the EEOC sought on grounds of its hostile environment allegation on behalf of Woods.[105] Boh Brothers failed to convince the court that there would be no future violations of Title VII. The court noted that "injunctive relief is mandatory in the wake of a Title VII violation 'absent clear and convincing proof of no reasonable probability of further noncompliance with the law.'"[106]

Most courts do not agree with the EEOC regarding acceptable grounds for allegations of sexual harassment when sexual orientation is the basis of the harassment.[107] Federal courts have refused to extend Title VII protections to individuals who claim they have been sexually harassed because they are gay or lesbian, citing Congress' intended meaning of the word "sex" and years of failed efforts by Congress to enact legislation that would specifically extend protection based on sexual orientation. For instance, in *Simonton v. Runyon*, the plaintiff, an employee of the U.S. Postal Service, sued under Title VII, claiming he suffered "abuse and harassment . . . by reason of his sexual orientation."[108] In rejecting his claim, the Second Circuit acknowledged the abuse the plaintiff suffered, but denied him relief under Title VII, stating:

> There can be no doubt that the conduct allegedly engaged in by Simonton's co-workers is morally reprehensible whenever and in whatever context it occurs, particularly in the modern workplace. Nevertheless, as the First Circuit recently explained in a similar context, "we are called upon here to construe a statute as glossed by the Supreme Court, not to make a moral judgment." When interpreting a statute, the role of a court is limited to discerning and adhering to legislative meaning. The law is well-settled in this circuit and in all others to have reached the question that Simonton has no cause of action under Title VII because Title VII does not prohibit harassment or discrimination because of sexual orientation.[109]

Although the Second Circuit refused to construe Title VII to include protection against discrimination based on sexual orientation, it did comment on Simonton's second argument, which was that he was harassed because he did not conform to a gender stereotype.

> Simonton next relies on *Price Waterhouse v. Hopkins* to argue that the abuse he suffered was discrimination based on sexual stereotypes, which may be cognizable as discrimination based on sex. We find this argument more substantial than Simonton's previous two arguments, but not sufficiently pled in this case. We express no opinion as to how this issue would be decided in a future case in which it is squarely presented and sufficiently pled.[110]

Some courts have ruled in favor of gay and lesbian plaintiffs when their complaints are based on gender stereotyping. For instance, Peter Terveer sued his employer, Billington (Librarian for the Library of Congress), arguing he was subjected to a hostile work environment based on his sexual orientation.[111] Due to his religious beliefs, Mech, Terveer's direct supervisor, objected to Terveer's homosexuality. Once Mech learned that Terveer was gay, he emailed him "photographs of assault weapons along with the tagline 'Diversity: Let's Celebrate It.'"[112] Mech also took every opportunity to deliver "religious lectures at the beginning of almost every work-related conversation to the point where it became clear that Mech was targeting [Plaintiff] by imposing his conservative Catholic beliefs on [Plaintiff] throughout the workday."[113] He also began receiving negative performance evaluations from Mech and was denied grade increases in his salary.

Terveer notified Mech's supervisor, Billington, of the harassment, but he was told by Billington that employees have no rights. The stress of the hostile work environment created health problems for Terveer, for which he took sick leave and then leave without pay. He was then notified that he would not be granted any further leave without pay and would be terminated for failure to return to work. He alleged in his suit that he was constructively fired because he could not return to work where he was constantly facing harassment.

In denying the defendant's motion to dismiss Terveer's sex discrimination claim under Title VII, the court accepted the plaintiff's argument that he was discriminated against because his homosexuality did not conform to his supervisor's ideas about being a man. The court stated:

> Here, Plaintiff has alleged that he is "a homosexual male whose sexual orientation is not consistent with the Defendant's perception of acceptable gender roles," that his "status as a homosexual male did not conform to the Defendant's gender stereotypes associated with men under Mech's supervision or at the LOC," and that "his orientation as homosexual had removed him from Mech's preconceived definition of male." As Plaintiff has alleged that Defendant denied him promotions and created a hostile work environment because of Plaintiff's nonconformity with male sex stereotypes, Plaintiff has met his burden of setting forth "a short and plain statement of the claim showing that the pleader is entitled to relief."[114]

Terveer v. Billington and *Simonton v. Runyon* exemplify the challenges that homosexuals face when they perceive they are being discriminated against in the workplace. Terveer's success in court was based on the Supreme Court's ruling in *Price Waterhouse,* in which the Court opined that sexual stereotyping is a form of sexual discrimination under Title VII.[115] Terveer clearly demonstrated that he suffered same-sex discrimination because he did not conform to his supervisor's notion of what is to be a man. Simonton was unsuccessful because he argued that he was discriminated against because of his sexual orientation, which federal courts have determined is not protected under Title VII.[116]

Discrimination based on transgender/transsexual identity under Title VII has been adjudicated in five federal Circuit Courts of Appeal since the *Price Waterhouse* decision.[117] In view of that decision, the First, Sixth, Ninth, and Eleventh Circuit courts concluded that the "because of sex" language of Title VII does offer discrimination protection for transgender/transsexual individuals. They determined that discrimination against transgender/transsexual individuals is based on gender nonconformity or sex stereotyping. As the Eleventh Circuit observed:

> A person is defined as transgender precisely because of the perception that his or her behavior transgresses gender stereotypes. "The very acts that define transgender people as transgender are those that contradict stereotypes of gender-appropriate appearance and behavior." There is thus a congruence between discriminating against transgender and transsexual individuals and discrimination on the basis of gender-based behavioral norms.[118]

The Tenth Circuit has not embraced this rationale and instead has upheld the pre-*Price Waterhouse* principle that "the plain meaning of 'sex' encompasses [no]thing more than male and female."[119] It determined that "transsexuals may not claim protection under Title VII from discrimination based solely on their status as a transsexual."[120]

The Seventh and Eighth Circuits have not adjudicated a claim regarding a transgender plaintiff since their pre-*Price Waterhouse* decisions. In *Ulane v. Eastern Airlines, Inc. (Ulane II)*, the Seventh Circuit ruled that "Congress never considered nor intended that this . . . legislation apply to anything other than the traditional concept of sex."[121] In *Sommers v. Budget Marketing, Inc.*, the Eighth Circuit similarly concluded that Title VII did not offer protection against discrimination for transgender individuals.[122]

A federal district court in Connecticut, which is in the Second Circuit Court's jurisdiction, recently ruled in *Fabian v. Hospital of Central Connecticut* that transgender individuals are protected against workplace sexual discrimination under Title VII.[123]

While the EEOC has moved forward aggressively to push for equal protection for LGBT employees under Title VII, Congress has not come to a consensus on this issue. Numerous LGBT and other civil rights groups have been lobbying Congress to address this gap in Title VII protections for several decades. Congress first considered an amendment to the Civil Rights Act of 1964 to add the language "affectional or sexual preference" in 1975, but it failed to pass.[124] The Employment Non-Discrimination Act (ENDA) was crafted to protect individuals from discrimination based on sexual orientation and gender identity, but has failed to pass although it has been introduced in multiple sessions of Congress.[125] The most recent attempt was in 2014 with the introduction of Senate Bill 815.[126] The Senate defeated a Republican filibuster and passed the legislation by a vote of 64-32, but House Speaker Boehner indicated that existing law already provides protection and that he had no intention of bringing it up for a vote in the House of Representatives.[127] As a result, the legislation died.

While the EEOC, Congress, and the courts wrangle over the meaning of the word "sex," there has been little change in how the courts evaluate allegations of sexual discrimination and harassment, retaliation, and liability under Title VII, Title IX of the Education Amendments of 1972, and the Fourteenth Amendment's Equal Protection Clause. It will be up to Congress to determine whether to extend protection against discrimination based on sexual orientation.

Recommendations for Practice

Standards for sexual harassment in the workplace are the same for both public and private employers. As evinced in *Ellerth* and *Faragher,* the employer may have vicarious liability for severe or pervasive conduct of employees in supervisory positions, but may offer an affirmative defense if the plaintiff employee has suffered no tangible adverse effect on his or her employment. An important component of the affirmative defense is demonstrating the existence and dissemination of an anti-sexual harassment policy. With this in mind, the following recommendations are made. The local school board should:

1. Develop, review, and disseminate a strong workplace policy prohibiting sexual harassment. Preferably there should be a mechanism for the faculty and staff to contribute to and ultimately endorse the policy, and to help monitor it.
    a. The policy should contain a statement explaining why it is important to prevent sexual harassment.
    b. Included in this policy should be a clear description or explanation of the prohibited behaviors. Generally speaking, these behaviors are unwarranted or unwanted sexual attention from peers, subordinates, supervisors, customers, clients, or anyone the employee must interact with in order to fulfill the duties of the job or school, where the employee's responses might be restrained by fear of reprisals. The range of behaviors includes but is not limited to leering, pinching, unnecessary touching or patting, verbal comments, subtle pressure for sexual activity, rape, and attempted rape.
    c. There should be clear assurances in the policy that an employee who files a harassment complaint or who provides information related to such a complaint will be protected from retaliation. There should also be assurances that to the degree possible, the employer will protect the confidentiality of those who file harassment complaints.

     d.   The policy should outline procedures for filing a complaint and should describe the employer's process for investigating and responding to a complaint. The process should include the following: the timeline for the investigation; suggestions for possible informal resolution of the problem; and assignment of complaint managers who are represented by the employees, are sensitive to the issue, and able to empathize with the victim.[128]

2.   The school board should adopt, publicize, and enforce penalties for violations of the policy.[129] The board should keep written records. However, it should take precautions to protect confidentiality. [130]

3.   The school board should publish results of resolved complaints, but should protect the identity of the individuals involved.[131]

4.   Measures should be taken to facilitate employees' awareness of the EEOC sexual harassment guidelines and alertness to the problem.

     a.   It is advisable that employers conduct periodic training for administrators and others in supervisory positions, teachers, and staff to ensure all employees understand and comply with the policy.

     b.   Orientation programs for new faculty and staff should include discussion of the sexual harassment policy and EEOC guidelines.

5.   The school board should include all policies related to sexual harassment in faculty, staff, and student handbooks.

What the future holds for LGBT employment protections is unclear. But, in light of the U.S. Supreme Court's decision providing marriage equality to same-sex couples and of more accepting attitudes regarding sexual orientation and gender identity nationally, it only seems logical that Employment Non-Discrimination Act (ENDA) or something similar will eventually be enacted. In the meantime, local school boards should be cognizant of evolving legal trends regarding sexual harassment based on sexual orientation and gender identity. The following suggestions are offered to school district authorities who want to be proactive and minimize liability in light of the EEOC's stance on LGBT protections.[132]

1.   Review the district's equal employment opportunity statement and other policies prohibiting discrimination and harassment to ensure those policies include protections based on sexual orientation and gender identity.

2.   All employee and supervisor training should address prohibitions against discrimination and harassment based on sexual orientation and gender identity, with case scenarios specific to those protections.

3. Complaints of harassment based on perceived sexual orientation and gender identity should be taken seriously and investigated in the same manner as other forms of sexual harassment.

4. If evidence indicates that an employee has been discriminated against, appropriate corrective action must be taken.

5. Employers also should be prepared for gender transitions in the workplace.

6. Transitions should be handled on a case-by-case basis, considering the preferences of the transgender employee where possible and, at a minimum, should include discussions with the employee regarding transition issues such as dress code and restroom use, informing coworkers, and informing customers.

7. Employers should approach each case in a way that ensures the transgender employee is treated with dignity and respect.[133]

Endnotes

[1] Paul Farhi, *Former Fox Host Gretchen Carlson settles Sexual Harassment Lawsuit Against Roger Ailes for $20 Million,* Washington Post, September 6, 2016, https://www.washingtonpost.com/lifestyle/style/former-fox-host-gretchen-carlson-settles-sexual-harassment-lawsuit-against-roger-ailes-for-20-million/2016/09/06/f1718310-7434-11e6-be4f-3f42f2e5a49e_story.html

[2] Lisa Rein, *As National Park Service Confronts Sexual Harassment, this Dysfunctional Park Is Exhibit A*, Wash. Post, July 4, 2016, https://www.washingtonpost.com/news/powerpost/wp/2016/07/02/as-national-park-service-confronts-a-sexual-harassment-this-dysfunctional-park-is-exhibit-a/

[3] *Id.*

[4] Tom Jackman, *Fairfax Fire Department Tolerated Sexual Harassment, Federal Jury Rules,* Wash. Post, May 26, 2016, https://www.washingtonpost.com/local/fairfax-fire-department-tolerated-sexual-harassment-federal-jury-rules/2011/05/26/AGDu5JCH_story.html

[5] *See* Peggy Fox, *A Fairfax Firefighter Is Alleging Sexual Harassment in a Lawsuit*, WUSA*9, May 11, 2016, http://www.wusa9.com/news/local/fairfax/fairfax-firefighter-alleges-sexual-harassment-by-fire-captain/185707861; Curt Varone, *Fairfax County Fire Sued Again for Sexual Harassment*, July 19, 2016, http://www.firelawblog.com/2016/07/19/fairfax-county-fire-sued-sexual-harassment/

[6] EEOC Press Release: *LensCrafters Sued by EEOC for Sexual Harassment by Woman against Male Co-Worker*, July 7, 2009, https://www1.eeoc.gov/eeoc/newsroom/release/7-9-09.cfm?renderforprint=1

[7] David Jamieson, *LensCrafters Settles Female-on-Male Sexual Harassment Case*, The Huffington Post, June 20, 2011, http://www.huffingtonpost.com/2011/06/20/lenscrafters-settles-fema_n_880709.html. See also EEOC Press Release: Regal Entertainment Group to Pay $175,000 for Sex Harassment of Man by Female Co-Worker, July 11, 2009, https://www.eeoc.gov/eeoc/newsroom/release/11-9-09a.cfm

[8] Catharine A. MacKinnon, Sexual Harassment of Working Women: A Case of Sex Discrimination (1979).

[9] From testimony of Anita Hill and Clarence Thomas on nationally televised Senate confirmation hearings for United States Supreme Court nominee, Clarence Thomas, October 10-13, 1991.See Maritza I. Reyes, *Professional Women Silenced by Men-Made Norms*, Akron L. Rev. 897 (2015).

10 *See, e.g.,* Price Waterhouse v. Hopkins, 490 U.S. 228, 237 (1989) (concluding that even when an employer illegally discriminates against an employee, the employer may escape liability by providing "clear and convincing evidence" that it would have taken the same action based on lawful reasons.

11 42 U.S.C.A. § 1981a. The Civil Rights Act was amended to include this language in 1991.

12 42 U.S.C. § 2000e-2(a)(I).

13 42 U.S.C. § 1981a.

14 29 C.F.R. § 1604.11(a) (1986).

15 *See* Harris v. Forklift Sys., Inc., 114 S.Ct. 367, 370 (1993).

16 *See* Meritor Sav. Bank, FSB v. Vinson, 106 S.Ct. 2399, 2404-2405 (1986).

17 *Id.*

18 *Id.* at 2406.

19 *Supra*, note 15

20 *Id.* at 369.

21 *Id.*

22 *Id.* at 371.

23 *Id.* at 370.

24 *Id.*

25 *Id.*

26 *Id.*

27 118 S.Ct. 2275 (1998).

28 *Id.* at 2261. *Also see* Pennsylvania State Police v. Suders, 542 U.S. 129, 124 S.Ct. 2342 (2004). In this case, a former female employee resigned, claiming that she was sexually harassed, which created a severe hostile work environment. She argued that the employer should be strictly liable for its supervisors' behavior because her resignation was effectively a constructive discharge and, therefore, an adverse employment action. The defendant employer argued it was not liable because the plaintiff "unreasonable failed" take advantage of its procedures for reporting harassment. The appellate court held that the affirmative defense is never available in constructive discharge cases, but the Supreme Court ruled that there were insufficient facts to determine the extent of official employer action in creating or tolerating a hostile work environment that led to the constructive discharge. It remanded the case for further proceedings.

29 *Supra*, note 27.

30 *Id.* at 2277.

31 *Id.* at 2278.

32 *Id.* at 2279.

33 *Id.*

34 *Id.* at 2279.

35 Vance v. Ball State University, 133 S.Ct. 2434 (2013).

36 *Id.* at 2439.

37 *See* EEOC, *Enforcement Guidance: Vicarious Employer Liability for Unlawful Harassment by Supervisors,* no. 915.002, endnote 7 (June 18, 1999).

38 121 S.Ct. 1508 (2001).

39 Harris v. Forklift Sys., Inc., 114 S. Ct. 367 (1993), *quoted in* Faragher, 118 S.Ct. at 2283.

40 42 U.S.C.A. § 2000e-3(a).

41 Burlington N. & Santa Fe Ry. Company v. White, 126 S. Ct. 2405, 2410 (2006).

42 42 U.S.C.S. § 2000e-2(a).

43 Tugmon v. Independent Sch. Dist. #23 of Mayes Co., OK, 2015 WL 1482524, 3 (2015). See *also* Terveer, note 107, 118-121.

44 Scrivner v. Socorro Indep. Sch. Dist., 169 F.3d 969 (5th Cir. 1999).

45 *Id.* at 970.

46 *Id.* at 971.

47 *Supra*, note 41.

48 *Id.* at 2409.

[49] *Id.*

[50] *Id.*

[51] *Id.* at 2415.

[52] *Id.* at 2407.

[53] *Supra*, note 43.

[54] *Id.* at *2.

[55] Smothers v. Solvay Chem., Inc. 746 F.3d 530, 539 (10th Cir. 2014).

[56] *Supra*, note 43, *3.

[57] *Id.* at *4.

[58] *Id.*

[59] *Id.*

[60] Univ. of Tex. Southwestern Med. Ctr. v. Nassar, 133 S.Ct. 2517 (2013). In this instance, Nassar, who was a faculty member of the medical school and a hospital staff physician, sued, alleging (1) job discrimination based on his ethnicity and religion and (2) retaliation for complaining about the discrimination. The Supreme Court ruled that the causation test for the job discrimination claim differs from the causation test for the retaliation claim. The first Title VII violation, discrimination based on an individual's race, color, religion, sex, and national origin, referred to by the Supreme Court as "status-based discrimination" requires a showing that "the motive to discriminate was one of the employer's motives, even if the employer also had other, lawful motives that were causative in the employer's decision" (at 2522). The second violation, retaliation, requires proof that "the desire to retaliate was the but-for cause of the challenged employment action" (at 2528).

[61] 20 U.S.C. § 1681.

[62] North Haven Bd. of Educ. v. Bell, 102 S. Ct. 1912, 1914 (1982).

[63] 34 C.F.R. Part 106; Title (X Legal Manual, U.S. Department of Justice, Civil Rights Division (2001).

[64] 112 S. Ct. 1028 (1992).

[65] *Id.* at 1030-1031.

[66] 864 F.2d 881 (1st Cir. 1988).

[67] *See* Susan Strauss, *Sexual Harassment in the School: Legal Implications for Principals,* 72 NASSP Bulletin 93 (March, 1988).

[68] *Id.*

[69] Jackson v. Birmingham Bd. of Educ., 125 S.Ct. 1497 (2005).

[70] *See, e.g.,* Singleton v. Chi. Sch. Reform Bd. of Trs. of the City of Chi., 2002 WL 2017082 (N.D. Ill.), (concerning a teacher's claim under Title VII, Title IX, First Amendment, and Equal Protection. Summary judgment was granted to the school board on all counts.

[71] 799 F.2d 1180 (7th Cir. 1986).

[72] Had the plaintiff filed a hostile environment claim instead of a retaliation claim under Title VII, she probably would have been successful. However, the lower court denied her the opportunity to amend her complaint and the appellate court ruled the lower court did not abuse its discretion in doing so.

[73] *Id.* at 1085.

[74] *Id.*

[75] Trautvetter v. Quick, 916 F.2d 1140 (7th Cir. 1990).

[76] *Id.* at 1151.

[77] EEOC, *Sex Discrimination Harassment*, https://www.eeoc.gov/laws/types/sex.cfm.

[78] *See Sexual Harassment Charges: EEOC & FERPAs Combined: FY 1997-FY 2011*, https://www.eeoc.gov/eeoc/statistics/enforcement/ sexual_harassment.cfm and *Charges Alleging Sexual Harassment: FY 2010-FY 2015*, https://www.eeoc.gov/eeoc/statistics/enforcement/sexual_harassment_new.cfm

[79] *See* Jessie Cardinale., Sexual Harassment Complaints by Males on the Rise: 2012 EEOC Enforcement and Litigation Statistics, Outten & Golden, LLP. Blog (April 29, 2013) at http://www.employmentlawblog.info/2013/04/sexual-harassment-complaints-by-males-on-the-rise-2012-eeoc-enforcement-and-litigation-statistics.shtml; The Washington Post, More Men File

Workplace Sexual Harassment Claims, (March 4, 2010) at http://www.washingtontimes.com/news/2010/mar/4/more-men-file-workplace-sexual-harassment-claims/

[80]   118 S.Ct. 998 (1998)

[81]   *Id.* at 1002.

[82]   *Id.*

[83]   *Id.*

[84]   EEOC, *Fact Sheet: Recent EEOC Litigation Regarding Title VII and LGBT-Related Discrimination*, July 8, 2016, https://www.eeoc.gov/eeoc/litigation/selected/lgbt_facts.cfm

[85]   In addressing discrimination against homosexuals, the U.S. Supreme Court observed that "proposals to ban such discrimination under Title VII have repeatedly been rejected by Congress." Lawrence v. Texas, 539 U.S. 558, 602 (2003).

[86]   *Id.* Case No. 1:16-CV-00595 (D. Md.). Settled June 28, 2016.

[87]   *Id.*

[88]   *Id.*

[89]   *Id.* Case No. 8:14-cv-2421 (M.D. Fla.). Settled April 9, 2015.

[90]   *Id.*

[91]   *Supra* note 10.

[92]   *Id.* at 235.

[93]   *Id.*

[94]   *Id.* at 256.

[95]   *Id.* at 251.

[96]   731 F.3d 444 (5th Cir. 2013).

[97]   *Id.* at 449-450.

[98]   *Id.* at 458.

[99]   *Id.* at 469.

[100]   *Id.*

[101]   *Id.* at 459-462.

[102]   *Id.* at 467. *See also* 42 U.S.C. § 1981a(b)(1).

[103]   *Id.* at 469.

[104]   *Id.*

[105]   *Id.* at 470.

[106]   *Id.* at 469-470.

[107]   *See, e.g.,* Schroeder v. Hamilton Sch. Dist., 282 F.3d 946, 951 (7th Cir. 2002) (declaring that "Title VII does not ... provide for a private right of action based on sexual orientation discrimination. As such, to the extent [the plaintiff] seeks to have this court judicially amend Title VII to provide for such a cause of action, we decline to do so. It is wholly inappropriate, as well as constituting a clear violation of the separation of powers, for this court, or any other federal court, to fashion causes of action out of whole cloth, regardless of any perceived public policy benefit."); Rene v. MGM Grand Hotel, 243 F.3d 1206 (9th Cir. 2001) (affirming district court's ruling that Title VII does not apply to discrimination based on sexual orientation); Hively v. Ivy Tech Cmty. College, 2016 U.S. App. LEXIS 13746 (7th Cir. 2016) (declaring that discrimination based on sexual orientation were not cognizable under Title VII); Dingle v. Bimbo Bakeries USA/Entenman's, 624 Fed. Appx. 57 (2d Cir. 2015) (upholding a lower court's decision to dismiss Title VII hostile work environment claim based on plaintiff's perceived sexual orientation). For greater in-depth discussion on the limits of Title VII with regard to sexual orientation, see Jeff Brodin, *Civil Rights Act: New Role of Title VII: Sexual Orientation and Gender Identity*, 51 AZ Attorney, 30 (2014, December); Brian Soucek, *Perceived Homosexuals: Looking Gay Enough for Title VII*, 63 Am. U.L. Rev. 715 (2014); Major Velma Cheri Gay, *50 Years Later . . . Still Interpreting the Meaning of "Because of Sex" within Title VII and Whether It Prohibits Sexual Orientation Discrimination*, 73 A.F. L. Rev. 61 (2015); Sasha Andersen, *That's What He Said: the Office, (Homo)Sexual Harassment, and Falling through the Cracks of Title VII.* 47 Ariz. St. L. J. 961 (2015, Fall).

[108]   232 F.3d 33, 34 (2d Cir. 2000).

[109] *Id.* at 35.

[110] *Id.* at 37.

[111] Terveer v. Billington, 34 F.Supp.3d 100 (D.D.C. 2014).

[112] *Id.* at 106.

[113] *Id.*

[114] *Id.* at 116.

[115] *Supra*, note 10.

[116] *Infra*, note 120.

[117] *See* Schwenk v. Hartford, 204 F.3d 1187 (9th Cir. 2000) (The Schewenk ruling abrogated the Ninth Circuit's pre-*Price Waterhouse* decision, Holloway v. Arthur Andersen & Co., 566 F.2d 659 (9th Cir. 1977), in which it had denied Title VII protection to transsexual individuals); Rosa v. Park West Bank & Trust Co., 214 F.3d 213 (1st Cir. 2000); Smith v. City of Salem, 378 F.3d 566 (6th Cir. 2004); Glenn v. Brumby, 663 F.3d 1312 (11th Cir. 2011); and Etsitty v. Utah Transit Authority, 502 F.3d 1215 (10th Cir. 2007).

[118] Glenn v. Brumby, 663 F.3d 1312, 1316 (11th Cir. 2011), citing Ilona M. Turner, Sex Stereotyping Per Se: Transgender Employees and Title VII, 95 Cal. L. Rev. 561, 563 (2007).

[119] Etsitty v. Utah Transit Authority, 502 F.3d 1215, 1221-1222 (10th Cir. 2007).

[120] *Id.* at 1222.

[121] Ulane v. Eastern Airlines, Inc. ("Ulane II"), 742 F.2d 1081, 1085 (7th Cir. 1984).

[122] Sommers v. Budget Marketing, Inc., 667 F.2d 748 (8th Cir. 1982).

[123] Fabian v. Hospital of Central Connecticut, 172 F.Supp. 3d 509 (D. Conn. 2016).

[124] Civil Rights Amendments Act of 1975, H.R. 166, 94th Cong. (1975). *See* Courtney Joslin, *Protection for Lesbian, Gay, Bisexual, and Transgender Employees under Title VII of the 1964 Civil Rights Act*, Human Rights Magazine (2004, Summer), http://www.americanbar.org/publications/human_rights_magazine_home/human_rights_vol31_2004/ summer2004/ irr_hr_summer04_protectlgbt.html

[125] *Supra*, note 110, Brodin, 30. See also Jennifer S. Hendricks, *Instead of ENDA, a Course Correction for Title VII*, 103 Northwestern U. L. Rev. Colloquy 209 (2008).

[126] (113th Congress).

[127] Sam Stein, *John Boehner Opposes ENDA, Dealing Blow to Bill's Chances*, The Huffington Post, Nov. 4, 2014, http://www.huffingtonpost.com/2013/11/04/john-boehner-enda_n_4212250.html

[128] *Supra*, note 70, at 97.

[129] Nebraska Association of School Boards, *12 Steps to Deal with Sexual Harassment in Schools*, NASB Employee Quarterly, (Summer 1993). Retrieved from http://www.nebr-schoolboards.org/12steps.htm.

[130] *Id.*

[131] *Id.*

[132] *Supra* note 110, Brodin, 37.

[133] *Id.*

Key Words

administrative remedies
adverse employment action
affirmative defense
but-for cause
Civil Rights Act
coach
confidentiality
damages
Department of Health and Human
  Services
Education Amendments of 1972
employer liability
Employment Non-Discrimination
  Act
Equal Employment Opportunity
  Commission (EEOC)
Equal Protection Clause
Fourteenth Amendment
gender identity
gender stereotyping
hostile environment harassment

intentional discrimination
LGBT
Office of Civil Rights (OCR)
prima facie case
quid pro quo harassment
retaliation (also see Antiretaliation)
same-sex harassment
sex discrimination
sexual innuendo
sexual orientation
Title IX of the Education Amendments Act of 1972
Title VII of the Civil Rights Act
training
transgender
transsexual
unwelcomed sexual advances
vicarious liability
workplace discrimination
workplace policy

Section II – Chapter 5

Federal Antidiscrimination Law

John E. Rumel*

Federal and state statutes shield employees from discriminatory treatment when that treatment is unlawfully motivated by the employee's race, color, religion, sex, national origin,[1] age,[2] disability,[3] or illness/medical condition, or the illness/medical condition of close family members.[4] These protections apply to many, if not most, employees at some time during their working lives. For this reason alone, administrators and school board members should become familiar with these provisions, which prohibit decisions to terminate, discharge, demote, or reassign an employee—or not renew an employment contract—based on discriminatory motivation or intent.

This chapter focuses on *federal* antidiscrimination statutes that apply to adverse employment decisions made in the context of K-12 educational institutions, both public and private. Many administrator or school board decisions about the nature of an employee's work might constitute an adverse action,[5] but most often the challenged decision is one that results in the employee's discharge, termination, or nonrenewal. Thus, this chapter will emphasize and discuss cases where terminated employees allege they were subject to adverse employment action because they are members of a protected class or status or they were retaliated against for opposing what they believed was discriminatory treatment against themselves or others.

Proof Structure

Discriminatory Treatment Claims

To prevail on a claim of discriminatory discharge, an employee must produce evidence that the administrative decision maker was motivated by animus or disdain for the employee's protected status. In other words, the employee must persuade the court that the cause of their termination was, in fact, unlawful discrimination or retaliation. Proving or disproving causation can be a sizeable hurdle. For this reason, court opinions and orders in these cases are often fact-intensive and frequently contain pages of factual background information. Moreover, discrimination law has evolved to recognize two primary methods of proving causation: direct evidence claims and indirect evidence claims.[6]

The distinction between direct and indirect claims is the type of proof required. Direct claims involve evidence that makes discrimination self-evident. For example, the statement "I can't possibly recommend your contract be renewed, you godless heathen," would be direct evidence of religious discrimination. Comments such as these suffice to show discriminatory animus when they are (1) related to the protected characteristics, (2) close in time to the adverse decision, (3) made by a person who controls or exerts influence over the decision, and (4) related to the decision at issue.[7] Direct claims have become increasingly rare, probably because employers have learned to avoid overt statements of discrimination.

Indirect claims of discriminatory discharge are more common. As such, school administrators must become familiar with the legal process employees invoke to show that a putatively nondiscriminatory reason is, in actuality, a pretext for discrimination. Indirect claims are evaluated using a burden-shifting analysis made famous in *McDonnell Douglas Corp. v. Green*.[8] Initially, terminated employees must demonstrate that they (1) belong to a protected class, (2) are qualified for the position they had, (3) suffered an adverse employment decision/action, and (4) that, after they were rejected, the position remained open and the employer continued to seek applications from persons of the rejected employee's qualifications.[9] This initial showing constitutes a prima facie case. The Supreme Court has explained that "these acts, if otherwise unexplained, are more likely than not based on the consideration of impermissible factors."[10] Once the plaintiff meets the initial burden, it shifts to the employer to otherwise explain the action with a legitimate, nondiscriminatory reason.[11] If the employer does this, the burden shifts back to the employee, who must then prove that the nondiscriminatory reason is pretextual, or unworthy of belief.[12]

The *McDonnell Douglas* framework was created in the context of a race-based Title VII claim. However, courts use the *McDonnell Douglas* framework to analyze indirect discrimination claims related to the Age Discrimination in Employment Act (ADEA), Section 504 of the Rehabilitation Act of 1973 (Section 504), and Americans with Disabilities Act of 1990 (ADA).[13] The burden-shifting analysis will be addressed repeatedly throughout the chapter, but it is interesting to note that at least one court abandoned the distinction between indirect and direct claims and subjects all claims of discrimination to the *McDonnell Douglas* framework.[14]

Cat's Paw Theory: Actions Based on Lower Management Decisions

In *Staub v. Proctor Hospital*, the United States Supreme Court resolved a question that had divided the lower courts, i.e., whether the discriminatory animus of a subordinate manager who influenced, but did not make, the ultimate adverse employment decision could render the employer liable under federal statutory antidiscrimination law. The Supreme Court, ascribing to a "cat's paw" theory, held that it could.[15]

Applying *Staub*, courts have reached varying results in the K-12 context. Two courts have held that school districts were not liable for discrimination in firing cases where the ultimate decision maker acted independently and did not rely solely on facts supplied by an administrator's recommendation in making its decision.[16] Two other courts have reached decisions favorable to school employees. Both held that, where biased school board members and biased administrators influenced school district decision makers concerning adverse employment decisions, the employer was or could be liable for discrimination.[17]

In many states, school boards take adverse employment action based on the recommendation of administrators, including superintendents and building principals. Likewise, employment decisions concerning non-certificated personnel, including custodians, bus drivers, aides and cafeteria workers, are often made by administrators based on recommendations from managers from the various departments in which those employees work. Given this decision-making structure, it can be anticipated that the Supreme Court's decision in *Staub* will frequently apply in cases involving school district employees.

Retaliation

In retaliation cases, the impermissible action is not based on animus toward a member of a protected class. Instead, retaliation involves an employee who engages in a protected activity when that employee believed discrimination was occurring. Thus, an employer who did not engage in discrimination might be liable for retaliation if it treated an employee adversely for complaining about perceived discrimination.

To prevail on a retaliation claim, an employee must prove "(1) that he opposed a practice made unlawful by Title VII; (2) that the employer took a materially adverse action against him; and (3) that the employer took the action 'because' the employee opposed the practice."[18] As to the second element, the Supreme Court, in *Burlington Northern & Santa Fe Ry. Co. v. White*,[19] made clear that a materially adverse employment action is one that would discourage or dissuade "a reasonable worker from making or supporting a charge of discrimination."[20] Under this standard, adverse employment action by an employer for purposes of retaliation claims is broader than for disparate treatment claims: adverse employment consequences in the retaliation context extend beyond employer conduct that affects terms and conditions of employment and, as such, might include employer conduct that occurs outside the workplace.[21] As to the third element, close temporal proximity between the protected activity and the adverse employment action, standing alone, will not typically prove the causation element.[22] However, unusually close temporal proximity will often raise a factual issue favoring the employee on causation,[23] while, conversely, attenuated proximity will often lead the court to resolve the issue in favor of the employer.[24] And, as with discrimination claims, the proof structure for Title VII retaliation claims applies to other federal retaliation claims as well.[25]

Third-Party Retaliation Claims

Within the past few years, the United States Supreme Court, in *Thompson v. North American Stainless*, decided that third parties who suffer adverse employment action and have a familial relationship with an employee who engages in protected activity under Title VII may have a retaliation claim of their own against the employer. In *Thompson*, the Supreme Court allowed Thompson, the fiancé of an employee Regalado, to proceed with a Title VII retaliation claim when the employer North American Stainless ("NAS") fired Thompson after Regalado filed a claim alleging that NAS had discriminated against her (Regalado) on the basis of gender.[26]

School districts often employ a substantial number of employees from the same or extended family.[27] There has been only one reported third-party retaliation claims under Title VII and *Thompson* in the K-12 setting involving husband or wife employees engaging in protected activity and the other spouse being subject to reprisal by the school district employer.[28] That number will almost certainly increase in the next few years, given the incidences of close family relationships among many school district employees.

Claims Arising under Title VII Based on Race and Color

Discriminatory Treatment

Most recently reported cases regarding race-based claims under Title VII proceed under an indirect evidence theory, which invites the courts to use the burden-shifting framework of *McDonnell-Douglas*. The employee's burden in raising a prima facie requires showing, by a preponderance of the evidence, that he or she (1) belongs to a particular race, (2) is qualified for a position, (3) has suffered an adverse employment decision (e.g., not hired, fired, demoted), and (4) has been treated worse than someone outside the racial group.[29] Because the prima facie requirements are typically easily met, most cases turn on whether the employee can prove the school district's proffered legitimate, nondiscriminatory reason for the adverse action is a pretext for discrimination.

Vessels v. Atlanta Independent School Systems raises several interesting issues concerning race-based claims in the public school employment context. In *Vessels,* a white male school psychologist claimed that he was passed over for an interim assignment in favor an African American female psychologist and that this amounted to reverse discrimination.[30] He also claimed that his eventual rejection for a permanent position constituted racial discrimination, because the candidate hired was also black. The court acknowledged that the employer's burden of merely articulating a legitimate, nondiscriminatory reason is very light: it requires the employer to produce a reason for the adverse employment action and does not require the employer to persuade the court that the reason is a good one.[31] In *Vessels*, the employee claimed that because senior district officials could not remember the reason they endorsed the immediate supervisor's recommendation, they had failed to meet their burden. In response, the court stated that because the immediate supervisor had posited nondiscriminatory reasons for preferring the black female candidate, the senior administrators' reliance on the recommendation, without changing or overruling it, was good enough.[32] The employee, however, was able to offer persuasive evidence of pretext such that summary judgment in favor of the school district was inappropriate. Specifically, the employee pointed to "evidence of racially tinged statements by AISS decision-makers, the relative superiority of [his] qualifications, [and] AISS's disregard of its own employment regulations," which, in the court's opinion, "raise[d] a genuine issue of material fact as to whether AISS's articulated reasons for rejecting Vessels for the interim position were pretextual."[33]

One common way for an employee to overcome a school district's proffered legitimate, nondiscriminatory reason is to identify other employees that were in "nearly identical" situations, but were treated better because they did not share the terminated employee's protected characteristic.[34] For example, a female African American teacher claimed her discharge for two Class C misdemeanor theft citations was discriminatory because four white employees who engaged in theft, sexual misconduct, and inappropriate use of credit cards were not terminated, but permitted to resign or transfer.[35] The court explained that relying on "[c]omparably serious misconduct, by itself, is not enough to make employees similarly situated.... Instead, the employees' circumstances must have been 'nearly identical in order to find them similarly situated.'"[36] Although the teacher's complaint lacked specific details concerning the dates of the comparators' misconduct, their responsibilities, and the outcome of their involvement in the criminal justice system (whether they were only arrested or charged or whether they were convicted) which prevented the court from being able to ascertain comparability, its allegations were enough to overcome the school district's motion to dismiss.[37] However, if an employee cannot show that the comparators have "similar performance records" or sufficiently similar circumstances, his or her claims of racial discrimination will fail.[38]

Retaliation

Courts have come to opposite conclusions concerning retaliation claims brought by teachers who had complained about racial discrimination.

In *Howard v. Board of Education of Memphis City Schools,* an African American teacher filed a complaint with Memphis Educational Association about how her principal had handled a student complaint against her, alleging that the school district had treated her unfavorably in the review on account of her race.[39] Thereafter, several troubling incidents happened to her—including a classroom transfer, increased scrutiny and monitoring, and multiple transfers—that taken together, the court noted, "might arguably give rise to actionable retaliatory harassment.[40]

The teacher then filed discrimination and retaliation claims under Title VII, which were both dismissed by the district court.[41] The Sixth Circuit affirmed the district court's decision in favor of the school district on the teacher's racial discrimination claim, but reversed on her retaliation claim.[42] Although the court of appeals did not expressly mention temporal proximity as a significant factor in the causation analysis, the court's focus on the above-noted events, occurring immediately after the teacher's complaint, indicates the importance of the timing/cause and effect factor.

In contrast, in *Broughton v. School Board of Escambia County*, an African American teacher brought a Title VII claim against her employer school district, alleging that the school district had retaliated against her by taking disciplinary action against her son (who was a student in the school district) in response to her previously having filed EEOC and judicial proceedings against it.[43] The Eleventh Circuit affirmed the district court's ruling against the teacher, concluding that (a) she had failed to demonstrate a causal connection between her having engaged in protected activities and the treatment of her son, and (b) the school district had demonstrated a legitimate, nondiscriminatory reason for disciplining him.[44] The court focused on the lack of temporal proximity between the teacher's complaints and the alleged retaliatory conduct, stating as follows:

> The alleged harassment and misconduct that occurred prior to her April 2010 EEOC complaint is so distant in time from her 2007 EEOC complaint that no reasonable jury could find causation without additional evidence, which Broughton did not submit.... Nor is that conduct—which began in December 2009—close enough in proximity to Broughton's lawsuits, which concluded in June of that year, to alone evidence causation.[45]

Claims Arising under Title VII Based on Religion

Discriminatory Treatment/Failure to Accommodate

School employees may be able to allege and prove they were treated discriminatorily or adversely because of their religious beliefs.[46] In addition, employees may also raise claims that their employer failed or refused to accommodate sincerely held religious beliefs. Failure to accommodate claims follow a modified burden-shifting framework. As to the prima facie case, employees must show they (1) hold sincere religious beliefs that conflict with work requirements; (2) informed the employer of the beliefs and conflict; and (3) were adversely affected for not following a work requirement. If they succeed, the employer can defend against the claim by showing the employee refused a reasonable accommodation, or that a reasonable accommodation was not possible without causing the employer an undue hardship.[47]

Various cases have examined what constitutes a religion or religious belief. In *Sidelinger v. Harbor Creek School District*, a teacher refused to comply with school board policy requiring employees to wear an identification badge at school because he had a "deep moral and religious" conviction against self-adornment.[48] When the school district insisted he wear the badge, the teacher experienced mental distress causing him to miss school; however, during that time he continued to communicate with administrators, but refused to explain his religious beliefs further. Eventually, the board terminated him for failing to follow the policy. The court ultimately decided the teacher's objection to self-adornment was not a sincerely held religious belief. The teacher lacked credibility, since he could not connect his belief against self-adornment to any established religious tenet,[49] and he never provided the court with sufficient information about how his belief came to exist, such that the court could not distinguish between religious conviction and "purely personal preference."[50] Moreover, the teacher failed to give the school district adequate notice of his belief and further failed to prove that the school district's nondiscriminatory reasons for terminating him (failing to follow the policy on reporting absences and showing administrators his gradebook) were pretextual.[51]

Retaliation

The results have been mixed concerning retaliation claims related to teachers asserting religious discrimination claims in the workplace. A Jewish teacher successfully defended against a summary judgment motion brought by a school district by presenting evidence that the school district allowed anti-Semitic workplace hostility to increase after the teacher had engaged in protected activity, i.e., the teacher lodged complaints about religious-based harassment by students.[52] Likewise, a court denied a school district's motion for summary judgment where a Muslim teacher raised genuine issues of material fact concerning whether (1) her suspension by the school district occurred because she had engaged in protected activity, i.e. she had complained to administrative agencies about alleged religious (and national origin) discrimination at the school district; and (2) the grounds for the school district's decision to suspend her, i.e. that she made a bomb threat, were false and, therefore, pretextual.[53]

However, school districts have successfully defended against religious retaliation claims. A court dismissed a teacher's retaliation claim where the teacher alleged that the district had retaliated against her because she had opposed discriminatory treatment based on her religion, but attempted to proceed under a liability theory predicated on her having claimed sexual harassment.[54] Likewise, a court granted summary judgment in favor of a school district and against a teacher on her retaliation claim where the teacher did not engage in any protected, oppositional activity concerning religious discrimination and did not suffer a material adverse employment action.[55] Courts have favored school districts where the evidence demonstrated the teacher's participation in protected activities concerning alleged religious discrimination was not known to school authorities and officials.[56] Teacher claims have also failed where other evidence of causation, including proximity between the time the teacher engaged in protected activity and the adverse employment action suffered by the teacher occurred, was lacking.[57]

Claims Arising under Title VII based on National Origin

Disparate Treatment

Employees who were born outside of the United States to non-citizen parents may claim discrimination based on national origin.[58] An individual born in the United States can also make national origin claims based on their ethnic heritage.[59] Cases involving national origin or ethnic heritage as a protected status follow the direct or indirect methods of proving discrimination.

Before the Seventh Circuit abandoned its distinction between direct and indirect discrimination claims, it had the opportunity to evaluate an appeal that relied solely on direct evidence. A nonrenewed Central Asian Indian teacher claimed her principal had told her to look for work on the "north side where most of the Indians go."[60] The court declined to find the statement was direct evidence of discrimination.[61] The comment allegedly was made ten months prior to the recommendation not to renew.[62] There was substantial evidence in the record that the reason for nonrenewal was poor classroom management.[63]

With regard to indirect claims, school employees who argue national origin-motivated adverse action against them have struggled to prove that nondiscriminatory reasons proffered by school districts were pretextual. In *Fong v. School Bd. of Palm Beach County, Florida*, a teacher of Chinese descent claimed the principal had rated her teaching as substandard because students could not understand her speech. [64] The teacher also pointed to an instance where the principal told the teacher her accent was difficult to understand.[65] The court of appeals initially explained that such cases are challenging because, although discrimination based on accent constitutes national origin discrimination, "an employee's heavy accent or difficulty with spoken English can be a legitimate basis for adverse employment action where effective communication skills are reasonably related to job performance, as they certainly are in a teaching position."[66] Ultimately, the court held that the remark about her accent "standing alone, is inadequate to support a finding of intentional discrimination."[67]

Retaliation

The Ninth Circuit considered both disparate treatment and retaliation claims in its decision *Raad v. Fairbanks North Star Borough School District.*[68] As discussed previously, the court of appeals ultimately concluded that the teacher had successfully raised a retaliation claim after she was disciplined and indefinitely denied a teaching position for an exchange she had with district employees who erroneously reported it as a bomb threat.[69] The teacher was a female, Lebanese substitute teacher who had been seeking full-time, permanent teaching positions.[70] After initially being passed over for five jobs, she met with the District EEO officer to complain of discrimination based on national origin and religion.[71] About a year later, she learned she was again passed over for a position for which she was well-qualified and again went to the district office to speak with the superintendent. In seeking to speak with the superintendent, the plaintiff made comments that her need to speak with him was a "matter of life or death," and that she was angry and did not want to "blow up."[72] The staff interpreted these comments, in light of the teacher's national origin, as a bomb threat. The court of appeals reversed the district court's grant of summary judgment because the teacher should have been given an opportunity to show that her discipline for the "bomb threat" could have been a "pretext for discrimination if she can demonstrate that the incident did not unfold as the District's witnesses allege and that the District knew or had reason to know of the falsity of those allegations."[73] In other words, the court was willing to presume national origin discrimination was the motivating factor if the bomb threat was manufactured to discipline the teacher.

As alluded to previously, one additional issue with regard to proving that adverse employment actions were taken because a teacher engaged in protected activity is the timing of the alleged retaliation. If the adverse action follows soon after the protected activity, the teacher can show that the protected activity was the likely cause. The courts have not identified a bright-line standard for how little time must pass to prove causation, but at least one court has suggested that five months is not too long.[74] In fact, a teacher prevailed on a retaliation claim by showing that his school changed the curriculum for his courses and assigned him to teach students with high absenteeism to make it more likely he would perform poorly. These actions occurred less than three months after he had filed a complaint with the EEOC. Because these actions were within the five-month threshold, the court had previously established, it found the temporal connection between the events to prove causation for purposes of overcoming a judgment on the pleadings.[75]

Claims Arising under Title VII Based on Sex or Gender

Disparate Treatment

Employment discrimination based on sex or gender (the terms are used interchangeably here), has evolved significantly since Title VII's passage in 1964. In response to a Supreme Court decision holding that discrimination against pregnant women was not sex-based discrimination,[76] Congress passed the Pregnancy Discrimination Act of 1978 which modified the definition of the word "sex" to expressly include pregnancy.[77] The Supreme Court has recently recognized that employers must accommodate pregnant employees the same way it might accommodate an employee who is disabled and "similar in their ability or inability to work."[78] Thus, if an employer offers light duty work to an employee because of a physical condition that is similar to pregnancy in its effect on ability to work, the pregnant employee should receive similarly modified duty. As one court explained, "Mrs. Herx's claim for pregnancy discrimination 'is a claim for gender discrimination, and the legal analysis for both claims is the same.'"[79] Thus, the *McDonnell Douglas* framework is equally applicable.

In addition, the Seventh Circuit recently has expanded the meaning of sex in Title VII to incorporate sexual orientation.[80] Although the court's holding is not applicable throughout the United States, it signals a growing movement that could potentially extend protection to school employees who identify as LGBTQ[81]—a subpopulation that has not been expressly included in Title VII protection. Sexual orientation claims as sex discrimination follow the traditional burden-shifting analysis.

An informative example of judicial treatment of disparate treatment claims is *Boutillier v. Hartford Public Schools.*[82] There, the teacher alleged she had been constructively discharged based on persistent hostility directed toward her by school administrators, which she asserted was based on her sexual orientation. The harsh personal treatment not only supported a harassment claim, but a disparate treatment claim as well, because the court acknowledged that a constructive discharge could constitute an adverse employment action.[83] A constructive discharge occurs when a supervisor makes the working environment so intolerable that a reasonable employee faced with those circumstances would have no choice but to quit.[84] The court also found that the evidence presented by the teacher (deposition testimony from other employees at the school) demonstrated that the purported nondiscriminatory reason given by the school district—she left employment for health reasons unrelated to her relationships with administrators—was pretextual.[85] The teacher's disparate treatment claim survived summary judgment.

Many sex-based discrimination claims relate to pregnancy. Some of the more interesting claims pertain to religious schools that have established policies against extramarital or premarital sex.[86] Courts have confirmed that religious schools may enforce such policies, but they must enforce them equally as between male and female teachers.[87] As with many indirect cases, employees struggle to show that nondiscriminatory reasons are pretextual,[88] but there are examples of success. One female teacher was able to marshal evidence of positive evaluations and financial benefits that would accrue to the school if she were discharged, such that court characterized the school's proffered nondiscriminatory justifications as "post hoc, provided in anticipation of litigation."[89]

Retaliation

Reverse discrimination claims from male teachers are rarely successful.[90] One case, however, stands out as a good example of a successful reverse discrimination claim premised on retaliation. In *Copeland v. Rosen*, an African American male teacher asserted that his termination from an alternative high school was based on race and gender.[91] His claim was bolstered by the fact that the school's director had only terminated three individuals during her tenure, all of whom were black men. Prior to his termination, the teacher had met with parents who were upset that one of the other teachers had been fired. The court found that the teacher's good faith belief that his colleague was fired for discriminatory reasons and his participation in the meeting of parents to oppose the firing constituted a protected activity.[92] Not long after the opposition meeting, he received a poor evaluation and was eventually terminated, both of which constituted an adverse employment action.[93] Finally, the school director's letter terminating him provided strong evidence of causation. In the letter, the director stated that she viewed his participation in the meeting as unprofessional and the reason for termination.[94] The statement in the letter also constituted sufficient evidence of pretext. Specifically, it overcame the director's argument, under what is known as the "same actor inference," that because she had hired the teacher, her decision to terminate him could not be discriminatory.[95] On this latter point, the court made clear that, although the same actor's participation in both the hiring and firing decisions may be evidence of non-discrimination, it is not in and of itself dispositive.[96]

Claims Based on Age Discrimination

Employers are barred from discriminating against employees over the age of 40 by the Age Discrimination in Employment Act of 1967 (ADEA).[97] The courts have applied the same legal framework used in Title VII cases to assess direct, indirect, and retaliatory claims of age discrimination.

Disparate Treatment

In *Hedgemon v. Madison Parish School Board*, a teacher was released as part of a budget-induced reduction in force, but claimed the true reason was age discrimination based on comments an administrator made that humiliated her and disparaged her age.[98] The court rejected the teacher's direct claim because the statements were not made close in time to the layoff and were unrelated to the employment decision at issue, even though the statements were age-related and made by an individual with authority for the employment decision.[99]

Indirect claims are resolved by the burden-shifting analysis articulated in *McDonnell Douglas*.[100] Employees will make out a prima facie case by showing they (1) are over age 40, (2) are minimally qualified for the position, (3) suffered an adverse employment action, and (4) that the action was the product of unlawful animus as demonstrated by the "cumulative weight of circumstantial evidence."[101] In showing the action was caused by unlawful animus, the employee must successfully argue age was the "but for" cause, not simply a motivating factor.[102] As with other discrimination claims, once the employee meets its initial burden, the employer must articulate a nondiscriminatory reason for the adverse employment decision. Once the employer sustains its burden, the employee must demonstrate that the reason was pretextual.

Employees with age discrimination claims most often struggle to show that age-related animus caused the discrimination,[103] and/or that the nondiscriminatory reason is pretextual.[104] Often evidence of causation and pretext comes down to employees being able to identify younger colleagues who were similarly situated.[105] For example, a principal who was demoted to a teaching position claimed that she was treated less favorably than younger principals in the same school district who had also had performance issues.[106] The court was unpersuaded because the principal failed to provide the ages of the comparators and could not claim that they were being scrutinized for the same type of misconduct.[107] However, an employee will be able to prevail if he or she can demonstrate "such weaknesses, implausibilities, inconsistencies, incoherencies, or contradictions in the employer's proffered legitimate reasons for its action that a reasonable fact finder could find them unworthy of credence."[108] This was the case in *Garcia v. Corpus Christi Ind. School Dist.,*[109] where a special education teacher was able to show that the school district's proffered reason, i.e. that she used inappropriate force with a student, was most likely untrue.[110] The teacher strengthened her case by pointing to comments made by district employees that she should retire if she felt tired and that it was impossible for her hair color to be natural at her age.[111]

Retaliation

Although the teacher prevailed on her indirect disparate treatment claim in *Garcia*, she was unsuccessful on her retaliation claim because she had not engaged in protected activity prior to the adverse employment action.[112] Another teacher encountered the same problem in *Klastow v. Newtown Friend Schools.*[113] There, the teacher had contested the treatment of a fellow teacher, who was over 40, by protesting the school district's placing the fellow teacher on the Teacher Assistance Track (TAT) and writing a letter to the school board challenging the district's eventual decision to terminate the fellow teacher. Because the objecting teacher had contested the fellow teacher's treatment, he argued that he had opposed a discriminatory practice and, therefore, had engaged in protected activity, prior to his own termination.[114] However, in neither case—in opposing the TAT placement, or in the letter to the board—did he raise the issue of age discrimination. For that reason, the court rejected his retaliation claim.[115] Moreover, even when teachers engage in protected activity, they must still show the cause of the adverse action was their participation in that activity. This can be challenging when a plausible nondiscriminatory reason, such as falsifying evaluation scores, is asserted as the reason for the adverse employment action by the school district.[116]

Claims Based on Disability Discrimination

Discriminatory Treatment/Failure to Accommodate

Adverse employment actions based on an employee's disability are made unlawful by two federal statutes: Section 504 of the Rehabilitation Act of 1973 ("Section 504"),[117] and the Americans with Disabilities Act of 1990 ("ADA").[118] Claims arising under these laws are "nearly identical," meaning that the elements of the claims are mostly the same.[119]

Those similarities notwithstanding, there are three important differences: (1) Section 504 only applies to employers receiving federal funds;[120] (2) Section

504 does not require exhaustion of administrative remedies; [121] and (3) Section 504 requires that an employee's disability be the "sole cause" of an adverse action, while the ADA only requires disability to be a "motivating factor."[122] Disability-based claims may be proved with direct or indirect evidence; however, the ADA and Section 504 also support failure-to-accommodate claims. Thus, in addition to showing unfavorable treatment because of disability, an employee might also argue that an employer refused to grant a reasonable accommodation.

The *McDonnell Douglas* framework is slightly modified for disability claims. An employee must show (1) the law applies to the employer (15+ employees); (2) the employee meets the definition of disabled; (3) the employee is otherwise qualified, meaning they "can perform the essential functions of the position with *or* without reasonable accommodations," and (4) the employer subjected the employee to an adverse employment action because of their disability.[123]

More often, an employee's prima facie case turns on whether they are actually qualified to perform their assigned essential job functions. Where a district court found that a preschool teacher's epilepsy constituted a disability, i.e. substantially limited one or more of the teacher's major life activities, and that the teacher could perform the essential functions of her teaching position, she was a qualified person with a disability such that the school district could not terminate her for that reason under the ADA.[124]

Similarly, where a school board refused to allow a teacher with rheumatoid arthritis to return to work because the board believed the teacher's physical restrictions would prevent her from maintaining order and student discipline in the classroom, the court held there were genuine issues of material fact precluding summary judgment on the issue of whether the teacher could perform the essential functions of her job.[125] Specifically, the court relied on evidence that the teacher had previously and successfully taught the class in a wheelchair. The court also doubted that the ability to physically intervene in student conflict was an essential function of the position.[126]

Conversely, if an employee attempts to claim their disability impacted their work, but in reality, there is no connection between the disability and work performance issues, courts find that the employee is not qualified. For example, where a teacher alleged that her multiple sclerosis made it difficult for her to walk, but the district terminated her for her inability to interpret psychological test results, poor organizational skills, and meeting attendance requirements, the court upheld the termination. Specifically, the court found and concluded that the teacher's poor mobility had no effect on her performance-related issues.[127] Likewise, an employee will not be considered qualified if the disabling condition causes objectionable conduct. Thus, where a teacher's post-concussive disorder contributed to her irritable and angry moods, that impairment could not excuse her threatening to kill students—a crime for which she was convicted.[128] Also, an employee's mental health might prevent him or her from performing with or without accommodation; in such cases, the teacher is not qualified.[129] Finally, one court rejected a teacher's contention that he was qualified where he only exhibited signs of disability when having to report to an aggressive and demanding supervisor.[130]

When employees assert they were denied a reasonable accommodation, they must offer different proof than is required of other disparate treatment claims. Specifically, employees must show that they informed their employer of the need for an accommodation (usually referred to as a request for an accommodation), but that a reasonable accommodation was not provided even after they engaged in an interactive process with the employer to determine what a reasonable accommodation might be. An employer can defend against failure to accommodate claims by showing a reasonable accommodation was offered but refused, or that there was no reasonable accommodation that would not produce an undue hardship on the employer. Teachers have failed to prevail in cases where they were given a reasonable accommodation, such as being given more time to complete their work, but still could not perform the essential functions of their job,[131] or failed to request an accommodation.[132] Conversely, school districts have lost failure-to-accommodate claims when it is obvious an accommodation is needed, and even though the employee does not request an accommodation, the school district does not engage in the interactive process required by the ADA.[133]

Retaliation

Requesting an accommodation is a protected activity, and employees are protected from adverse action for having made the request. The timing between an adverse employment action and the protected activity is circumstantial evidence of causation for disability retaliation claims.[134] Thus, a teacher prevailed on her retaliation claim when she argued that her reassignment to a teaching pool followed three weeks after she had complained about discriminatory treatment based on her disability.

Claims Based on Taking Leave for Medical Care

Interference/Disparate Treatment

The Family Medical Leave Act of 1993 allows eligible employees to take "unpaid, job-protective leave" without the loss of medical benefits for up to twelve weeks if they are taking the leave to provide care for themselves while suffering a serious health condition, provide care for a newly born or adopted child or a family member with a serious health condition, address their own or a family member's deployment or return from employment as a military service member.[135] The statute gives aggrieved employees two causes of action: interference and retaliation.[136] In some jurisdictions, an individual supervisor or administrator can be sued in their individual capacity under FMLA.[137] Significantly, employers can involuntarily place employees on leave under FMLA.[138]

To succeed on an FMLA claim regarding the right to take leave, an employee must establish the following prima facie case:

1. The employee is eligible to request the leave (has worked for the employer for twelve months, and within those twelve months worked at least 1,250 hours);
2. The employer is covered by FMLA (schools are covered regardless of how many people they employ, so this element is easily satisfied);
3. The employee was entitled to leave under the FMLA (e.g., newborn child, etc.);
4. The employee gave notice to the employer they intended to take the leave (adequate notice is typically thirty days, unless the serious health condition could not be anticipated); and
5. The employer interfered by (a) denying the leave, (b) failing to permit the full twelve weeks, or (c) failing to reinstate the employee to the same or equivalent position.[139]

Calculating the hours worked in the previous twelve months may make the difference concerning whether a district is liable. In one case, a teacher incurred significant absences during the 2008-2009 school year without taking FMLA leave, and when he finally did request leave in 2009-10, the court found he had not worked enough days.[140]

Issues also often arise concerning notice requirements. Courts have held that an employee need not invoke the FMLA by name,[141] and failing to use a form or protocol established by a school district to request the leave is not fatal to interference claims.[142] In fact, a school district should inquire more rather than summarily deny an imperfect application.[143] More important, school districts should have a notice requirement to inform employees of their rights under the law. If they fail to do so, they have engaged in actionable interference. One teacher was unaware that he could take leave for his ailments, and instead of taking the time necessary for his health to improve, he continued to struggle at work. He was late and ineffective, which caused his district to terminate him. The court held that the school district's failure to inform the teacher of his rights meant he could not meaningfully exercise them.[144] However, at least one court has required a teacher to show that the lack of information in fact interfered with the exercise of rights.[145]

Also common are claims that the district failed to reinstate the employee to the same or an equivalent position following the leave. If an employee cannot return to work after twelve weeks of leave, he or she is not entitled to the same or equivalent position.[146] However, if an employee informs the district that they can return to work with accommodations, the same job or an equivalent job must be tendered.[147] These cases often turn on causation, and overcoming a nondiscriminatory reason offered by the school district. For example, a teacher with significant performance issues was unable to adequately show that those issues were not the reason for her termination and placement in the reassigned teaching pool. Thus, the different placement was justified and not the product of FMLA interference.[148] Conversely, a teacher prevailed when she could show that, although the board claimed it fired her for insubordination, the board never addressed that reason in its meeting minutes and only focused on the teacher's alleged abandonment of contract; however, her alleged abandonment had been shown to be the result of a medical condition that qualified for FMLA leave.[149]

Retaliation

Employees may claim retaliation under FMLA if they can demonstrate they (1) exercised their FMLA rights, (2) were qualified for the position they left and desired to return, (3) suffered an adverse employment action, and (4) the adverse action was the result of retaliation for having taken leave.[150] Retaliation is easy to prove when the school district admits the termination was for taking leave, and one such district did so because it erroneously believed the leave was unauthorized. In that case, it denied the leave and then fired the teacher. The district denied the leave because they thought that the employee's mother falling and becoming injured did not entitle the employee to leave. The school district was wrong, and it lost both an interference claim and a retaliation claim.[151]

Most retaliation claims turn on the issue of causation. In other words, employees must persuade the court that the real reason for the adverse action was that they took leave. Teachers can often offer evidence of causation-based comments made by administrators that convey disdain for excessive absences when those comments follow requests for additional leave to care for others. For instance, teachers caring for sick children with medical conditions of indefinite duration have used terse comments about their absences as evidence of retaliation when they eventually lose their positions.[152] However, teachers have lost retaliation claims when they cannot show the board knew about their leave at the time they were terminated,[153] significant time has elapsed between the adverse employment action and the leave,[154] and the teacher could not return after twelve weeks.[155]

Rules Unique to Educators

Unlike any other federal antidiscrimination or accommodation law, the FMLA provides special rules for "instructional employees" employed at elementary and secondary schools.[156] The legislative intent behind these rules was to balance "both the educational needs of children with the family leave needs of teachers."[157] These special rules affect the ability of instructional employees to take intermittent leave or leave near the end of an academic term.[158]

Where an instructional employee requests intermittent FMLA leave to be able to care for a family member with a serious health condition, to care for his or her own serious health condition, or to care for a covered service member—with each case having foreseeable planned medical treatment, and where the intermittent leave would total more than 20% of the total number of working days in that period—the employer may require the employee to choose between two alternatives. [159] Specifically, the employer may offer the option to (1) take only a specific period of leave, which will not exceed the duration of the planned medical treatment; or (2) transfer to a different position offered by the employer which will better accommodate the recurring leave than the employee's current position, and for which the employee is qualified to work and will receive equal pay and benefits.[160]

The FMLA also provides special rules affecting the ability of instructional employees to take FMLA leave more than or less than five weeks before the end of an academic term and less than three weeks before the end of an academic term.[161] Under the FMLA's special rules, "academic term" means the school semester, with one typically ending near the end of the calendar year and the other near the end of spring each school year.[162] Accordingly, for purposes of the FMLA, no school may count more than two academic terms each academic year.[163]

Where an instructional employee needs to take FMLA leave more than five weeks prior to the end of the academic term for any qualifying event, "the employer may require the employee to continue taking leave until the end of the [academic] term . . . ." However, the employer may only require this "if (1) the leave will last at least three weeks, and (2) the employee would return to work during the three-week period before the end of the [academic] term."[164] It should be noted, however, that for this circumstance and each of the others discussed below, where an employer requires the instructional employee to stay on leave until the end of the term, "only the period of leave until the employee is ready and able to return to work shall be charged against the employee's FMLA leave entitlement."[165]

Similarly, if an instructional employee needs to take FMLA leave less than five weeks prior to the end of the academic term because of the birth of a child, the placement of a child for adoption or foster care, to care for a family member having a serious health condition, or to care for a covered service member, "the employer may require the employee to continue taking leave until the end of the [academic] term . . . ."[166] However, differing slightly from the requirements for leave taking place more than five week prior to the end of the term, the employer may only require this "if 1) the leave will last more than two weeks, and 2) the employee would return to work during the two-week period before the end of the [academic] term."[167]

Finally, where an instructional employee needs to take FMLA leave less than three weeks prior to the end of the academic term because of the birth of a child, the placement of a child for adoption or foster care, to care for a family member having a serious health condition, or to care for a covered service member, "the employer may require the employee to continue taking leave until the end of the [academic] term . . . ."[168] However, the employer may only require this if the leave will last more than five working days.[169]

Recommendations for Practice

1. Laws protecting against antidiscrimination are complicated, but as a general rule, if an employer has legitimate, nondiscriminatory reasons for taking an adverse employment action, courts will sustain the employment decision.

2. Administrators should be aware that federal antidiscrimination laws protect prohibit discrimination against "adverse employment actions." That term can have several meanings, not just termination. For example, demoting an employee could be an adverse employment action. And, if that action was taken for prohibited, discriminatory reasons, it could expose a school district to litigation under the federal laws discussed here.

3. Administrators should keep in mind that these laws apply to all employees, including non-tenured teachers and non-certificated/classified employees.

4. The law in this area is changing rapidly, especially in the area of what constitutes gender discrimination. Administrators should stay current with these changes through professional development.

5. Finally, superintendents should be sure that lower level administrators (principals, assistant principals) who have the day-to-day management of personnel are well aware of these laws. When school districts are sued under antidiscrimination laws, the actions of these managers are scrutinized closely.

Figure 1
The McDonnell Douglas Burden-Shifting Framework Illustrated

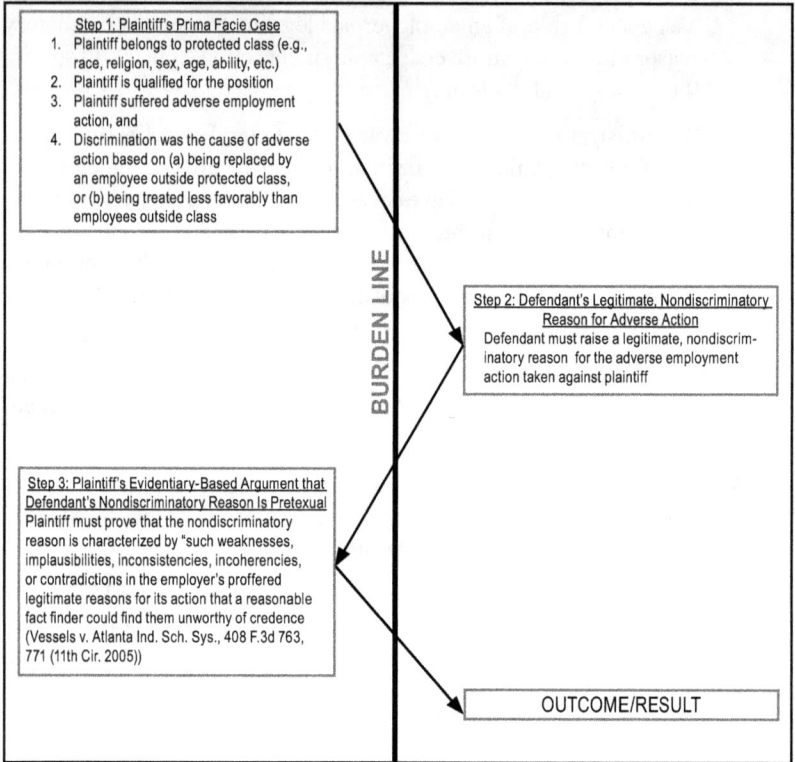

Step 1: Plaintiff's Prima Facie Case
1. Plaintiff belongs to protected class (e.g., race, religion, sex, age, ability, etc.)
2. Plaintiff is qualified for the position
3. Plaintiff suffered adverse employment action, and
4. Discrimination was the cause of adverse action based on (a) being replaced by an employee outside protected class, or (b) being treated less favorably than employees outside class

BURDEN LINE

Step 2: Defendant's Legitimate, Nondiscriminatory Reason for Adverse Action
Defendant must raise a legitimate, nondiscriminatory reason for the adverse employment action taken against plaintiff

Step 3: Plaintiff's Evidentiary-Based Argument that Defendant's Nondiscriminatory Reason Is Pretexual
Plaintiff must prove that the nondiscriminatory reason is characterized by "such weaknesses, implausibilities, inconsistencies, incoherencies, or contradictions in the employer's proffered legitimate reasons for its action that a reasonable fact finder could find them unworthy of credence (Vessels v. Atlanta Ind. Sch. Sys., 408 F.3d 763, 771 (11th Cir. 2005))

OUTCOME/RESULT

Table 1
Types of Claims a Terminated Employee May
Make Under Federal Civil Rights Statutes

Statute	Disparate Treatment Claims				Retaliation
	Direct	Indirect	Mixed Motive	Failure to Accommodate	
Title VII of the Civil Rights Act of 1964 - Race & Color	Y	Y	Y	N	Y
Title VII of the Civil Rights Act of 1964 - Religion	Y	Y	Y	Y	Y
Title VII of the Civil Rights Act of 1964 - National Origin	Y	Y	Y	N	Y
Title VII of the Civil Rights Act of 1964 - Sex	Y	Y	Y	N	Y
Age Discrimination in Employment Act of 1967 - Age	Y	Y	N	N	Y
Section 504 of the Rehabilitation Act of 1973 - Disability	Y	Y	P	Y	Y
Americans with Disabilities Act of 1990 - Disability	Y	Y	P	Y	Y
Family Medical Leave Act of 1993 - Family Leave	Y	Y	P	N	Y

Y = Yes   N = No   P = Possibly

Endnotes

[1] These characteristics and statuses are protected by Title VII of the Civil Rights Act of 1964, Pub. L. No. 88-352, 78 Stat. 241 (1964). *See* 42 U.S.C. § 2000e-2 (2012).

[2] Age discrimination is prohibited under the Age Discrimination in Employment Act of 1967, Pub. L. No. 90-202, 81 Stat. 602 (1967). *See* 29 U.S.C. §§ 621-634 (2012).

[3] Disability discrimination is prohibited by Section 504 of the Rehabilitation Act of 1973, Pub. L. No. 93-112, 87 Stat. 355 (1973) and the Americans with Disabilities Act of 1990, Pub. L. No. 101-336, 104 Stat. 327 (1990) as amended by ADA Amendments Act of 2008, Pub. L. No. 110-325, 122 Stat. 3553 (2008). *See* 29 U.S.C. §§ 794 – 794g (2012) and 42 U.S.C. §§ 12101 – 12213 (2012).

[4] Discrimination based on an employee's illness or medical condition or the illness or medical condition of a family member for whom the employee has responsibility to provide care is prohibited by the Family Medical Leave Act of 1993, Pub. L. No. 103-3, 107 Stat. 6 (1993). *See* 29 U.S.C. §§ 2601-2654 (2012).

[5] Whether a particular administrator or school board decision amounts to an adverse action is an issue that is often addressed by courts. *See* Carmellino v. Dist. 20 of N.Y.C. Dep't of Educ., 2006 WL 2583019, at **3-4 (S.D.N.Y. Sept. 6, 2006)

[6] *See generally* Marion G. Crane, Pauline T. Kim, & Michael Selmi, Work Law: Cases and Materials 567-69 (3d Ed. Matthew Bender and Co., Inc. 2015)

[7] *See* Hedgemon v. Madison Par. Sch. Bd., No. 14–0817, 2015 WL 4094701, at *5 (W.D. La. July 7, 2015).

[8] 411 U.S. 792 (1973).

[9] *Id.* at 802.

[10] Furnco Constr. Corp. v. Waters, 438 U.S. 567, 577 (1978).

[11] *McDonnell Douglas*, 411 U.S. at 802-03.

[12] *Id.* at 804. Sometimes the evidence presented will demonstrate that an employer's adverse employment action against an employee was based on both permissible *and* discriminatory reasons. To address these circumstances, Congress, in 1991 amendments to Title VII, formulated a mixed-motive proof structure. Civil Rights Act of 1991, 42 U.S.C. Sec. 2000e-2(m) and -5(g)(2)(B). In a mixed-motive case, an employee may establish an actionable discrimination claim under Title VII by demonstrating that his or her protected status or characteristic "was a motivating factor for any employment practice, even though other factors also motivated the practice." *Id.*, Section 2000e-2(m). Once an employee proves a violation under Section 2000e-2(m), the employer may avail itself of a limited affirmative defense restricting the remedies available to the employee if it can demonstrate that it would have taken the same action absent the impermissible motivating factor. Sec. 2000e-5(g)(2)(B). *See* Desert Palace, Inc. v. Costa, 539 U.S. 90, 94-95 (2003). Courts have applied this mixed-motive proof structure to Title VII cases in the K-12 school setting. Vereen v. Woodland Hills School Dist., No. CV-06-462, 2008 WL 79445, **18-20 (W.D. Pa. March 24, 2008); Louis v. East Baton Rouge Parish School Bd., 303 F.Supp.2d 799, 800-804 (M.D. La. 2003). The Supreme Court, however, has held that the mixed-motive burden shifting framework does not apply to age discrimination claims under the ADEA. Gross v. FBL Financial Services, Inc., 557 U.S. 167 (2009).

[13] *See, e.g.*, Carson v. Lake County, Indiana, 856 F.3d 526, 533 (7th Cir. 2017) (ADEA claims); Abilt v. Central Intelligence Agency, 848 F.3d 305, 315 (4th Cir. 2017) (Section 504 claims); Caldwell v. KHOU-TV, 850 F.3d 237, 241 (5th Cir. 2017) (ADA claims).

[14] Ortiz v. Werner Enters., Inc., 834 F.3d 760, 763–66 (7th Cir. 2016).

[15] 562 U.S. 411, 422 (2011). According to the Supreme Court: The term "cat's paw" derives from a fable conceived by Aesop, put into verse by La Fontaine in 1679, and injected into United States employment discrimination law by Posner in 1990. …In the fable, a monkey induces a cat by flattery to extract roasting chestnuts from the fire. After the cat has done so, burning its paws in the process, the monkey makes off with the chestnuts and leaves the

cat with nothing. A coda to the fable (relevant only marginally, if at all, to employment law) observes that the cat is similar to princes who, flattered by the king, perform services on the king's behalf and receive no reward. *Id.* at 415 n.1.

[16] Lawrence v. School Dist. No.1, 560 Fed. Appx. 791-795-796 (10th Cir. 2014); Wray v. School Dist. Of Philadelphia, Civil Action No. 14-5886, 2016 WL 427058, **3-4 (E.D. Pa. February 4, 2016).

[17] Johnson v. Camden City School Dist., 1:15-cv-01124-NLH-JS,2017 WL 1227925, **6-7 n.4 (D.N.J. April 3, 2017); Jackson v. Lowndes County School Dist., 126 F.Supp.3d 772, 783-84 (N.D. Miss. 2015).

[18] Robbins v. District of Columbia, 650 Fed.Appx. 37, 38 (D.C. Cir. 2016).

[19] 548 U.S. 68 (2006).

[20] *Burlington Northern*, 548 U.S. at 68.

[21] *Id.* at 60-63; Rodriquez v. Central School Dist. 13J, No. 12-CV-01223 –HU, 2013 WL 6576278, * 9 (D. Or. Oct. 4, 2013).

[22] Hernandez v. Yellow Transp., Inc., 670 F.3d 644, 658 (5th Cir. 2012).

[23] LeBoon v. Lancaster Jewish Community Center Ass'n, 503 F.3d 217, 232 (3d Cir. 2007).

[24] Liles v. C.S. McCrossan, Inc., 851 F.3d 810. 821 (8th Cir. 2017).

[25] Kessler v. Westchester County Dept. of Social Services, 461 F.3d 199, 205-06 (2d Cir. 2006) (ADEA claims); Mogehan v. Napolitano, 613 F.3d 1162, 1166 (D.C. Cir. 2010) (Section 504 claims); Hennagir v. Utah Dept. of Corrections, 587 F.3d 1255, 1266 (10th Cir. 2009) (ADA claims); Breneisen v. Motorola, Inc., 512 F.3d 972, 979 (7th Cir. 2008).

[26] 562 U.S. 170 (2011).

[27] Because school districts are often one of the largest employers in a community, and because dual-income spouses are increasingly necessary to maintain a reasonable standard of living, it is not uncommon for spouses and other family members to work for the same school district. *See, e.g.,* http://schoolboardnews.nsba.org/2011/01/nsba-high-court-ruling-may-lead-to-more-employee-lawsuits/.

[28] Prew v. Llano Independent School Dist., No. A-13-CA-144-SS, 2013 WL 3994188, *3 (W.D. Tex. Aug. 2, 2013).

[29] The prima facie case under *McDonnell Douglas's* fourth element can vary based on the circumstances of the employee. "Generally, the fourth prong of the McDonnell Douglas prima facie case requires a plaintiff to show either that (i) he was replaced by someone outside the protected class or (ii) other similarly situated employees outside the protected class were treated more favorably under nearly identical circumstances. *Okoye*, 245 F.3d at 512–14. However, the prima facie case framework "was never intended to be rigid mechanized, or ritualistic." Suggs v. Lowndes Cty. Sch. Dist., 804 F.Supp.2d 510, 515-16 (N.D. Miss. 2011) (*quoting* Furnco Constr. Corp. v. Waters, 438 U.S. 567, 577 (1978)).

[30] *Id.* at 768-69.

[31] *Id.* at 769-70.

[32] *Id.* at 770.

[33] *Id.* at 772.

[34] Brown v. Bd. of Trs. Sealy Ind. Sch. Dist., 871 F.Supp.2d 581 (S.D. Tex. 2012)

[35] *Id.* at 592-93.

[36] *Id.* at 593 (citing Perez v. Tex. Dep't of Crim. Justice, 395 F.3d 206, 213 (5th Cir. 2004)).

[37] *Id.* at 595-96. *see also* Fortes v. Boyertown Area Sch. Dist., No. 12-6063, 2014 WL 3573104, at *8-9 (E.D. Penn. July 18, 2014).

[38] *See* Preddie v. Bartholomew Consol. Sch. Corp., 799 F.3d 806, 816 (7th Cir. 2015). *See also* Suggs v. Lowndes Cty. Sch. Dist., 804 F.Supp.2d 510, 515-16 (N.D. Miss. 2011).

[39] *Howard*, 70 Fed.Appx. 272, 275-77 (6th Cir. 2003).

[40] *Id.* at 283.

[41] *Id.* at 274.

[42] *Id.* at 283-84.

[43] 540 Fed. Appx. 907 (11th Cir. 2013).

[44] *Id.* at 912.

45 *Id.*

46 *See e.g.,* Raad v. Fairbanks North Star Borough School Dist., 323 F.3d 1185, 1195-96 (9th Cir. 2003); Raheim v. N.Y.C. Bd. of Educ., Nos. 95-CV-4599, 97-CV-3687, 2006 WL 2385428 (E.D.N.Y. Aug. 17, 2016).

47 Sidelinger v. Harbor Creek Sch. Dist., No. CIV 02-62 ERIE, 2006 WL 3455073 (W.D. Penn. Nov. 29, 2006).

48 *Id.* at *2.

49 *Id.* at *12-15.

50 *Id.* at *24.

51 *Id.* at *26-27.

52 Berger-Rothberg v. City of New York, 803 F.3d 155, 165-67 (E.D. N.Y. 2011).

53 Raad v. Fairbanks North Star Borough School Dist., 323 F.3d 1185, 1196-97 (9th Cir. 2003); *see infra* notes 68-73 and accompanying text.

54 McDonough v. Nassau County Board of Co-op. Educational Services, No. 05CV2507(JG), 2007 WL 3124550, *9 (E.D. N.Y. 2007); *see also* Sancho v. Anderson School Dist. Four, C.A. No. 8:15-1353-HMH-KFM, 2016 WL 4123910, *6 (D.S.C. 2016).

55 Greene v. School Board of Broward County, No. 13-62644-CIV, 2014 WL 3950387, **3-5 (S.D. Fla. 2014).

56 *Raad,* 323 F.3d at 1197; Price v. Warrensville Heights City Schools, No. 1:09 CV 01052, 2013 WL 133713, *6 (N.D. Ohio 2013).

57 Cherabori v. City of Quincy, 213 F.Supp.3d 264, 277 (D. Mass. 2016); Herling v. New York City Dept. of Education, No. 13-CV-5287, 2014 WL 1621966, *10 (E.D. N.Y. 2014)

58 *See* Dass v. Chi. Bd. of Educ., 675 F.3d 1060 (7th Cir. 2012).

59 *See* Vega v. Hampstead Union Free Sch. Dist., 801 F.3d 72 (2d Cir. 2015).

60 *Dass,* 675 F.3d at 1072.

61 *Id.*

62 *Id.*

63 *Id.*

64 590 Fed.Appx. 930 (11th Cir. 2014).

65 *Id.* at 932.

66 *Id.* at 933 (*quoting* Jiminez v. Mary Washington Coll., 57 F.3d 369, 380 (4th Cir. 1995)).

67 *Id.* at 937.

68 323 F.3d 1185 (9th Cir. 2003); *see supra* note 53 and accompanying text.

69 *Id.* at 1196-97.

70 *Id.* at 1189.

71 *Id.* at 1190.

72 *Id.*

73 *Id.* at 1197.

74 *Vega,* 801 F.3d at 90.

75 *Id.* at 92.

76 General Elec. Co. v. Gilbert, 429 U.S. 125 (1976) (The Court declined to extend the meaning of "sex" to include pregnancy and held that GE disability benefits plan's exclusion of pregnancy did not violate Title VII.)

77 42 U.S.C. § 2000e(k) (2012), Pregnancy Discrimination Act of 1978, Pub. L. No. 95-955, 96 Stat. 2076 (1978).

78 Young v. United Parcel Serv., Inc., 135 S.Ct. 1338, 1354 (2015). *See also* EEOC, No. 915.003, ENFORCEMENT GUIDANCE ON PREGNANCY DISCRIMINATION AND RELATED ISSUES (2015), https://www.eeoc.gov/laws/guidance/upload/pregnancy_guidance.pdf.

79 Herx v. Diocese of Ft. Wayne-South Bend Inc., 48 F.Supp.3d 1168, 1173 (N.D. Ind. 2014) (quoting Serednyj v. Beverly Healthcare, LLC, 656 F.3d 540, 547 (7th Cir.2011)).

80 *See* Hively v. Ivy Tech Comm. Coll. of Ind., 853 F.3d 339 (7th Cir. 2017).

81 *See* Boutillier v. Hartford Pub. Schs., 221 F.Supp.3d 255 (D. Conn. 2016).

82 *Id.*

83 *Id.* at 271-72

84 *Id.* at 272 (quoting Petrosino v. Bell Atlantic, 385 F.3d 210, 229 (2d Cir. 2004)) ("An employee is constructively discharged where an employer intentionally creates a work atmosphere so intolerable that she is forced to quit involuntarily.")

85 *Id.*

86 *See* Cline v. Catholic Diocese of Toledo, 206 F.3d 651 (6th Cir. 2000); Boyd v. Harding Acad. of Memphis, Inc., 88 F.3d 410 (6th Cir. 1996).

87 Cline v. Catholic Diocese of Toledo, 206 F.3d 651 (6th Cir. 2000) .

88 *See, e.g.,* Silverman v. Bd. of Educ. of City of Chi., 637 F.3d 729 (7th Cir. 2012) *abrogated on other grounds by* Ortiz v. Werner Enters., Inc., 834 F.3d 760, 763–66 (7th Cir. 2016); Weisbecker v. Sayville Union Free Sch. Dist., 890 F.Supp.2d 215, 237-38 (E.D.N.Y. 2012) (Teacher failed to show nondiscriminatory reason, i.e. that she failed to complete her gradebook and report cards before departing on maternity leave, was pretextual); Heaphy v. Webster Cent. Sch. Dist., 761 F.Supp.2d 89, 93 (W.D.N.Y. 2011) (School district prevailed by showing that its decision to not renew a teacher's contract because of consistent poor performance which was shared before and after maternity leave. Moreover, "mere inquiry into plaintiff's maternity leave plans does not, as plaintiff assumes, suggest a discriminatory motive…[plaintiff] does not dispute that [administrator] has responded the *same way* to all teachers for whom an extended leave of absence is expected, regardless of the reason.") (emphasis added).

89 Johnson v. Sch. Union, No. 107, 295 F.Supp.2d 106, 112 (D. Me. 2003).

90 *See* Koerdt v. Sheridan Sch. Dist., 5:13CV00360JM, 2015 WL 13264433 (E.D. Ark. Mar. 17, 2015); *see also* Deshler v. Pinon Unified Sch. Dist., No. CIV 04-1554 PCT MEA, 2006 WL 988139 (D. Ariz. Apr. 11, 2006).

91 38 F.Supp.2d 298 (S.D.N.Y. 1999)

92 *Id.* at 306-07 (quoting Galdieri-Abrosini v. National Realty & Dev. Corp., 136 F.3d 276, 292 (2d Cir. 1998)).

93 *Id.* at 307.

94 *Id.* at 308.

95 *Id.*

96 *Id.*

97 29 U.S.C. §§ 621-634 (2012). The ADEA was amended by the Older Workers Benefit Protection Act of 1990, Pub. L. No. 101-433, 104 Stat. 978 (1990), and the Civil Rights Act of 1991, Pub. L. No. 102-166, 105 Stat. 1071 (1991).

98 Hedgemon v. Madison Par. Sch. Bd., No. 14-0817, 2015 WL 4094701, at *3 (W.D. La. July 7, 2015) (The superintendent pointed at the plaintiff while repeating the adage "something old, something new" and also later stated "why do we have all these retired people working for the school board?").

99 *Id.* at *5.

100 *See* Klastow v. Newtown Friends Sch., 515 Fed.Appx. 130, 132-34 (3d Cir. 2013); Reeder v. Wasatch Cty. Sch. Dist., 359 Fed. Appx. 920, 923 (10th Cir. 2009); Galabya v. N.Y.C. Bd. of Educ., 202 F.3d 636 (2d Cir. 2000); and Carmellino v. Dist. 20 of N.Y.C. Dep't of Educ., 2006 WL 2583019 (S.D.N.Y. Sept. 6, 2006).

101 *Carmellino*, 2006 WL 2583019 at *3 (quoting Carlton v. Mystic Transp., Inc., 202 F.3d 129, 135 (2d Cir.2000))

102 *See* Reeder v. Wasatch Cty. Sch. Dist., 359 Fed.Appx. 920, 923 (10th Cir. 2009); Gould v. Omaha Pub. Schs, No. 8:14CV258, 2014 WL 6950263 at *3 (D. Ne. Dec. 8, 2014).

103 *Gould*, 2014 WL 6950263 at *3.

104 *Klastow*, 515 Fed.Appx. at 132-34.

105 Aberman v. Bd. of Educ. of City of Chi., No. 12–cv–10181, 2017 WL 1036487, at *12 (N.D. Ill. March 17, 2017) ; *see also* McDowell v. Indianapolis Pub. Schs., No. 1:14–cv–00479–SEB–TAB, 2015 WL 7016497, at *8 (S.D. Ind. Nov. 12, 2015).

106 *McDowell*, 2015 WL 7016497, at *8.

107 *Id.*

[108] Nore v. Fulton County School Dist., No. 1:08-CV-00311-JTC/AJB, 2009 WL 10666308, at *9 (N.D. Ga. July 17, 2009) (quoting Vessels v. Atlanta Ind. Sch. Sys., 408 F.3d 763, 771 (11th Cir. 2005)).

[109] Garcia v. Corpus Christi Ind. Sch. Dist., 866 F.Supp.2d 646, 653 (S.D. Tex. 2011).

[110] *Id.*

[111] *Id.* at 655.

[112] *Id.* at 658-59.

[113] 515 Fed.Appx. 130, 132-33 (3d Cir. 2013).

[114] *Id.* at 132.

[115] *Id.* at 133.

[116] Gould v. Omaha Pub. Schs., No. 8:14CV258, 2014 WL 6950263, at *3 (D. Ne. Dec. 8, 2014).

[117] 29 U.S.C. §§ 794 – 794g (2012). Section 504 of the Rehabilitation Act of 1973, Pub. L. No. 93-112, 87 Stat. 355 (1973). Regulations for applying Section 504 to educational institutions are codified at 34 C.F.R. Part 104. *See* U.S. DEP'T OF EDUC., PROTECTING STUDENTS WITH DISABILITIES (Oct. 16, 2015), https://www2.ed.gov/about/offices/list/ocr/504faq.html.

[118] 42 U.S.C. §§ 12101-12213 (2012), Americans with Disabilities Act of 1990, Pub. L. No. 101-336, 104 Stat. 327 (1990) as amended by ADA Amendments Act of 2008, Pub. L. No. 110-325, 122 Stat. 3553 (2008).

[119] *See* Aberman v. Bd. of Educ. of City of Chi., No. 12–cv–10181, 2017 WL 1036487, at *15 (N.D. Ill. March 17, 2017) (citing Silk v. City of Chicago, 194 F.3d 788, 798 (7th Cir. 1999)).

[120] *See id. See also* Paul A. Race & Seth M. Dornier, *ADA Amendments Act of 2008: The Effect on Employers and Educators*, 46 WILLAMETTE L. REV. 357, 362-63 (2009).

[121] *See* Cooper v. Henderson, 174 F.Supp.3d 193 (D.D.C. 2016); Gore v. Cedar Hill Ind. Sch. Dist., No. 3:15-cv-3963-M-BN, 2016 WL 4597513 (N.D. Texas July 26, 2016) (citing Dao v. Auchan Hypermarket, 96 F.3d 787, 788-89 (5th Cir. 1996); Johnson v. Bd. of Trs. of Boundary Cty. Sch. Dist., No. 101, 666 F.3d 561, 564 n. 1 (9th Cir. 2011).

[122] *See* Valenzisi v. Stamford Bd. of Educ., 948 F.Supp.2d 227, 242 (D. Conn. 2013).

[123] Siudock v. Volusia Cty. Sch. Bd., 568 Fed.Appx. 659, 662 (11th Cir. 2014); see *also Valenzisi*, 948 F.Supp.2d at 240.

[124] Susie v. Apple Tree Preschool and Child Care Center, Inc., 866 F.Supp.2d 390, 395-97 (N.D. Iowa 1994).

[125] Ross v. Board of Educ. of Prince George's County, 195 F.Supp.2d 730, 735 (D. Md. 2002).

[126] *Id.*

[127] King-Hardy v. Bloomfield Bd. of Educ., No. Civ. 3:01CV979, 2002 WL 32500923, *7 (D. Conn. 2002); *see also* Moore-Fotso v. Bd. of Educ. of the City of Chi., 211 F.Supp.3d 1012, 1018; 1026-28 (N.D. Ill. 2016).

[128] Macy v. Hopkins Cty. Bd. of Educ., 429 F.Supp.2d 888, 892, 899 (W.D. Ky. 2006) ("The ADA protects only 'qualified' employees, that is a teacher qualified to do the job for which she is hired; and threatening to kill students disqualifies Macy from being a teacher.")

[129] *See* McGill v. Williamson Cty. Schs., 2013 WL 5346273, at * 1, 6 (M.D. Tenn. 2013) (The teacher's treating physician ruled out her qualification by writing "it is my opinion she will be unable to return to teaching in the future."); Roark v. LaGrange Sch. Dist., No. 10 C 7220, 2012 WL 1080368, at *4 (N.D. Ill. Mar. 30, 2012) (After a teacher left school suffering from anxiety and inability to focus, he never returned and the court concluded he had "a mental impairment of indefinite duration that rendered him unable to perform the essential functions of his teaching job with or without reasonable accommodation.")

[130] Unal v. Los Alamos Pub. Schs., No. 1:13-cv-00367 LAM/WPL, 2015 WL 13260396 (D. N.M. Mar. 6, 2015).

[131] *Ortega*, 2015 WL 4036016, at *18 (Teacher received an extension to complete assignment grading by the end of the week but missed the deadline. The teacher could not show this accommodation was unreasonable in light of the circumstances).

[132] *See* Preddie v. Bartholomew Consol. Sch. Corp., 799 F.3d 806, 813-15 (7th Cir. 2015)

[133] *Wanamaker*, 11 F.Supp.3d at 78 (noting that school reassigned teacher to a classroom position rather than a computer lab [stationary] position, and never engaged in figuring out what accommodations would allow her to be successful in the classroom position.).

[134] *Ortega*, 2015 WL 4036016, at *19-20.

[135] 29 U.S.C. §§ 2601-2654 (2012). Family Medical Leave Act of 1993, Pub. L. No. 103-3, 107 Stat. 6 (1993). *See also* U.S. Dep't of Labor, Wage and Hour Division (WHD), Family Medical Leave Act, https://www.dol.gov/whd/fmla/. (last visited July 26, 2017).

[136] 29 U.S.C. § 2615(a)(1)-(2) (2012).

[137] Ainsworth v. Loudon Cty. Sch. Bd., 851 Supp.2d 963, 972 (E.D. Va. 2012).

[138] Gore v. Cedar Hill Ind. School Dist., No. 3:15-cv-3963-M-BN, 2016 WL 4597513, at *6 (N.D. Tx. July 26, 2016) ("Plaintiff's allegation that Defendants violated his statutory rights by 'plac[ing] [him] on involuntary FMLA [leave]' is without merit as a matter of law.").

[139] *See generally* Chadwell v. Brewer, 59 F.Supp.3d 756, 766 (W.D. Va. 2014); Wanamaker v. Westport Bd. of Educ., 899 F.Supp.2d 193, 205 (D. Conn. 2012); Ainsworth v. Loudon Cty. Sch. Bd., 851 Supp.2d 963, 975 (E.D. Va. 2012); *see also* U.S. Dep't of Labor, WH1506, Need Time? The Employee's Guide to the Family Medical Leave Act (2015), https://www.dol.gov/whd/fmla/employeeguide.pdf.

[140] McArdle v. Town of Dracut/Dracut Pub. Schs., 732 F.3d 29 (1st Cir. 2013)

[141] *Preddie*, 799 F.3d at 816-17.

[142] Ozolins v. Northwood-Kensett Comm. Sch. Dist., 40 F.Supp.2d 1055 (N.D. Iowa 1999).

[143] *Id.* at 1064.

[144] Ruder v. Pequea Valley Sch. Dist., 790 F.Supp.2d 377, 394 (E.D. Penn. 2011); *see also* De Oliveira v. Cairo-Durham Cent. Sch. Dist., 634 Fed. Appx. 320, 322 (2d Cir. 2016).

[145] Holmes v. Board of Educ. of West Harvey-Dixmoor Sch. Dist. No. 147, No. 03 C 6897, 2006 WL 1843393, **12-13 (N.D. Ill. June 30, 2006).

[146] *Ainsworth*, 851 F.Supp.2d at 975.

[147] *Wanamaker*, 899 F.Supp.2d at 206.

[148] Aberman v. Bd. of Educ. of City of Chi., No. 12–cv–10181, 2017 WL 1036487, at *16 (N.D. Ill. Mar. 17, 2017)

[149] *Holmes*, 2006 WL 1843393, at *9-10.

[150] *See generally Wanamaker*, 899 F.Supp.2d at 207; *Ainsworth*, 851 F.Supp.2d at 976; Washington v. Houston Ind. Sch. Dist., No. H–05–3119, 2006 WL 6576892, at *3 (S.D. Tx. July 26, 2006).

[151] Ozolins v. Northwood-Kensett Comm. Sch. Dist., 40 F.Supp.2d 1065 (N.D. Iowa 1999).

[152] *See Preddie*, 799 F.3d at 816-17; *Wanamaker*, 899 F.Supp.2d at 208-09.

[153] Caldwell v. Clayton Cty. Sch. Dist., 604 Fed.Appx. 855, 860-863 (11th Cir. 2015).

[154] *Id.*

[155] Gore v. Cedar Hill Ind. Sch. Dist., No. 3:15-cv-3963-M-BN, 2016 WL 4597513, *7 (N.D. Tex. July 26, 2016)

[156] 29 U.S.C.A. § 2618 (2009); 29 C.F.R. § 825.600(a) (2016). In the handful of cases which cite to the FMLA's special rules for instructional employees, courts have held that those rules did not apply to the employees on the facts of the particular case, Bellone v. Southwick-Tolland Regional School Dist., 748 F.3d 418, 425 (1st Cir. 2014); Romano v. Board of Education for Bloom Township High School Dist., No. 14-cv-9095, 2016 WL 2344581, *3 (N.D. Illi. 2016); Holmes v. Fulton County School Dist., No. 1:06-CV-2556-CC-AJD, 2007 WL 9650147, *10 n.26 (N.D. Ga. 2007), or that the employee waived the claim by arguing it for the first time on appeal. *Bellone*, 748 F.3d at 425.

[157] Merrick T. Rossein, § 30:30 Generally, Special Rules for Educational Institutions, Family and Medical Leave Act of 1993, Westlaw (updated June 2017).

[158] 29 C.F.R. § 825.600(a) (2016).

[159] 29 C.F.R. § 825.601(a) (2016); 29 U.S.C.A. § 2618 (2009).

[160] *Id.*

[161] 29 U.S.C.A. § 2618(d) (2009).

[162] 29 C.F.R. § 825.602(b) (2016).

[163] *Id.*

[164] 29 C.F.R. § 825.602(a)(1) (2016).

[165] 29 C.F.R. § 825.603(b) (2016).

[166] 29 C.F.R. § 825.602(a)(2) (2016); 29 U.S.C.A. § 2618(d)(2) (2009).

[167] 29 C.F.R. § 825.602(a)(2) (2016); 29 U.S.C.A. § 2618(d)(2) (2009).

[168] 29 C.F.R. § 825.602(a)(3) (2016); 29 U.S.C.A. § 2618(d)(3) (2009).

[169] 29 C.F.R. § 825.602(a)(3) (2016); 29 U.S.C.A. § 2618(d)(3) (2009).

* The author would like to thank third-year law student Jacob Johnson for his valuable research and writing assistance.

Key Words

accommodation

administrative remedies

adverse employment action

age discrimination

Age Discrimination in Employment Act/ADEA

Americans with Disabilities Act/ADA

animus

bomb threat

burden shifting

but for cause

cat's paw theory

causation

constructive discharge

direct and indirect claims

disability claims

discharge

discriminatory treatment

disparate treatment

failure to accommodate

Family Medical Leave Act/FMLA

federal funds

harassment

instructional employee

insubordination

interference

leave

legitimate, nondiscriminatory

LGBTQ

major life activities

McDonnell Douglas

medical care

mental health

Muslim

national origin discrimination

nonrenewal

notice requirements

Pregnancy Discrimination Act

pretextual

prima facie

protected class/status/activity

racial discrimination

religious discrimination

retaliation

reverse discrimination

same actor inference

Section 504

sex/gender discrimination

similarly situated

temporal proximity

termination

third-party claim

Title VII of Rehabilitation Act

Section III – Chapter 6

Evaluations

Lynn Rossi Scott

Introduction

In most schools and districts—whether by statute, regulation, negotiated labor agreement, or customs of practice—responsibility for evaluating teachers typically is assigned to principals. While others in the district may also be involved in conducting teacher evaluation, this chapter focuses on the principal's role. Unfortunately, and somewhat ironically, the evaluation of employees is among the most difficult of a principal's various functions. Since most principals are former classroom educators, they tend to adhere to one of the basic philosophical beliefs that "All Children Can Learn." A dedicated educator believes that if a child has not learned something, it is more a reflection of the teacher's ability to teach than it is a reflection on the student's ability to learn. Therefore, the dedicated educator will reteach, repeat, or try different manipulations of the environment, different instructional strategies, or different presentation methods, all in an effort to ensure that a child learns. The evaluation of employees requires the same mindset, at least to some degree, since evaluation at a fundamental level is a form of teaching. However, it is not the responsibility of the supervisor, evaluator, or administrator to manipulate the environment, to change the employee's job description, or to reteach the employee until the employee learns how to master his or her job. At some point, after the supervisor has given the employee full notice of job expectations and performance deficiencies, it is the employee's responsibility to perform that job at an acceptable level; it is not the supervisor's responsibility to change the job so that the employee is successful.

Conversely, educators who correct and guide students' work every day sometimes react negatively to correction and guidance from their supervisors. What must be communicated to these reluctant learners is that constructive evaluations enable employees to become even better at their jobs. Evaluations allow employees to better understand the expectations on which they are judged. Most professionals would not knowingly continue doing things that disturb their supervisors. Only through evaluations, or some other remediation attempts, however, can professionals know what their supervisors find disturbing.

Without open and honest evaluation of job performance, the possibility exists that a professional will continue to act in a manner that is intolerable to a supervisor, ultimately destroying their working relationship.

This chapter will discuss statutory and judicial guidance regarding the elements of appropriate evaluation systems, as well as practical advice to avoid legal claims.

Legal Issues

Goals and Functions of Evaluation

An appropriately conducted evaluation process facilitates open, honest, and effective communication between the supervisor and the employee, making clear the supervisor's expectations for job performance and the supervisor's methods of evaluating that job performance. The evaluation process then provides the employee with notice of strengths, weaknesses, and required improvements in job performance. It may also provide timelines for corrections of behavior and methods by which behavior must be corrected. This notice then becomes an effective tool to manage employee behavior. In the vast majority of cases, the outcome of an appropriate evaluation system is improved employee performance.

Legal Intervention

In the rare situations when improved performance does not occur, the ultimate outcome of an evaluation process may be reassignment, demotion, the termination or nonrenewal of employment, or the recognition by the employee that it is time to seek other employment. Adverse employment decisions are often litigated. At the time that a state or federal court steps in to review an employer's actions regarding an employee's job performance, the court is not in a position to view a teacher in a classroom or a custodian in a hallway. Rather, the judge or jury must rely on complete written evaluation documents drafted by the supervisor and others with evaluative responsibilities. Evaluations become critical evidence when employers must justify adverse employment decisions in court. Judicial intervention in an employee evaluation or termination often requires that the court interpret statutory language, regulatory provisions, board policies, collective bargaining agreements, contract language, and the evaluation instruments themselves. Therefore, it is essential that these potential pieces of evidence be understandable to non-educators and be direct, clear, and capable of withstanding such judicial scrutiny.

Indeed, it is becoming more and more common for state statutes to require that employment termination and contract nonrenewal decisions be based on written evaluations that point out specific job performance deficiencies, and for courts to overturn employment termination decisions when evaluations are either not provided or are improperly provided.[1]

For example, school districts in Alaska require that each nontenured teacher receive at least two observations per year.[2] Each tenured teacher and administrator must receive an annual evaluation.[3] Oklahoma has established the Oklahoma Teacher and Leader Effectiveness System, which requires annual teacher evaluations.[4] Florida public school district employees must all receive annual evaluations, except new teachers, who must receive two evaluations their first year.[5] West Virginia's statute states that its mandatory evaluation system for professional personnel shall serve the following purposes:

1. Serve as a basis for the improvement of the performance of the personnel in their assigned duties.

2. Provide an indicator for satisfactory performance for individual professionals.

3. Serve as documentation for a dismissal on the grounds of unsatisfactory performance.

4. Serve as the basis for programs to increase the professional growth and development of professional personnel.[6]

The West Virginia statute further contains a plan for performance improvement:

> A professional whose performance is considered to be unsatisfactory shall be given notice of deficiencies. A remediation plan to correct deficiencies shall be developed by the employing county board of education and the professional. The professional shall be given a reasonable period of time for remediating the deficiencies and shall receive a statement of the resources and assistance available for the purposes of correcting the deficiencies.[7]

Finally, West Virginia's statute establishes outcomes for performance improvement and for lack of improvement:

> Any professional whose performance evaluation includes a written improvement plan shall be given an opportunity to improve his or her performance through the implementation of the plan. If the next performance evaluation shows that the professional is now performing satisfactorily, no further action may be taken concerning the original performance evaluation. If the evaluation shows that the professional is still not performing satisfactorily, the evaluator either shall make additional recommendations for improvement or may recommend the dismissal of the professional in accordance with the provisions of section eight §18A-2-8 of this article.[8]

Mandatory statutory notice of performance deficiencies prior to adverse employment action is also becoming more common, for the simple reason that it appears fair to employees and to the legislatures that create such laws.

That is not to say that the absence of a poor evaluation grade will necessarily destroy an employment termination case. In fact, even in some states in which performance evaluations or written records of notice of unsatisfactory work performance are required by law, there is an acknowledgment that certain conduct is non-remediable or uncorrectable and, therefore, does not require a remediation attempt. Such non-remediable conduct can include intentionally harmful conduct, insubordination, intemperance, dishonesty, immorality, misrepresentation, fraud, and other intentional misconduct such as abuse or battery.[9] Often, evaluations are also unnecessary when employment is terminated for budgetary or financial exigency reasons unrelated to an employee's job performance, and when the reduction-in-force system does not consider performance as a criterion for selection of employees subject to reduction in force.[10] Finally, evaluations are often unnecessary for those employees who are at-will employees, such as auxiliary staff, noncertified administrators, and others without contracts, who can be fired or who can resign for any reason.[11] In the majority of cases, however, a proper evaluation system, correctly implemented, is essential.

The Importance of Appropriate Evaluation Systems

A proper evaluation can make a termination or nonrenewal case pass judicial muster. On the contrary, a poorly drafted evaluation, or the lack of an evaluation, can sometimes destroy the possibility of a successful termination or nonrenewal case. For example, consider two adverse employment actions which, after judicial review, resulted in very different outcomes based on the evaluations provided by supervisors.

The Supreme Court of Appeals in West Virginia reviewed a termination action of a thirteen-year employee of a school district who had an exemplary record until her campus got a new principal.[12] After their relationship quickly became strained, the principal started keeping records, ultimately listing ten incidents of the teacher's improper behavior, involving such things as the teacher throwing bookbags; crying and stating that she wished she would die when she was upset about a classroom scheduling issue; telling the principal that if she was having a bad day, she might jump out a window and give the proceeds to her children; calling her principal "Napoleon"; failing to maintain classroom discipline; taking all of her students with her on an out-of-class errand; moving a heavy locker by herself; and falling to her knees during a parent-teacher conference in which she was explaining how the parent's special education student received red marks around his neck.[13] However, the principal did not share any of his written documentation or any warning, criticism, or concern with the teacher until he wrote five of the incidents on the teacher's otherwise excellent classroom observation a number of months later. The principal then presented the evaluation to the teacher with a needs assessment and asked her to sign it, without allowing any meaningful discussion. She refused because she did not understand his needs assessment. Four months later, he again observed her classroom performance, again noting exemplary classroom teaching, and again attached his criticisms regarding the teacher's prior acts. At the summative evaluation conference, after the principal read his criticisms, he again did not allow discussion. Instead, he asked the teacher to immediately sign the evaluation documents, and she refused. Two days later, the principal once more asked her to sign the evaluation, again without giving her an opportunity to discuss his comments. When she refused to sign a second time, her principal told her that she would be called to appear before the school board in Welch, West Virginia, regarding her refusal. She responded by telling her principal that she would draw a map for him to get to Welch.

The situation continued to escalate. Days later, the teacher, without prior warning, was driven to the superintendent's office to discuss the principal's concerns about her job performance and her refusal to sign her evaluation. Again, however, in the meeting with the superintendent, assistant superintendent, and the principal, she was not given an opportunity to respond to her principal's criticisms, but was just asked to sign the documents or face discipline. Feeling like a "caged animal," she told the principal that she should have blown his head off with a shotgun. After hearing the teacher's comment, the superintendent called 911 and told her that he was recommending termination of her employment because her comment confirmed that the principal's allegations were legitimate and she was insubordinate.[14]

The teacher filed suit after her employment was terminated for insubordination, which by that state's statute does not require remediation. The West Virginia Supreme Court of Appeals ultimately remanded the case for further consideration. Describing the situation as a personality conflict that "escalated grievously," the court characterized the teacher's conduct as performance-related rather than insubordinate, and then criticized the principal for his failure to constructively communicate legitimate job-performance concerns with the teacher. The court held that the teacher's job performance and communication with her supervisor should have been "meaningfully deliberated upon," and the district should have analyzed whether or not the teacher's conduct was correctable before terminating her employment. Because neither occurred, the court, without sanctioning the teacher's behavior, determined that she should have been given a remediation attempt and an improvement period, if her behavior was remediable. Therefore, in spite of clearly unprofessional conduct by the teacher, the case was remanded to determine whether the teacher's conduct was correctable, with the likelihood being that the teacher would reclaim her job.[15]

On the other hand, consider the teacher in the Houston Independent School District in Texas who had a continuing contract with the district and whose performance was evaluated numerous times during two school years. Evaluations of the teacher's performance included both written assessments and videotapes of the teacher's classroom performance. The videotapes were used so that the teacher could more easily follow and understand the evaluation team's observations and criticisms. At the termination hearing, the school board heard testimony from the teacher's supervisors and reviewed approximately one hundred documents regarding the teacher's classroom performance. The board also viewed a thirty-minute videotape, which included excerpts from five separate videotapes made of the teacher's classroom performance. The court held that both the written evaluation and the videotapes revealed numerous problems with the teacher's performance. The teacher was told of these problems, but did not correct and improve her performance. Therefore, the court upheld the board's employment termination decision.[16]

Judges are not educators, nor are they education evaluators. As such, when there is an evaluation or assessment procedure, when that procedure appears to have been followed, and when there is concrete evidence of an evaluation or other evaluative materials, judges have shown a great deal of deference to educational administrators in determining the appropriate standards of performance of education professionals and other school employees. As stated by one court, public schools need not be "married to mediocrity" when setting standards for the evaluation of professional employees.[17] What school administrators must do, however, is communicate those standards and notify those who do not meet the standards. Where evaluations are mandatory under state statute, regulations, local policies, or contracts, the courts appear to afford a great deal of protection to employees, requiring that the employees be properly evaluated and informed regarding problems with their job performance so that their deficient performance can be corrected.[18]

Furthermore, when those evaluations are statutorily required, and those evaluations are properly performed, courts are much more likely to conclude that an employee "cannot complain" about notice of job performance concerns and the remediation opportunity that notice provides, even when the employee fails to understand the remediation required or the consequences of a failure or refusal to remediate job performance.[19]

It is incumbent upon a board to develop sound policies with regard to evaluations. It is further incumbent upon the campus administrator to follow the evaluation policies and procedures that are developed. It is then necessary that specific job-related performance criteria, those that are valid and observable, be used in the evaluation of an employee's performance such that it is clear to the employee that the performance level expected by a supervisor will enable the employee to achieve success in that workplace. Further, it is highly recommended that employees be given advance notice of performance criteria, the priorities and expectations of the administrator, and the procedures that will be followed, to minimize the degree of uncertainty in the process and to make clear that the process is as objective and nondiscriminatory as possible.

Implementation of Evaluation Policies

A number of cases have considered whether a failure to comply with evaluation procedures is a constitutional defect violative of the due process clause of state constitutions. These cases tend to reflect that problems with an evaluation do not rise to the level of a constitutional violation. Courts often find property rights in continued employment, based on either state statutes or contracts.[20] However, the same does not hold true in finding a property right to a particular evaluation. A statutory right to receive an evaluation does not normally create a protected property right to continued employment, although some courts have held that a teacher is entitled to a hearing, complete with cross-examination, regarding whether the statutory criteria were followed in assessing a teacher.[21] The typical due process notion of notice and a hearing before deprivation of a property right, therefore, seldom applies to an evaluation. Courts have held that federal procedural due process does not entitle any employee to an evaluation or any related procedures, although that could be required under state law or board policy.[22] Even if a statutory evaluation process creates a protected property interest, however, an "unsatisfactory" evaluation does not normally constitute egregious official misconduct sufficient to trigger a violation of substantive due process.[23] In addition, stigmatizing comments on a performance evaluation do not normally implicate an employee's liberty interests, because evaluation comments are not normally made public and, therefore, do not impair an employee's rights to a good name, reputation, honor, or integrity, as required to support a liberty interest due process claim.[24] The courts have even held that an evaluation policy that is established by a school district board of education does not create a right to reemployment by a nontenured teacher,[25] although the evaluation procedure itself may be subject to mandatory negotiation in a collective bargaining state.[26]

That does not mean, however, that those conducting evaluations need not follow procedures. The responsibility to implement evaluation policies and to document compliance with those policies is typically the responsibility of the principal. In general, the courts adopt a standard called "substantial compliance" in determining whether or not a principal complied with required procedures.[27] This standard of "substantial compliance," as opposed to "full and complete compliance," attempts to avoid placing an undue burden on a school administrator.[28] When different courts have used a substantial compliance standard, they have explained that supervising administrators are not required to ensure that every employee fully understands every suggestion for improvement or the means by which an employee might obtain assistance in making required improvements.[29] However, failures to comply with essential elements of evaluation policies can result in reinstatements for school employees when it is determined those employees have been improperly subjected to inadequate, incomplete, or prejudicial performance evaluations, or when an essential criterion for assessment, such as student performance, has not been considered.[30] Furthermore, a violation of an evaluation statute has, in at least one situation, resulted in reinstatement of a school employee, when it was impossible to evaluate the employee because she was off work on approved medical leave.[31]

Legal Challenges to Evaluation Systems

In order to avoid later contentions that an evaluation system is arbitrary or capricious, it is essential that evaluation criteria be valid, observable, and directly related to the job.[32] A hotly debated topic is whether student achievement should be used to evaluate teacher performance. No Child Left Behind, a 2002 federal law designed to improve public education, contained very high-achieving goals for making students college- and career-ready. Because the goals were so high as to be unattainable, a waiver provision was added to allow states to seek waivers of goals.[33] Since 2011, the U.S. Department of Education allowed states to obtain waivers of some of the more onerous expectations of NCLB. However, to receive the waivers, states were required to develop rigorous and comprehensive plans to address what the U.S. Department of Education perceived to be critical areas to improve educational outcomes for students. One of those requirements was that states, through their legislatures or state education agencies, set basic guidelines for teacher/principal evaluations that used multiple measures, including student growth.[34] Under the waivers, student growth was typically measured by standardized test results. The new teacher/principal evaluation systems under the waivers were due to be implemented by 2014–2015, so that personnel decisions could be made during the 2015–2016 school year.[35]

In the meantime, greatly concerned about the concept of over-testing students, the U.S. Congress passed the Every Student Succeeds Act (ESSA), which severely limited federal involvement in teacher evaluations. ESSA, enacted in 2015, leaves more decisions about the content of teacher and principal evaluations to the states.[36] It does, however, provide that school districts "may include a rigorous, transparent, and fair evaluation and support system for teachers, principals, or other school leaders that is based, in part, on evidence of student achievement, which may include student growth; and shall include multiple measures of educator performance and provide clear, timely, and useful feedback to teachers, principals, or other school leaders."[37] Recognizing that states have spent years enacting legislation designed to incorporate student progress into teacher evaluations to obtain previously requested waivers, it remains unclear what states will do—eliminate recently enacted legislation to incorporate student progress into the evaluation system, go back to more traditional models that focus on characteristics of a good teacher, or create new, innovative evaluation models. What is clear is that the movement to incorporate student growth into teacher evaluations sparked a great deal of legislation and a multitude of lawsuits.

A number of states have now enacted laws incorporating student test performance into teacher evaluations. As examples, Florida requires that at least one-third of a performance evaluation be based on student growth and achievement data.[38] [39] Beginning with the 2015–2016 school year, Michigan required that 25% of a teacher's evaluation be based on student growth and assessment data. Beginning in the 2018–2019 school year, 40% of a teacher's evaluation in Michigan will be based on student growth and assessment.[40]

When the New Mexico legislature failed to act in compliance with an NCLB waiver and pass the Teacher and School Leader Effectiveness Act—which would have incorporated student growth into evaluations—the state's Secretary of the Public Education Department created and published regulations for teacher evaluations that emphasized teacher effectiveness and student achievement growth.[41] Not unexpectedly, litigation ensued, although the Secretary's right to implement the regulations was upheld by the court in a mandamus proceeding.[42]

Florida's Student Success Act mandated that for purposes of teacher and principal evaluations, student learning growth must have been originally measured by statewide assessments in the areas covered by statewide assessments and by school district assessments in the areas not covered by statewide assessments—a so-called "value-added model."[43] It analyzed student test scores from prior and current years, the number of subject-relevant courses in which a student was enrolled, and attendance, and then output the teacher's contribution to student success and the school's contribution to student success (principal leadership, neighborhood effects, etc.). As a result of a dearth of statewide assessments, evaluation standards differed greatly between school districts. In some cases, teachers were evaluated based on students' test scores in classes the teachers did not teach. The statute required that teacher pay, promotion, assignment and retention be based on the evaluations. Teachers from several school districts sued the Florida Commissioner of Education alleging substantive due process violations, equal protection claims, and state law violations. The federal district court, while finding the system unfair, held that it passed constitutional muster because the court found a conceivable rational basis to support the system; i.e., that it is rational to believe the policies advanced a legitimate state interest in increasing student learning growth, teachers positively influence student learning growth, student growth can be factored into teacher evaluations, and such inclusions can lead to improved teacher performance.[44] In another attack on the statute, this time in state court, the court held that the statute did not unconstitutionally delegate core legislative authority to the state's Board of Education.[45] The statute has since been amended to allow the Commissioner of Education to approve formulas to measure individual student learning growth on statewide standardized English language arts and math tests, but to also consider student attendance, disability, and English language proficiency as factors. The Commissioner will also add new formulas as new statewide assessments are implemented.[46]

In 2011, a group of parents sued the Los Angeles Unified School District, as well as the teachers' union and the administrators' union, alleging that the district's students were being "deprived of their Constitutional right to basic educational equality and opportunity to learn" by the district's failure to use student progress as a measure for evaluating teachers and administrators.[47] The California "Stull Act" requires that school boards consider "the progress of pupils towards [board-adopted standards of expected student achievement] and, if applicable, the state-adopted academic content standards as measured by state-adopted criterion-referenced assessments" when evaluating its teachers and administrators.[48] At the time the lawsuit was filed, the district was using an evaluation system that primarily focused on a teacher's use of instructional methods. The district argued that the evaluation system indirectly measured student progress because teachers were rated based on their ability to use periodic student testing data to guide classroom instruction. Determining that an evaluation of a teacher's instructional technique was not direct enough to make the required connection between student progress and teacher evaluation, the court issued an order directing the district to evaluate the performance of its professional employees as it "reasonably relates to pupil progress towards [district and state standards]." However, the court's order stated that the district still had the discretion to determine: (1) the means of measuring student performance that will be used in the evaluation; (2) how the student performance criteria will be incorporated into teacher and administrator evaluations; (3) the importance of student progress in relation to other factors on which the employees would be evaluated; and (4) the training requirements for principals in how to use student progress in teacher evaluations. The court's ruling will potentially change the criteria used by many California school districts to evaluate professional employees.

California litigation over teacher quality continues. In 2014, a state court judge ruled as unconstitutional five of California's teacher tenure and dismissal laws, which resulted in 1–3%, or 2,750–8,250 teachers, who were considered to be grossly ineffective still having protected jobs.[49] However, a three-judge panel of the appellate court reversed the trial court's decision and held that the teacher tenure, layoff, and dismissal statutes were not unconstitutional. Lawyers for parents requested that the California Supreme Court reverse the Court of Appeals' decision, but the state's highest court declined to hear the case.[50]

In yet another case addressing California Stull Act, parents sued thirteen school districts seeking to compel them to formally evaluate teachers based, in part, on student standardized test performance. The court, however, concluded that the Stull Act, in its discussion of teacher evaluations, is not that clear. The court determined that the Stull Act does not require school districts to evaluate each teacher in a summative evaluation with consequences based on students' standardized test scores.[51]

Other courts, while acknowledging the flaws and unfairness of teacher evaluation systems based on student growth, especially to teachers in areas in which student growth is not measured on standardized tests, have held the statutes to be constitutional.[52]

Individual cases based on value-added measurement models appear to be especially problematic for courts. One court analyzed a teacher's evaluation score of "ineffective," even though her high-achieving students scored very similarly to her students in years past, when she received "effective" ratings. The court was especially concerned with what the court described as the "VAM bias against teachers at both ends of the spectrum," the inability of high-achieving students to demonstrate as much growth as that achieved by low-performing students, the swing in the teacher's scores from one year to the next with similarly achieving students, and the school district's imposition of a Bell curve that places teachers in four categories regardless of whether student performance rose or fell. The court concluded that the teacher's growth score and rating was "indisputably arbitrary and capricious," and so vacated and set aside her evaluation.[53]

Elements of Appropriate Evaluation Systems

The most effective evaluation environment is that in which the supervisor develops a pattern of continual feedback regarding the employee's job performance, so that nothing on a summative performance evaluation comes as a surprise to the employee. This can be done informally, by discussing situations as they arise, or on a more formal basis, through appropriate documentation. While not always essential, employees should also receive advance notice of potential consequences of good and of bad evaluations.[54] While it can certainly be argued that employees know the consequences of good and bad evaluations, because different systems result in different management decisions based on evaluations, employees should understand the consequences of failing to improve job performance after receiving poor evaluations in their school systems.

A good evaluation system starts with a pre-observation conference, at which a supervisor informs the employee of the supervisor's criteria, the supervisor's priorities and expectations, and the procedure that will be used for the evaluation. This conference should be documented so that it is clear that the pre-observation conference occurred. At this point, it is appropriate for the employee to have input into the evaluation process. This participation can come in the form of a pre-observation discussion of expectations, plans and goals, or warnings, and should give the employee the opportunity to inform the evaluator of any special circumstances that the evaluator may observe. The pre-observation conference can also help to insure that an employee understands what conduct will be assessed and how it will be assessed, so that both the evaluator and the employee can focus on the appropriate elements of the employee's performance.[55]

After the supervisor has observed employee performance, timely notice of specific performance deficiencies that are related to the employee's job performance should be provided to the employee. Those deficiencies should be consistent with the job-related evaluation criteria that were originally established. If they are not, then either those deficiencies do not hinge upon appropriate job performance, or the criteria upon which the evaluation is based should be revised.[56] This timely notice should be in written form, but should also be presented orally to the employee so that frank, person-to-person communication can occur, misunderstandings can be corrected, and expectations can be clarified.[57]

The written document should be closely edited to insure that there are no typographical, factual, or other embarrassing errors that could distract from the purpose of the evaluation, discredit the evaluator, be used as evidence in any administrative or judicial proceeding, or made public through some other means. A post-observation evaluation conference should also provide an employee an opportunity to respond to the comments that were made by the evaluator. After the conference, the employee should be provided with an opportunity to respond in writing to an unsatisfactory performance evaluation, and the supervisor should review that response so that errors can be corrected and all sides of a story can be considered.[58] In some jurisdictions, the employee is allowed to grieve that performance evaluation to the board or beyond, or to have some other measure of oversight, such as a second appraiser or a rebuttal right.[59]

If a campus principal is concerned that an employee will allege that the principal has shown bias in the evaluation of the employee, it is always a good idea for the campus principal to bring in objective third parties to also observe the teacher's performance. These observation evaluations by trained evaluators can confirm deficiencies discovered by the principal and can provide additional assistance to the employee in remediating improper job performance. Further, these outside evaluators will not be perceived as having the same alleged bias as an on-campus professional; they can strengthen evidence that may be presented in any later proceeding.[60] It is likely that a school board or a court would rely to a greater degree on multiple reports by different evaluators that confirm a specific performance deficiency of an employee. Of course, the supervisor does run the risk that a different evaluator may find an employee's performance to be satisfactory, which could jeopardize any future remediation attempts or adverse employment actions contemplated by the supervisor. Should such an evaluation occur, it is incumbent upon the campus administrator to seriously review his or her evaluation of the employee's performance to determine whether or not bias does, in fact, exist.

Remediation of Employee Job Performance

It is essential that all employees be evaluated in a uniform manner and that they be given an opportunity to remediate perceived correctable performance deficiencies. In a Fifth Circuit termination case, an employer was held liable for race discrimination against a minority employee who was given consistently good evaluations and pay raises in spite of performance deficiencies. The employee's supervisor stated that the good evaluations were given in an effort to avoid any confrontations with the employee about her work. The supervisor further admitted that he instructed other employees to give her good evaluations in order to avoid charges of race discrimination by the employee. The Fifth Circuit held that by ignoring its own evaluation procedures, the employer discriminated against the employee by not giving her the same opportunity to improve her job performance as the employer did of white employees who received honest evaluations.[61]

A remediation plan for the improvement of an employee's job performance should be developed in cooperation with the employee. The remediation plan should note the specific deficiencies that are being targeted, methods by which the employee can remediate the specific job performance areas, and objective criteria for determining whether or not the employee has accomplished the goal of remediating his or her job performance. Finally, a remediation plan should include a timeline for remediation of the performance.[62] A reasonable time period for an employee to complete a remediation plan should be allowed.

The nature of the performance deficiencies, the nature of the employment, the extent of the person's education and experience, and the egregiousness of the conduct all factor into the amount of time that is required for remediation of performance.[63] For example, it may only take one day to learn to stand at the classroom door and greet students with a smile when they enter. On the contrary, it may take a year to perfect implementation of a new computer curriculum.

What if an employee refuses to cooperate in the development of a growth plan or objects to the supervisor's expectations? As long as the supervisor is consistent in his or her expectations, it is within the supervisor's discretion to require certain job performance standards. Therefore, while a certain amount of "give and take" is to be expected in the development of a growth plan, a supervisor ultimately can, and should, set job-performance standards and expect those standards to be met consistently.

Prior to making an adverse employment decision to nonrenew, nonextend, terminate, or demote an employee, it is recommended that all anecdotal records regarding previous job performance issues, including classroom observations and complaints by parents or fellow workers, be compiled. These anecdotal records and formal and informal reports contribute to the overall weight of the evidence to be accorded an unsatisfactory job evaluation.[64] They will form the basis of any adverse employment action.

Avoiding Legal Claims

Courts have frequently considered whether poor performance evaluations constitute "adverse employment actions" sufficient to present discrimination or retaliation claims in court, most often requiring tangible changes in working conditions or duties, or material changes in salary or position, before an actionable adverse employment action is found.[65] On the other hand, a negative evaluation that results in denial of a raise could constitute an adverse employment action sufficient to maintain a discrimination or retaliation claim.[66]

The very nature of an employee evaluation system requires that the supervisor discriminate between effective and ineffective employees. It is very important, however, that a supervisor be careful not to discriminate illegally against any employee. Furthermore, it is incumbent upon a supervisor to refrain from any sort of retaliation, especially when an employee has exercised a constitutional or statutory right.

Federal protections against illegal discrimination and retaliation include free speech as a private citizen on matters of public concern;[67] illegal discrimination on the basis of race, national origin, religion, and/or sex or sex stereotypes;[68] illegal discrimination on the basis of age;[69] or illegal discrimination on the basis of disability, pregnancy, or genetic information.[70] The supervisor must also avoid discrimination or retaliation on the basis of pension interests,[71] wage and hour complaints,[72] workplace safety,[73] garnishment of indebtedness,[74] refusal to submit to a polygraph test,[75] union membership or political party membership,[76] medical leave for family or self,[77] or bankruptcy,[78] among others. Depending on the state, numerous state protections and common law protections also exist to protect an employee against illegal discrimination or retaliation.

To avoid potential state defamation claims, evaluations must also be truthful and accurate, and the negative comments made in evaluations should be kept confidential from all except the employee being evaluated. As long as comments in an evaluation are truthful and are not made public to third parties, an employee will not be able to claim that he or she was defamed or that his or her good name and reputation was impaired.[79] In fact, in some states, teacher evaluations are expressly made confidential by law.[80]

Recommendations for Practice

1. Develop sound evaluation policies and procedures and follow them.

2. Apply specific job-related performance criteria that are valid, observable, and related to an employee's job performance.

3. Give advance notice of performance criteria, priorities, expectations, and the procedures that will be used.

4. Give advance notice of potential consequences of good and bad evaluations.

5. Consider employee input.

6. Develop a pattern of continual feedback regarding job performance.

7. Proofread all documentation before presentation to the employee.

8. Timely inform the employee of specific evaluation problems, orally and in writing.

9. Allow the employee to respond to evaluations orally, in writing, or through a grievance, appeal, or arbitration process.

10. Evaluate all employees in a uniform manner to avoid the inference of discrimination.

11. Ensure that evaluations are truthful and accurate.

12. Keep evaluations confidential from all except the employee being evaluated.

13. Do not use an evaluation to retaliate against any employee for any legally protected conduct, or to discriminate based on any legally protected status.

14. Develop a remediation plan in cooperation with the employee, if necessary. Follow up on the remediation plan with periodic checkups.

15. Provide a reasonable time for the employee to correct deficiencies, with activities designed to correct performance problem areas.

16. Allow more than one evaluator to observe an employee if there are concerns regarding objectivity or bias.

17. Make all employment decisions based on job performance as a whole, using all available documents, including evaluations.

18. If making an adverse employment decision, follow all constitutional, statutory, and contractual procedures.

Endnotes

[1] Simmons v. New Pub. Sch. Dist. No. 8, 574 N.W.2d 561 (N.D. 1999); Fla. Stat. Ann. § 1012.34 (West, current through 2016 2nd R.S. of the 24th Leg.); Tex. Educ. Code Ann. § 21.203(a) (West, current through the 2015 R.S. of the 8th Leg.).

[2] Alaska Stat. §14.20.149 (West, current through the 2016 1st R.S. of the 29th Leg.).

[3] *Id.*

[4] Okla. Stat. Ann. tit. 70, § 6-101.16 (West, current through the 2016 2nd R.S. of the 55th Leg.).

[5] Fla. Stat. Ann. § 1012.34 (West, current through 2016 2nd R.S. of the 55th Leg.).

[6] W. Va. Code Ann.. § 18A-2-12(e)(3)(A)-(D) (2012) (West, current through the 2016 R.S.).

[7] W. Va. Code Ann. § 18A-2-12(f) (2012) (West, current through the 2016 R.S.).

[8] W. Va. Code Ann. § 18A-2-12(h) (2012) (West, current through the 2016 R.S.).

[9] West v. San Jon Bd. of Educ., 79 P.3d 842 (N.M. Ct. App. 2003); Harjo v. Bd. of Educ. of Indep. Sch. Dist. No. 7 of Seminole Cnty., 976 P.2d 1096 (Okla. Civ. App. 1999); W. Va. Code R. § 18A–2–8 (West, current through the 2016 R.S.).

[10] Savre v. Indep. Sch. Dist. No. 283, 642 N.W.2d 467 (Minn. Ct. App. 2002).

[11] Gonzalez v. State Operated Sch. Dist. of Newark, 784 A.2d 101 (N.J. Super. Ct. App. Div. 2001).

[12] Maxey v. McDowell Cnty. Bd. of Educ., 575 S.E.2d 278 (W. Va. 2002); *See also*, Boss v. Filmore Cnty. Sch. Dist. No. 19, 559 N.W.2d 448 (Neb. 1997).

[13] *Maxey* at 281.

[14] *Id.*

[15] *Id.*

[16] Roberts v. Houston Indep. Sch. Dist., 788 S.W.2d 107 (Tex. App. 1990).

[17] Briggs v. Bd. of Dirs. of Hinton Comm. Sch. Dist., 282 N.W.2d 740, 743 (Iowa 1979); Bd. of Dir. of Ames Cnty. Sch. Dist. v. Cullinan, 745 N.W.2d 487 (Iowa 2008).

[18] Chicago Bd. of Educ. v. Smith, 664 N.E.2d 113 (Ill. App. Ct. 1996); Farmer v. Kelleys Island Bd. of Educ., 630 N.E.2d 721 (Ohio 1994) (opinion clarified by 638 N.E.2d 79 (Ohio 1994)); Hellman v. Union Sch. Dist., 170 S.W.3d 52 (Mo. Ct. App. 2005).

[19] Hoffner v. Bismarck Pub. Sch. Dist., 589 N.W.2d 195 (N.D. 1999); Dakos v. Lorain City Sch. Dist. Bd. of Educ., No. 01–CA–007888, 2002 Ohio App. Lexis 93 (Ohio Ct. App. Jan. 16, 2002).

[20] Bd. of Regents of State Colleges v. Roth, 408 U.S. 564 (1972).

[21] Yates v. District of Columbia, 224 F. Supp. 2d 68 (D.D.C. 2002), *aff'd on other grounds*, 324 F.3d 724 (D.C. Cir. 2003); Witgenstein v. Sch. Bd. of Leon Cnty., 347 So. 2d 1069 (Fla. Dist. Ct. App. 1977)

[22] Atencio v. Bd. of Educ. of Penasco Indep. Sch. Dist. No. 4, 658 F.2d 774, 779 (10th Cir. 1981); Wood v. Indep. Sch. Dist. No. 141 of Pottawatomie Cnty., 661 P.2d 892 (Okla. 1983); Goodrich v. Newport News Sch. Bd., 743 F.2d 225 (4th Cir. 1984); Hibbits v. Buchanan Cnty. Sch. Bd., No. 1:09CV00073, 2010 U.S. Dist. Lexis 62422 (W.D. Va. June 23, 2010).

[23] Yates v. District of Columbia., 324 F.3d 724 (D.C. Cir. 2003).

[24] Echtenkamp v. Loudon Cnty. Pub. Schs., 263 F. Supp. 2d 1043 (E.D. Va. 2003).

[25] King v. Jefferson Cnty. Bd. of Educ., 659 So. 2d 686 (Ala. Civ. App. 1995).

[26] *In re* Pittsfield Sch. Dist., 744 A.2d 594 (N.H. 1999).

[27] McKenzie v. Webster Parish Sch. Bd., 653 So. 2d 215 (La. Ct. App. 1995); Thomas v. Bd. of Educ. of Newark City Sch. Dist., 643 N.E.2d 131 (Ohio 1994); White Mountain Reg'l Sch. Dist., 908 A. 2d 790 (N.H. 2006).

[28] Thomas, 643 N.E.2d at 134.

[29] Dakos, 2002 Ohio App. Lexis 93.

[30] Snyder v. Mendon-Union Local Sch. Dist. Bd. of Educ., 661 N.E.2d 717 (Ohio 1996); Sherrod v. Palm Beach Cnty. Sch. Bd., 963 So. 2d 251 (Fla. Dist. Ct. App. 2006).

[31] Skilton v. Perry Local Sch. Dist. Bd. of Educ., No. 2001–L–140, 2002 Ohio App. Lexis 6470 (Ohio Ct. App. Dec. 6, 2002), aff'd by 807 N.E.2d 919 (Ohio 2004).

[32] Meyer v. Bd. of Educ. of Charlotte Valley Cent. Sch. Dist., 581 N.Y.S.2d 920 (N.Y. App. Div. 1992).

[33] 20 U.S.C. § 7861 (West).

[34] June 18, 2013 Policy Letter from U.S. Secretary of Education Arne Duncan.

[35] Id.

[36] ESSA, 20 U.S.C.A. § 6613 (West).

[37] 20 U.S.C. § 6613(b)(3) (2016).

[38] Fla. Stat. Ann. 1012.34(3)(a)(1) (West, current through 2016 R.S. of the 29th Leg.).

[39] Fla. Stat. Ann. § 1012.34(7) (West, current through 2016 R.S. of the 29th Leg.)

[40] Mich. Comp. Laws Serv. 380.1249(2)(1)(i).

[41] 6.69.8 N.M. Admin. Code (2012).

[42] New Mexico v. Skandera, 346 P.3d 1191 (N.M. App. 2015).

[43] Fla. Stat. Ann § 1012.34(3)(1)(West, current through the 2016 2nd R.S. of the 24th Leg.).

[44] Cook v. Stewart, 28 F. Supp. 3d, 1207 (N.D. Fla. 2014).

[45] Robinson v. Stewart, 161 So. 3d 589 (Fla. App. 1 Dist. 2015).

[46] Fla. Stat. Ann. § 1012.34(7) (West current through the 2016 R.S. of the 29th Legis).

[47] Tentative Decision on Petition for Writ of Mandate, Doe v. Deasy, No. BS 134604 (Cal. Super. Ct. June 5, 2012.), See also, Los Angeles Unif. Sch. Dist. v. Superior Court, 228 Cal App. 4th 222 (2012).

[48] Cal. Educ. Code § 44662(b) (West, current through 2016 R.S.).

[49] Vergara v. Cal., 246 Cal. App. 4th 619 (Sup. Ct. of Cal. (August 27, 2014)).

[50] Vergara v. State (Cal. Ct. App. 2016) 209 Cal.Rptr.3d 532, 556, rehg den. (May 3, 2016), review den. (Aug. 22, 2016).

[51] Opinion & Order, Doe, et al. v. Antioch Unified Sch. Dist., et al., No. MSN 15-1127 (Cal. Super. Ct. Contra Costa County Sept. 19, 2016).

[52] Wagner v. Haslam, 112 F. Supp. 3d 673 (M.D. Tenn. 2015).

[53] In re Lederman v. King, Index No. 5443-14; RJ1 No. 01-14-ST6183 (N.Y. S.Ct. Albany Cnty. May 10, 2016).

[54] McQuinn v. Douglas Cnty. Sch. Dist. No. 66, 612 N.W.2d 198 (Neb. 2000).

[55] Crump v. Durham Cnty. Bd. of Educ., 327 S.E.2d 599 (N.C. Ct. App. 1985).

[56] Iversen v. Wall Bd. of Educ., 522 N.W.2d 188 (S.D. 1994); Hendrickson v. Spartanburg Cnty. Sch. Dist. No. 5, 413 S.E.2d 871 (S.C. Ct. App. 1992).

[57] Maxey, 575 S.E.2d at 278.

[58] In re Lincoln-Woodstock Coop. Sch. Dist., 731 A.2d 992 (N.H. 1999).

[59] Homan v. Blue Ridge Sch. Dist., 405 A.2d 572 (Pa. Commw. Ct. 1979); 19 Tex. Admin. Code § 150.1004(a),(c) (West 2012).

[60] Cliff v. Bd. of Sch. Comm'rs of Indianapolis, 42 F.3d 403 (7th Cir. 1994); Spry v. Winston-Salem-Forsyth Cnty. Bd. of Educ., 412 S.E.2d 687 (N.C. Ct. App. 1992), aff'd 422 S.E.2d 575 (N.C. 1992) (superseded by statute on other grounds).

[61] Vaughn v. Edel, 918 F.2d 517, 523 (5th Cir. 1990).

[62] Kurey v. New York State Sch. for the Deaf, 642 N.Y.S.2d 415 (N.Y. App. Div. 1996); Newcomb v. Humansville R-IV Sch. Dist., 908 S.W.2d 821 (Mo. Ct. App. 1995); Thomas Cnty Sch. Dist, v. Bd. of Educ. of Newark, 643 N.E.2d at 134.

[63] Gayno v. Indep. Sch. Dist. No. 832, 311 N.W.2d 497 (Minn. 1981); Mason Cnty. Bd. of Educ. v. State Superintendent of Schs., 274 S.E.2d 435 (W. Va. 1980).

[64] Seifert v. Lingleville Indep. Sch. Dist., 692 S.W.2d 461 (Tex. 1985); Aigner v. Cass Sch. Twp. of LaPorte Cnty., 577 N.E.2d 983 (Ind. Ct. App. 1991); Beck v. James, 793 S.W.2d 416 (Mo. Ct. App. 1990).

[65] Weimann v. Indianola Cmty. Sch. Dist., 278 F. Supp. 2d 968 (S.D. Iowa 2003).

[66] Crawford v. Carroll, 529 F.3d 961 (11th Cir. 2008).

[67] Pickering v. Bd. of Educ. of Twp. High Sch. Dist. 205, 391 U.S. 563 (1968); Levich v. Liberty Cent. Sch. Dist, 361 F. Supp. 2d 151 (S.D.N.Y. 2004); Morey v. Somers Cent. Sch. Dist., No. 06 Civ. 1877 (WCC), 2007 U.S. Dist. Lexis 20265 (S.D.N.Y. Mar. 21, 2007).

[68] 42 U.S.C.S. § 2000e *et seq.* (2016); 42 U.S.C.S. § 1981 (2016); Burlington N. & Santa Fe Ry. Co. v. White, 548 U.S. 53 (2006); Price Waterhouse v. Hopkins, 490 U.S. 228 (1989).

[69] 42 U.S.C. § 2000e *et seq.* (2016).

[70] 29 U.S.C. § 793 *et seq.* (2016); 42 U.S.C. § 12101 *et seq.* (2016); 42 U.S.C. § 2000e(k)(2016); 42 U.S.C. § 2000ff (2016).

[71] 29 U.S.C. § 1140 *et seq.* (2016).

[72] 29 U.S.C. § 215 (2016).

[73] 29 U.S.C. § 660 (2016).

[74] 15 U.S.C. § 1674(a) (2016).

[75] 29 U.S.C. § 2001 *et seq.* (2016).

[76] 29 U.S.C. § 158 (2016); Alaniz v. San Isidro Indep. Sch. Dist., 742 F.2d 207 (5th Cir. 1984).

[77] 29 U.S.C. § 2601 *et seq.* (2016).

[78] 11 U.S.C. § 525(a) (2016).

[79] *Echtenkamp*, 263 F. Supp. 2d at 1043.

[80] Tex. Educ. Code Ann. § 21.355 (West, current through the 2015 R.S. of the 8th Leg.).

Key Words

constitutional
adverse employment action
anecdotal records
arbitrary and capricious
collective bargaining
correctable
defamation claims
deficiencies
discrimination
documentation
due process
evaluation criteria
Every Student Succeeds Act (ESSA)
feedback
free speech
growth plan

hearing
insubordination
intentional misconduct
liberty interest
litigation
needs assessment
No Child Left Behind
nonrenewal
observation
performance criteria
policies
procedure
professional growth
property right
remediation
retaliation

Section III – Chapter 7

Documentation

Kelly Frels, Janet L. Horton, and Lisa R. McBride

Introduction

The primary objective of a school district's employee evaluation system is to improve employees' performance so they can become successful and contribute to achieving the district's goals. If the evaluation process does not produce this positive result, the employee must be replaced, either by resignation or termination. The district's evaluation system thus serves a secondary function—the removal of the unsatisfactory employee.

Depending upon the nature of the employee's relationship or contract status with a school district, the district must observe various degrees of procedural due process before relieving an employee of his or her position. In many situations, this process culminates with a hearing before the board of education or a hearing officer to determine whether cause exists to terminate the employee.

In school employee termination hearings, principals are often faced with the claim that there is too little documentation or evidence of help being given to the employee and, as such, the principal has not done a sufficient job in working with the employee to remediate weaknesses. In other cases, the aggrieved employee claims that the principal has developed so much documentation that the employee has been harassed. At other employee termination hearings, the employee complains that the process is unfair and that he or she did not know what was expected in the performance of his or her duties. As a result of these assertions, there has been a noticeable unwillingness on the part of principals and other supervisors to bring recommendations for termination to the superintendent or the board of education. In most situations, the supervisor worries that he or she, rather than the employee, will be put on trial at a hearing.

In an effort to provide support for the supervisor, especially principals, and to help ensure the fair treatment of employees who are evaluated, a simple but effective system of communication founded in documentation has been developed which can be used in conjunction with virtually any school district's evaluation system, as well as with a variety of contractual schemes authorized by state statutes. This documentation system is founded on the concept of communication; its goal is to humanize the evaluation and documentation process, with the ultimate objective of improving an employee's performance to an acceptable level. If an employee's performance does not improve, the system is designed to provide an incentive for voluntary resignation or, if voluntary resignation is not received, to provide the necessary documentation for the supervisor to have confidence in recommending the employee's termination.

For simplicity, and to provide focus, this chapter will discuss teachers as the representative employee group. It follows then that the chapter discusses principals as supervisors. Although this chapter primarily refers to the teacher/principal relationship in a school context, the content is equally applicable to the relationship between a school employee and supervisor at any level, including colleges and universities. This chapter will also refer to memoranda not just as written documents, but also with the intention that the comments are equally applicable to emails (or other writing designed to memorialize facts and circumstances for later reference), where there is often less opportunity to analyze the impact of what one has written.[1]

Legal Issues

This communication and documentation system becomes an essential ingredient in preparing the district's principals and supervisors not only for a hearing before a hearing officer or the board of education, but also for appeals and lawsuits filed with a state commissioner of education, an arbitrator, or a court. The system can also provide the necessary documentation to sustain the termination if the employee files a discrimination complaint with the Equal Employment Opportunity Commission or the Department of Education. Furthermore, adherence to a system of this nature can help avoid First Amendment or whistleblower problems from becoming significant issues. If there is systematic documentation of poor performance before an employee engages in a protected speech activity, the performance deficiency may continue to be addressed as needed, and termination recommended if required. In contrast, the absence of such documentation prior to an employee's engaging in a protected speech activity could brand the employee as legally untouchable because the documentation may appear to be retaliation for the employee's speech.

Much has been written about the due process requirements involved in the termination process. Because that process varies by state and the nature of the employment relationship with a district, this chapter will not include a review of the procedural requirements necessary to effect a termination. Instead, it will provide practical advice to principals and other supervisors concerning the documentation that should be generated and used in the evaluation process and presented at any required hearing to support a recommendation for termination. It is important to remember that the due process rights of employees do not shield them from termination. Incapable or insubordinate employees can, and should, be terminated. Due process requirements simply prescribe procedures that must be followed in effectuating those terminations. Of course, the allowable grounds for termination will usually be enunciated in state law, an employment contract, and/or a collective bargaining agreement. Thus, educational administrators should examine these sources to determine the criteria under which employees should be judged and evaluated.

The Documentation System

The documentation contemplated in a teacher evaluation system involves the use of several types of written memoranda. First, *memoranda to the file* should be used sparingly to serve as a supervisor's memory keys for less-significant infractions or deviations by a teacher. Second, specific incident memoranda should be used to record conferences with a teacher concerning significant events. Third, summary memoranda should be used to record conferences with a teacher in which several incidents, problems, or deficiencies are discussed. Fourth, visitation memoranda should record observations made of a teacher's on-the-job performance. Fifth, an assessment instrument should be used to evaluate the teacher's overall performance.

Documentation concerning a teacher can and should be used for several purposes. First, it allows the principal to follow a teacher's actions and performance, thus enabling the principal to pinpoint weaknesses and problem areas. Second, it informs the teacher of any problems or deficiencies and provides valuable information concerning the necessary corrective steps the teacher must take to improve. Third, if a teacher's performance does not improve, it serves as concrete evidence to support a recommendation for termination.

The process outlined below should keep the volume of documents to a minimum, yet meet the need for full and complete documentation. This documentation system anticipates that a district has an evaluation system and it attempts to take into account the practicalities of the time constraints placed on school principals and other supervisors. By following the suggested documentation process below, the goals of improving employee performance or removing an unsatisfactory teacher should be attainable. Care must be taken, however, to ensure that this process conforms with state law, school board policies, and/or any applicable collective bargaining agreement.

Memoranda to the File

Whenever a principal observes an incident or behavior that is not serious enough to warrant an immediate conference with the teacher, but which should ultimately be considered in the teacher's evaluation or discussed at a general conference with the teacher, the principal should prepare a short memorandum to the file. These file memoranda can be in various forms, such as a notation on a calendar, in a notebook with separate pages designated for specific individuals, or in a teacher's folder in a secure electronic data system. These file memoranda should include the name of the teacher, the name or initials of the principal, the date of the occurrence, and the facts of the event observed. These file memoranda can be used as memory keys, generally for the following limited purposes:

1. Conference with the teacher concerning the incident or incidents;
2. Assessment of the teacher's performance; and
3. Refreshing the memory of the principal for testimony at any proceeding or hearing relative to the teacher's performance if the relevant incidents have not been incorporated into summary memoranda or other evaluative documents.

Most administrators find it counterproductive to keep the existence of these file memoranda secret from the teachers. In fact, most administrators find it helpful to make all employees aware that these memoranda are kept and actually encourage the employees to review any file memoranda made concerning their performance. Openness is important to successful communication.

Copies of these file memoranda normally need not be given to the teacher unless the teacher requests them under a state's freedom of information act. However, if the copies are not given to the teacher upon request, they should not normally be used in a subsequent hearing as evidentiary documentation to establish facts. In fact, in some states, documents not shown to the teacher may not be considered in that state's formal evaluation process. The best practice is to incorporate the contents of these file memoranda into a summary memorandum or an assessment instrument that is given to the teacher after a conference. If a summary memorandum includes the information contained in the file memoranda, the file memoranda should never have to be used again. Whether these documents must be retained, and if so, for how long, is controlled by each state's records retention laws.

Even though it may not be the intention of the principal to use these documents as future evidence or to share the file memoranda with the teacher, the memoranda should be written with the knowledge that copies may be introduced in a future proceeding or made available to the teacher through a request under most states' freedom of information acts. For example, if file memoranda are being used to refresh a principal's memory at a hearing, most state laws entitle the attorney for the teacher to see copies of the documents. Thus, a principal should exercise care not to write or record anything in a manner that could cause future embarrassment. A good practice is to record facts rather than conclusions or opinions in file memoranda.

File memoranda should be used sparingly and only for minor matters. If an incident is in any way serious, the specific incident memorandum should be used following a conference with the teacher.

Specific Incident Memoranda

If the principal observes an incident or behavior, or has a significant complaint from a third party, the principal should consider sending the teacher a specific incident memorandum. This memorandum should be sent only *after* the principal holds a conference with the teacher at which the incident is discussed and the teacher's viewpoint is considered. The specific incident memorandum should summarize the complaint (whether originating from a third party or from the principal's observation(s)); the teacher's response; the principal's decision regarding the matter; and any directives, corrective action, or reprimands to the teacher. If the incident is so serious it warrants recommending immediate termination, the memorandum should so state. While many administrators might like to avoid talking with a teacher about an incident in the hope that it will go away, such an attitude is self-defeating and naive. These incidents should be faced head-on as they occur. Teachers generally want to know of problems immediately to avoid their recurrence. The conference should be held as soon after the incident or complaint as possible. Thirty minutes spent conferencing with a teacher following an incident may provide the spark to help the teacher improve, and by doing so, avoid a two-day hearing or a week-long trial at some later date.

Moreover, the failure to confront problems, infractions, and deficiencies at the time they occur can weaken a later case for termination. For example, suppose several incidents occur in the fall of a school year, but the principal does not discuss them with the teacher. An attempt to use those incidents to support a proposed termination in the spring of that school year may prove difficult. The teacher will claim that he or she is being treated unfairly, or that the reasons are a pretext for discriminatory motives, because the reason(s) for termination were not discussed with the teacher earlier in the school year when they occurred. Not dealing with the problems as they occur makes the principal appear arbitrary or devious, and may taint a proposal to terminate.

If the specific incident concerning the teacher comes from a third party, such as a parent or student, the principal must fully investigate the facts and determine whether the third party's information is correct. It is improper and potentially disastrous to base a decision to terminate on information from a third party when the truthfulness of the allegation has not been established. Upon receiving a third-party complaint, the principal should request the informant submit the complaint in writing and conduct an investigation. Some school district policies or collective bargaining agreements require that third-party complaints be in writing before any employment action can be taken. But, be cautioned: If the complaint concerns suspected child abuse or neglect, many states' laws require that suspected child abuse or neglect be reported within certain time limits, regardless of whether the information is received in writing.

The principal should arrange a conference with the teacher to obtain the teacher's side of the story. If there is a discrepancy between the third party's allegations and the teacher's explanations, the principal should interview any witnesses and attempt to determine what occurred. It may be necessary to have the teacher confront the complainant in an informal conference to determine what actually occurred. The principal should advise the third party that if adverse action is taken against the teacher based on the incident, the third party must be available to testify before the board, a hearing officer, an arbitrator, or a court. If the third party will not agree to appear as a witness, other independent evidence must be available to establish the relevant facts at a hearing. Otherwise, action adverse to the teacher should not be taken, because there will be no evidence to support the action.

In many cases, it simply will not be possible for the principal to have everyone agree on what happened, so the principal has to act as a judge and decide whose story to believe. If the parties can eventually reach agreement, or if the principal has enough information to make a factual determination, a specific incident memorandum can be prepared. Such a memorandum should explain the findings made by the principal and the reasons for those findings. Specific directives or suggestions to the teacher should be included in the memorandum, as appropriate. If the principal, in the course of his or her investigation, cannot determine what exactly occurred, the principal should not issue corrective or disciplinary action, but can still issue a specific incident memorandum containing the findings he or she was able to make and also a directive to the teacher, if the investigation shows behavior by the teacher is questionable or indicates poor judgment.

It is important to establish on the face of the specific incident memorandum that the teacher received a copy of the document. In teacher termination hearings, disputes often arise over whether the teacher ever received a copy of a particular document. It is essential, therefore, to have the teacher sign the memorandum acknowledging its receipt. If a teacher refuses to sign, the principal should have an adult witness, other than the principal, sign and date a copy of the document, verifying that the teacher was given a copy of the memorandum, but refused to sign an acknowledgement of its receipt. It should be made clear to the teacher (either on the face of the document or orally) that the teacher's signature only verifies that a copy of the memorandum has been received, and does not constitute agreement with the memorandum's contents.

It is important that the teacher has the opportunity to respond to any memorandum. This can be accomplished by inviting the teacher to make a written statement concerning any differences of fact or opinion expressed by the principal in the memorandum by a certain date or within a given number of days. For example, the final paragraph of a memorandum might conclude, "If you disagree with the facts or conclusions stated in this memorandum, please advise me in writing no later than (date) so we can meet and work out any differences." By so doing, any disagreement can be noted and the differences perhaps resolved immediately. In serious situations where the employee has proven recalcitrant or dishonest, one might consider a final sentence such as "If you do not respond, I can only assume you agree with the facts stated in this memorandum." A statement of this nature should be used sparingly because it tends to polarize the positions of the administrator and the employee, thus making future communications more difficult.

Giving the teacher an opportunity to submit a written response disagreeing with the contents of the memorandum puts the teacher on notice of the facts and findings stated in the memorandum. If no disagreement is noted in writing by the teacher, most reasonable people presume that the contents of the memorandum accurately reflect the facts. Members of a jury, a hearing officer, or a judge examining this situation will normally take the view that a reasonable person who received such a memorandum, and who disagreed with the facts, would prepare a written response to the items with which the individual disagreed. If the teacher does not respond within the time stated in the memorandum, the teacher appears less credible if he or she later argues at a termination hearing that he or she disagrees with the content of the memorandum, or disagreed when the memorandum was written.

Visitation Memoranda

In some school districts, it is a common practice for principals to summarize their visits to a teacher's classroom. If visitation forms or checklists are used, or if visitation memoranda are prepared, their contents should be reviewed with the teacher, and the teacher should be given a copy. Suggestions for improvement or any specific directives should be made in a conference and noted in the memorandum. A visitation memorandum may be used in a termination proceeding, but the results of a visitation are normally reviewed in a summary memorandum or in the evaluation document.

Summary Memoranda

Summary memoranda are ideal ways to outline the results of conferences concerning several incidents, classroom visitations, or conferences regarding general teacher performance. Through such memoranda, the principal may incorporate matters referred to in the file memoranda (which may not have been given to or discussed with the teacher previously) as well as matters not reflected in other memoranda. The summary memorandum should be used to issue directives to the teacher, reach understanding, establish standards, provide evidence that a conference was held, and confirm the subjects discussed. A copy of each summary memorandum should be given to the teacher, and the teacher should acknowledge receipt by signing a copy.

The teacher should also be given an opportunity to offer any written responses disputing the facts and conclusions stated in the memorandum. If a teacher disagrees with the facts stated in the memorandum and files a response, a subsequent conference should be held with a follow-up memorandum to try to resolve any differences that may exist. The same comments applicable to the specific incident memoranda reviewed above are also applicable to summary memoranda, with the major difference being that summary memoranda are designed to cover general conferences with the teacher on several matters rather than only a specific incident.

The Assessment or Evaluation Document

The assessment or evaluation document should be completed as prescribed by the policies and procedures of the district and by any state laws or regulations. A summary narrative should be considered for each negative assessment noted in the document. This can be done on the assessment document or on an attachment to the evaluation. If the assessment is such that the teacher might be terminated if no improvement is shown, the teacher should be advised that failure to improve could result in a recommendation for termination. Furthermore, it is wise to include instructions or specific directives for improvement. Doing so is not only helpful to the teacher, but it also strengthens the argument that the teacher has been treated fairly, if the principal's actions are later questioned. The evaluation document should be signed by the teacher as well as the principal. Through the use of such evaluation documents, the teacher will be put on notice that there are deficiencies that could result in a proposal to terminate, should those deficiencies not be remedied according to the instructions given for improvement. All identified deficiencies of the teacher, as well as any problems that have been encountered during the assessment period, should be included in the assessment document. If the teacher has not remedied a deficiency from previous years, it should be noted on the assessment. A deficiency, once identified and not corrected, never becomes stale if the deficiency is appropriately carried forward in documentation.

In order to avoid difficulties with ratings on the evaluation, a teacher should not be rated too highly or too positively when he or she is initially employed or assigned to a school and before the administrator has an in-depth and accurate picture of the teacher's skill, talent, and capability; rather, a straightforward and truthful evaluation should be made. It is much easier to raise evaluation scores in subsequent years than it is to lower previous inflated assessments. Furthermore, a fair system of evaluation requires the setting of standards and expectations at the beginning of the school year, with the principal following through with the implementation of those standards through the evaluation process.

Teachers who continuously fail to implement directives issued by principals in other memoranda may need to be placed on a growth plan (also known as a professional improvement plan, intervention plan, prescriptive plan for assistance, etc.). In conjunction with a teacher's formal evaluation, a growth plan may be necessary to address specific problems with classroom performance. A school district or a state may require an evaluation system that includes a specific form for a growth plan. Whatever the form, it is important for the growth plan to clearly identify the concern with the teacher's performance, include useful and reasonable sources of education and support to help solve the deficiencies, specify the change that is expected to occur in the teacher's performance, and set reasonable timelines for completion. It is important that progress toward completion of the growth plan is monitored periodically. If the problems are not rectified, the growth plan can be extended, or it may be time to consider termination.

When placing a teacher on a growth plan, the principal should hold a conference with that employee and then issue a growth plan conference memorandum, which is similar to the summary memorandum discussed above. This conference memorandum should state the focus area or areas that will be addressed by the growth plan, the specific evidence collected (by the principal or other administrators) that causes concerns with regard to the focus areas, and the action steps and professional development activities that the teacher must complete. The memorandum should also state that completing the action steps and professional development activities will not be sufficient to close out the growth plan, and that the teacher must incorporate the activities into his or her regular classroom routines. The principal should inform the teacher that the growth plan is a living document that may be modified at any time to address either the teacher's improvement or need for additional remediation. The principal or other administrator should monitor the teacher throughout the growth plan. A growth plan should be for a set period of time, after which it can either be extended or closed out, based on the evidence collected relating to the teacher's progress in the focus areas. The principal should have a conference with the teacher when extending or closing out the growth plan, and should provide the teacher a growth plan conference memorandum afterward.

The Close-out Memorandum

Occasionally, a teacher will write a response to the administrator's memorandum if he or she disagrees with the facts, conclusions, or directives in it. If a teacher does respond to the memorandum, it is essential that the administrator carefully review the response. If the teacher disagrees with the principal's statement of facts in the original memorandum and offers specific information in his or her defense, the principal may need to further investigate the matter. Sometimes in the response a teacher may accuse the administrator of discriminatory conduct or motives. Such accusations should not be ignored, but should be addressed specifically by the principal in a follow-up conference. A teacher's response may also indicate that he or she is confused about a directive or corrective action. After reading the response, the administrator should not hesitate to hold another conference with the teacher to resolve any issues created by the teacher's response.

The results of this follow-up conference should be recorded in a specific incident or summary memorandum sent by the principal. If the communication in the conference is effective and is properly reflected in the memorandum, a teacher will rarely have reason to respond again. However, a second response from the teacher sometimes does occur, and another conference may be necessary. At some point, however, the memorandum writing must be brought to a close and in normal circumstances, sending the follow-up memorandum to this conference may be an appropriate time. A close-out memorandum may be written. The language inviting a response from the teacher used in prior memoranda is not included, and the teacher is advised that the matter should be considered closed.

General Guide for Email Communication

Email communication is faster and more convenient than scheduling face-to-face meetings to discuss minor or less-important matters, but principals should not become used to using email as a complete substitute for in-person meetings, especially for important or evaluative discussions. These days, it is very common for principals to communicate with school staff and personnel via email, and many principals do so without a second thought. Many principals also use mobile devices, such as smartphones, that allow them to send emails instantly from wherever they are. However, using email is not recommended for important discussions, for several reasons.

First, it can be very difficult to properly evaluate the tone of an email. This can cause the email to be misconstrued by the recipient when it is originally sent, and can also cause the email to be misinterpreted by a school board, hearing officer, judge, or other outside party, at a subsequent time. Second, a principal should never assume that emails are confidential, or that the matters or identity of individuals discussed in the email will stay between the principal and the email's intended recipient. There is no guarantee that the email's recipient will not forward the communication to another individual, or include another recipient on a response email; also, the email would likely have to be turned over to the other side during discovery, if there were ever a lawsuit relating to matters discussed in it. Members of the public might be able to request copies of the email through the state open records law.

Individuals sending emails, especially when using their smartphones, are much less likely to proofread those emails than they would be to proofread a more formal memorandum or letter. Additionally, because emails are a faster, and sometimes more informal, mode of communication, they can be sent in the heat of the moment without deliberation. Finally, and just as importantly, every time a principal sends important or sensitive information via email, there is the possibility that he or she might accidentally send that information to an unintended recipient.

For all these reasons, it is recommended that important documentation and sensitive information not be transmitted using the school district's email system, especially if the sender is on the go.

Principals should also resist the temptation to send any of the documents discussed in this chapter via email because it is important to have the teacher sign every issued memorandum at the bottom, indicating that he or she has received it. Although email is generally a reliable method of delivering documents to employees, not all jurisdictions find delivery of documents by email to be legally conclusive. If an employee never opens the email, or chooses not to send a "read receipt," even if one is requested by the principal, it may prove difficult to demonstrate at a later hearing that the employee did, indeed, receive the memorandum at issue.

Additionally, if employee performance is serious enough to warrant documentation, it is serious enough to warrant a conference and the formality of a memorandum placed on letterhead and officially signed by the supervisor.

Informal emails typically do not have the same persuasive impact as more formal documentation when reviewed by the school board, hearing officer, or judge.

Documentation, Discipline, and Social Media

The news is increasingly full of stories about teachers being suspended or terminated for improper conduct on social media, including posting inappropriate or explicit photographs to various internet sites such as Facebook, Twitter, Instagram, MySpace, and so on. Many school districts now have policies regulating the nature of contact with students by school staff using social media. Staff should be educated about the requirements of those policies and expected to comply. While the issue of disciplining teachers or other school employees for their social media activities has not yet been taken up by the Supreme Court, various state and federal courts across the country have affirmed the ability of principals to discipline teachers (including issuing write-ups, suspensions, and recommending terminations) for teachers' off-campus internet activities, under certain circumstances.

If a principal receives a complaint about a teacher posting inappropriate content, or about a teacher engaging in inappropriate activities that are potentially disruptive to the teacher's ability to teach and the school's ability to operate, the principal should follow the same steps outlined in the specific incident memoranda section above. Inappropriate content may include explicit, pornographic, or highly offensive photographs or comments, especially if the content can be viewed by the teacher's students or the general public. Inappropriate activities may include engaging students in unprofessional, unethical, or sexual conversations, or encouraging students to act violently, unlawfully, or contrary to the code of conduct. Even if the principal receives photographic documentation of what appears to be an inappropriate social media post by a teacher, he or she should nonetheless follow the guidelines and recommendations outlined in the sections above.

The principal should not request that the third party making the complaint, or another employee with access to the content, provide his or her login user name and password so that the principal may personally access the website. Instead, if the principal does not have direct access to the content in question, he or she should request that the third party making the complaint take a screen shot of the content and either email the screen shot, or print it out and bring it to the principal. If the principal has personal access to the social media content in question—either because the principal is connected to the teacher on the social media website, or because the content can be viewed by the general public—the principal should print the entire webpage on which it appears, if possible. Alternatively, the principal should take a screen shot of the content (not copy and paste it) and save or print the screen shot. This is necessary if the principal wishes to base a memorandum or any corrective action on the content, should the webpage become unavailable or the content later be removed or hidden by the teacher.

The principal should be cautious about recommending a teacher for termination based on a single inappropriate use of social media. Termination may be appropriate if sufficient previous documentation supports such a recommendation, or the teacher's social media activities are directly and unambiguously disruptive to school activities.[2] For example, if the teacher solicits a sexual relationship with a student over the internet, recommendation for immediate termination would be appropriate.

Principals should take care when disciplining a teacher for his or her social media use. The principal should consider factors such as a history of problems or shortcomings, whether the teacher's social media use is visible to his or her students or the general public, or whether it is carefully restricted to only the teacher's personal friends. If the teacher's social media use does not actually impact the teacher's ability to effectively perform his or her job, attempts to discipline the teacher may argue that his or her First Amendment rights have been violated. Principals who first effectively document a teacher's inappropriate social media use, warn the teacher about the inappropriate internet conduct, and give the teacher an opportunity to correct his or her behavior (through a growth plan, if necessary), are more likely to have their decisions to discipline a teacher for the use of social media later upheld by the board of education, independent hearing officer, or judge.

If a teacher's use of social media or other internet activities could arguably be related to a "matter of public concern," this may give rise to additional constitutional concerns.[3] For example, if a teacher posts on Twitter about the working conditions of, or rights to collective bargaining for all teachers at a given school, the teacher may assert that his or her actions are protected under the First Amendment and that the principal is retaliating against the teacher, especially if the social media activities in question happened before the principal issued the teacher any corrective memoranda. Principals have less to worry about if the social media activities relate only to the teacher's private interests or concerns. It will be much more difficult for a teacher to link posting lewd or drug-related photographs on Instagram, or posting a Facebook status that is offensive or insulting to the teacher's students, to any First Amendment rights. This does not mean that a principal cannot discipline or document the deficiencies of a teacher who has posted on social media about a possible "matter of public concern"—only that it is especially important for a principal to be consistent with all employees and diligently address, through documentation, all problems and issues as they arise.

Recommendations for Practice

1. Memoranda should recite specific facts and circumstances. Conclusory statements, especially when unsupported by facts, should be avoided. For example, in a classroom visitation memorandum, a statement that the teacher's classroom was disorderly, without any explanation, is neither specific nor effective. Rather, the memoranda

should note, for example, that three children were observed talking during class and one child was playing in the back of the room. The memoranda should note that the stray conversations and play went unnoticed and were not corrected by the teacher.

2.   In preparing a memorandum, avoid inflammatory words which may promote unnecessary animosity and, as with the above, are neither specific nor effective. For example, rather than characterize an act as insubordinate, referred to specific acts as failure to comply. In describing the act the memorandum should specifically identify which rules, policies, procedures, or directives the act disobeyed or disregarded.

3.   Memoranda should explain instructions or directions in positive, specific, and jargon-free language. When directing a sometimes-tardy teacher, instead of saying "You may not be late any further," one might state, "You are required to be at school by (a specific time), and you will be expected to have signed in by that time." Instead of directing, "Your lesson plans are due once a week," one might write, "Beginning this Friday, I expect your lesson plans to me emailed or in my office mailbox by 4:00 p.m. on each Friday." When written in a constructive manner, precise directives tend to avoid real or imagined confusion about what is expected.

4.   The specific incident memorandum, the summary memorandum, the visitation memorandum, and the assessment document should be personalized. Ambiguous references such as "we" or "they" should be avoided unless there are two or more people involved. When multiple individuals are involved, each should be identified by name.

5.   Care should be taken to treat all teachers alike, especially when dealing with absences and tardiness. In a termination case that involves tardiness and absences, it is embarrassing and counterproductive when a teacher or a teacher's attorney presents a school's sign-in sheet as evidence that other teachers have more tardies or absences than the teacher in the case at hand.

6.   Never send a memorandum while upset or angry. It is better to reflect for a day or more before proceeding. Another strategy when a case has provoked strong emotions is to consult with colleagues, attorneys, or others prior to sending. By doing so, a memorandum will be less likely to include statements that may be regretted later.

7.   Prepare and send a memorandum soon after the incident and conference it memorializes. Timely communication will be more effective than delayed communication.

8.   Memoranda should be accurately dated. Backdating a memorandum may be regarded as contractual violations or fraud.

9. State explicitly in the memorandum, and verbally, any adverse employment actions that may result in the absence of improvement or correction.

10. Request that recipients sign for or electronically acknowledge receipt of the memorandum. Ensure that the opportunity to acknowledge receipt does not constitute agreement with its contents. Invite a written response and set a specific time for the response to be provided. If the recipient refuses to acknowledge receipt, prepare a supplemental memorandum to the file of that document's delivery (similar to an affidavit of service). Consider also having an adult witness sign documents that confirm delivery.

11. The evaluator should be careful to ensure that the teacher believes he or she has been treated fairly. One should remember that if the teacher's performance does not improve and a recommendation for termination is made, the fairness of the process will be judged by the members of the board or a hearing officer and, possibly, by the state's commissioner of education, an arbitrator, a judge, or jury. In ensuring that a teacher has been treated fairly, one should attempt to conduct an evaluation from the perspective of a reasonable person who, after receiving all the facts, could determine that the process was fair. Work toward ensuring that all parties were treated as the evaluator would like to have been treated, had the circumstances been reversed.

12. If the teacher does not receive a copy of a memorandum to the file, it should not be used as evidence at a hearing but should be used only when necessary to refresh the principal's memory while testifying concerning the specific facts of an event. For example, normally the only documents that would be used as documentary evidence at a termination hearing would be the summary memoranda and the evaluation or assessment instruments. Occasionally, specific incident and visitation memoranda would be included; however, these specific incident and visitation memoranda should be reviewed and included in a subsequent summary memorandum or evaluation instrument.

13. Be sure to include in-person meetings. This documentation system can be utilized in an electronic personnel record system but, especially given the impersonal nature of electronic or written communication, no documentation system can replace in-person meetings. Maintaining the personal touch in communication is essential to the successful use of this documentation system.

Conclusion

Like all other personnel-related activities, this simple system of communication and documentation is not fail-safe. It must be implemented by humans, and it is subject to error. This system does, however, provide an opportunity for a principal to demonstrate leadership and to communicate effectively with teachers while developing the proper documentation for improvement or termination. In working with this system, the members of the board of education, hearing officers, the state commissioner of education, arbitrators, judges, or juries will evaluate the termination recommendation on the basis of fairness and reasonableness. In the implementation of this system, a principal should be guided by the standard of treating the teacher as the principal would like to be treated if the principal were in the teacher's position. The principal should also strive to establish and maintain a climate where the employee can maintain his or her personal dignity. Use of this fair and effective documentation system should result in the improvement of most personnel problems, and the efficient resolution of major or persistent problems through termination.

Endnotes

[1] Pickering v. Bd, of Educ., 391 U.S. 563, 88 S.Ct. 1731 (1968); Munroe v. Cent. Bucks Sch. Dist., 805 F.3d 454 (3rd Cir. 2015)

[2] Pickering v. Bd, of Educ., 391 U.S. 563, 88 S.Ct. 1731 (1968); Connick v. Myers, 461 U.S. 138, 103 S.Ct 1684 (1983); Munroe v. Cent. Bucks Sch. Dist., 805 F.3d 454 (3rd Cir. 2015)

[3] For a more complete treatment of documentation, including sample memoranda and a checklist, see K. FRELS, J.L. HORTON, L. MCBRIDE, I. FELDSHEROV, A DOCUMENTATION SYSTEM FOR TEACHER IMPROVEMENT OR TERMINATION (7th Ed., 2014).

Key Words

adverse employment action
assessment document
close-out memorandum
conclusory statement
conference
contract status
directives
discipline
documentation system
e-mail communication
electronic personnel record
   system
evaluation
fair treatment
file memorandum/memorandum
   to the file

First Amendment
growth plan
hearing
memoranda
procedural due process
remediation
reprimand
social media
specific incident memorandum
summary memorandum
termination
third-party complaint
visitation memorandum
webpage
write-up

Section III – Chapter 8

Teacher Dismissal

Evan G. Mense, Nathan M. Roberts, and Kenneth E. Lane*

Introduction

Because education was not mentioned in the United States Constitution, the governmental function was reserved for the states.[1] Consequently, each state has ultimate control over education, which makes education a game in the eyes of some politicians. Centralized control at the state level has appeal for many politicians, demonstrated by the dramatic growth of state control over education during the last two decades.[2] Since the *A Nation At Risk* report in 1983, education has become the object of reform, reinvention, renewal, and revival—all without appreciable change.[3]

The federal government has become more involved in facilitating changes by states and local governing agencies with the implementation of the key initiative, *No Child Left Behind*, and subsequently, The Race-to-the-Top.[4] The No Child Left Behind Act of 2001 (NCLB) was the reauthorization of the Elementary and Secondary Education Act of 1965 (ESEA), the first major incursion of the federal government into public K-12 education. The primary premise of NCLB was that all traditional public school students reach academic proficiency by the 2013–14 academic year.[5] U.S. government and state regulators monitor district and school progress toward meeting academic proficiency through Adequate Yearly Progress (AYP) calculations. AYP was designed to showcase minimum competency performance targets that had to be met by districts and schools to avoid penalties.[6]

With these legislative mandates, one of the many contentious issues is the concept of teacher quality. Teacher quality has been defined in numerous ways by many different associations, groups, researchers, and individuals.[7] However, the most important concept of teacher quality is how to deal with those who are not of sufficient quality to remain in the profession.[8] Although few agree on what constitutes quality teaching and how quality teaching is evaluated, most educators and the public can agree on what constitutes poor teaching.[9] Such is the topic of this chapter: how to dismiss teachers who should not be in the teaching profession.

Background

Teacher dismissal has taken on the mantra of other educational reforms and concerns in the recent decade.[10] The U.S. President and Congress have enacted legislation to impact the way teachers are evaluated, retained, and dismissed.[11] Grants have been offered to and accepted by the states to respond to enticements for changing teacher evaluation systems.[12] When a state accepts these grants, the state agrees to tie teacher evaluations with student performance—not student achievement, but student performance on mandatory tests.[13] In a study published in in 2103, The Center for Public Education found that:

- Forty-seven states require or recommend that stakeholders, including teachers, provide input into the design of new evaluation systems. Such input is important to gaining broad-based support.

- Forty-six states require or recommend that evaluations include measures on how teachers impact their students' achievement.

- Classroom observations are a component of every state's evaluation system; about a third (thirty-three) of them require or recommend all teachers be observed at least once a year.

- Forty-one states require or recommend teachers be evaluated on multiple measures as a more complete and accurate gauge of performance. No state evaluates teachers on test scores alone.

- Most states are primarily focused on using evaluation for the purpose of raising teacher performance, but also use the results to inform personnel decisions.

- More than half of states use evaluation results to target professional development opportunities for individual teachers.

- Teachers can be dismissed due to poor evaluations in thirty-two states. However, typically teachers are not *eligible* to be dismissed until they have been rated as low-performing over multiple years, and only after being provided interventions to improve. Even if the teacher fails to improve, in most states the decision to dismiss is left up to the discretion of the school district.

- Local school districts need flexibility in designing and implementing teacher evaluation systems so they are aligned to the needs of the district, but they also need strong support from their states.

- Seventeen states provide districts flexibility as well as support in developing evaluation systems, while twenty-one states leave almost all the responsibility for developing an evaluation system in the hands of districts.[14]

With the passage of the ESSA, it is likely that some states will reconsider their teacher evaluation systems. The new law loosens the review of teachers and places less emphasis on the evaluation of teachers. Several states, including New York, Oklahoma and South Carolina, were already reconsidering their teacher evaluation systems.[15] The trend of addressing teacher evaluations will likely continue as states review ESSA and the resulting regulations.

Currently, nearly half of states link teacher evaluations to student achievement test scores.[16] These states are linking pay to performance reviews, continuing employment, or changing the concept of tenure, making it more difficult to keep and obtain teachers. In addition, reduction-in-force policies have changed from systems of last in–first out, to systems that link reduction to student performance; Indiana, Michigan, and Louisiana[17] are examples of this action.[18] Accountability specified in state assessments and federal assessments under the No Child Left Behind Act (NCLB) and the Race-to-the-Top demands that teachers and administrators alike demonstrate proficiency in the improvement of student learning.[19] Evaluation systems are now being used to assess teacher and principal performance. For example, the new "school reform" efforts emphasize the term "value-added" that refers to a growth model used to analyze student assessment data.[20] The resulting "value" that a school contributes to student performance during a particular time also relates to teacher performance and evaluations. "Value-added" could potentially lead to the reduction in job security for teachers, although tenure provides due process protection against arbitrary teacher dismissal.

At least twenty-three states and the District of Columbia now evaluate public school teachers in part using student standardized test data.[21] Colorado law requires that 50% of a teacher's evaluation must be based on student test results. A principal must address poor teaching and poor leadership, or student learning will suffer.[22] Almost all state legislatures have passed statutes that provide consequences for teachers who fail to meet specified targets of student performance.[23]

Legal Issues

Teacher Contracts and Dismissal

Corbin defines a contract as "a promise enforceable at law directly or indirectly."[24] The enforceable promise is important for local school districts as contracts may arise in two basic settings, employment and general services. Important to this discussion is the setting of employment. Principals are part of this setting and must be familiar with the state laws of certification, contract law, and the local rules for employment.[25]

Employment of a teacher is generally governed in part by state licensure requirements and the local school's collective bargaining contract. In states or districts without collective bargaining, state law will dictate employment guidelines. Each state has its own requirements, including certification and educational requirements. The district contract or collective bargaining agreement describes the duties and responsibilities of a teacher.[26] A lack of knowledge of contract language and expectations cannot be used, by teachers and principals alike, as a defense in dismissal cases. All of them are charged with the responsibility of knowing what is in the contract.[27]

Several elements of a contract ordinarily must be present to have a legally enforceable contract:

1.   The parties must have the legal authority to enter into a contract;
2.   There must be an offer and an acceptance of the contract;
3.   The contract must contain valid and adequate consideration; and
4.   The contract must generally be documented in writing and signed.
     [Note: In some cases, a verbal agreement may be enforceable as a contract, particularly if the term of performance is less than a year.]

The legal authority to enter contracts is typically found in state statutes that allow local districts to enter into agreements for employment.[28] In most states, local boards of education have the legal authority to enter into contracts with individuals for educational services. Offer and acceptance are made in writing when a person is offered a position and he or she agrees to the terms of the offer and signs the contract.[29] Local schools offer salary, working conditions, and fringe benefits for consideration by the teacher. In return, the teacher promises to perform the requirements of the job for the length of the contract.[30] It is important to note that assignments of job duties made in addition to the regular contract may be governed by amendments or supplements to the regular contract.[31] Collective bargaining agreements may also supplement a regular contract.

The failure of a teacher to fulfill a contractual duty may constitute a breach of contract; more specifically, a teacher has an absolute and immediate duty to perform substantial work obligations under the terms of the contract.[32] Contracts can be breached in several ways. For example, a teacher may leave in the middle of the contract, or fail to fulfill obligations such as arriving on time, supervising students, or attending mandatory training. Some teachers receive better offers before the year begins and choose to break their contract. However, the school board then has the legal right to file a grievance with the state agency handling teacher certification to prevent the breaking of the contract or to suspend or revoke the teacher's certification. It is best to seek a release of the contract from the school board. While local school districts can seek damages or performance, they must consider the financial cost of pursuing an alleged breach of contract case through the court system. If the alleged breach is for serious misconduct, as opposed to the teacher leaving the district to accept a position in another school district, and it is determined the district is at fault, the district may be required to reinstate the teacher and provide past wages.[33]

A contract is not valid unless the teacher holds a legal certificate of qualification at the time the contract period begins.[34] A contract must contain clear and definite language. In the case of teacher dismissal without cause, most states' due process laws have been interpreted to include the identification of alleged deficiencies and efforts of remediation attempted. For example, a teacher may not properly supervise students in the class, or provide adequate lesson plans to the principal, or conduct appropriate parent conferences. These identified deficiencies and remediation methods to correct must be clear and in definitive language to ensure that a teacher understands the level of performance required to remain employed as a teacher in the local school district.[35]

The standard written contract outlines the rights and duties of the teacher.[36] It is important to note, however, that a contract may be more than the expressed contractual writings. First, unwritten clauses or implied contract requirements may be inferred. Second, contracts often incorporate the language of other policies and documents, obligating employees under those contracts to also comply with the provisions of those external policies and documents.[37] In other words, general rules and regulations adopted by the school board and the relevant state statutes may be included in the contract by implication.[38] In the case of implied requirements, contractual implications can be created "as a matter of reason and justice from the acts or conduct inferred from the intentions of the parties as evidenced by circumstances and ordinary course of dealing and common understanding...."[39] Alternatively, contracts may contain an "integration" clause stating that only the expressed contractual writings are included in the contract, absent a written amendment by the parties named in the contract.[40]

The court case interpretations cited in the preceding paragraph should not be taken to mean that any additional requirements can be proclaimed as inferred contractual agreements. This is particularly true when a new requirement for a teacher's job duties seeks to void written contractual agreements and state requirements. For example, the continuation of work by a nontenured teacher for the remainder of one's contract, when that contract will not be renewed and the teacher has been so notified, does not constitute a change in contract.[41]

Termination

Typically, both the teacher and a school board can mutually terminate an employment contract. However, the termination of a contract is not always mutual and voluntary; for example, when a teacher does not perform in accordance with the job duties described in the contract and without good reason. In such cases, the teacher's contract with the school may be terminated, nonrenewed, or suspended.[42] In more serious cases, the teaching certificate or license may be revoked.[43] Three actions of discharge have been identified to address the permanent or temporary severance in employment:

1. **Dismissal.** This discharge refers to termination for cause of any school professional under contract. This includes both tenured and nontenured teachers.

2. **Nonrenewal.** This discharge refers to the decision not to renew a nontenured teacher, a tenured teacher who is not under some form of continuing contract law, or a teacher who fails to improve adequately on previously identified need for improvement.[44]

3. **Suspension.** This discharge refers to the removal of a school professional from his or her duties for a limited period of time, and includes both tenured and nontenured contracts.[45]

Principals need an understanding of the implications of these actions and the appropriateness of these actions as they apply to the immediacy of a disciplinary action. They should not hesitate due to concerns of high legal cost.[46]

Legal Status of Dismissal for Tenured and Nontenured Teachers

Once a teacher has received tenure, many assume that they cannot be dismissed; however, this is not true. A teacher, regardless of his or her tenure status, has an absolute and immediate duty to perform under the contract. If such duty has not been discharged, then the failure of that party to meet the agreed-upon obligation may lead to dismissal.[47] A contract termination implicates both liberty and property rights, as recognized by the Fourteenth Amendment Due Process Clause. Any violation of a teacher's constitutional rights may afford the teacher full due process rights under the law.[48] The amount of due process afforded depends on the level of deprivation of rights. In the case of a termination, liberty rights (in good name, reputation, honor, and the right to enter into contract and to pursue professional work) and property rights (in the existing contract and its wages and benefits) are implicated.

The discharge of a teacher varies based upon the status of the teacher in tenure law. Generally, tenure is granted to a teacher who has successfully completed a probationary period of one to three years in a school.[49] Tenured teachers are viewed as having a greater right to due process than nontenured teachers. However, due process is a flexible concept, varying by seriousness of infraction and penalty and by whether a teacher is tenured or nontenured. For example, both tenured teachers and nontenured teachers must be afforded notice and hearings before termination during the period of a contract. The type of notice and level of hearing may vary.

In the case of a nonrenewal of a nontenured teacher, only liberty interests are implicated, because he or she does not have a reasonable expectation of continued employment constituting a property interest. It is here where the primary distinction between tenured and nontenured teachers can be made. Tenured teachers cannot have their contracts nonrenewed without due process, while nontenured teachers can. Termination and suspension, however, apply to both tenured and nontenured teachers alike. In all discharge cases, a clear link should be established between the teacher's actions and the impact upon the school setting.

The Tenured Teacher

Tenure is a provision statutorily or contractually created to provide a teacher with certain rights and privileges. For the purpose of clarity, tenure in public school systems is a continuing contract law. The purpose of tenure rights is to protect teachers from abuses or whims of principals and other administrators, while protecting the public's interests in academic freedom in schools.[50] A broad purpose of tenure is to provide protection for teachers with a vested right in their employment, thus establishing a state property right that ensures due process proceedings when dismissal actions occur. Tenure rights vary by state, but most states have determined that teachers with tenure (also called continuing contract teachers) are entitled to full due process rights prior to termination or nonrenewal.[51] Full due process procedures are usually outlined in state tenure statutes and generally follow the pattern of:

1. Notice of the possible infraction and intention to terminate;
2. A written statement with specifics of the charges prior to dismissal;
3. A hearing on the charges;
4. Assistance of legal counsel;
5. Evidentiary procedures; and
6. The right to judicial review.[52]

Tenure is a status conferred upon a certified or licensed teacher who has served a probationary period, usually one to three years; however, some states have eliminated tenure and the state of Louisiana now requires a teacher be rated "highly effective" for five years within a six-year period, pursuant to the performance evaluation program, to earn tenure[53]. Tenure is usually not transferable to another state or another school district, but some states allow tenure to be earned in a shorter period of time if simply moving from district to district.[54] Tenure guarantees a teacher the right to continued employment. Usually, the acquired tenure is in the area(s) of certification and the area of probation[55] Generally, the area of probation refers to whether the district employee was hired at the entry level as a teacher, counselor, or principal and, therefore, would not necessarily have the right to take a position in another level if removed from the current level. Tenure does not guarantee a particular position, location or indefinite employment. It does offer an expectation of employment if a teacher performs well and the position continues to exist. Many of the specific rights to tenure are found in state law, the teacher's individual contract, and local school district's collective bargaining agreements, if applicable. Tenure policies in many states are also being challenged or changed. In states such as Florida and Idaho, tenure for new teachers has ended. Colorado and Nevada developed rules for teachers who receive consecutive ineffective ratings, ensuring their tenure status would be lost. In Louisiana, tenure for new teachers has been significantly altered to make the status much more difficult to obtain[56]

Causes for Termination

State statutes describe the causes for termination; generally, they are incompetency, insubordination, immorality, good cause, as well as reduction of force. These are all conclusions that the school board must determine based on facts contained in the charges and proved at a hearing. Accordingly, the school board hears evidence on the charges and, if found valid, the board must then decide if the charges amount to incompetency, insubordination, immorality, or good cause.

Incompetency

The courts have given a broad interpretation to incompetency. Because professional training and certification identify competent teachers, the school board needs to show incompetence of a teacher in the performance of duties in regard to parents, students, and supervisors. Incompetency as defined by Black's Law Dictionary, is the "lack of ability, legal qualification, or fitness to discharge the required duty."[57] Some situations where incompetency has been found include off-campus conduct that impacts the capacity of the teacher to conduct an effective classroom;[58] failure of students to make normal progress when compared to another classroom;[59] physical or psychological disabilities that threaten the health, safety, and welfare of students;[60] and the failure to maintain proper classroom discipline.[61] Some states have also used failure to meet continuing education or certification requirements as a component of incompetency.[62] With the advent of the use of student performance written into teacher evaluations, one can be sure that this will be added to the list of reasons leading to dismissal for incompetence. Generally, a warning should precede charges for the dismissal of a teacher for incompetence, and the teacher should be given the opportunity to improve on the reason for the charges. Dismissal proceedings and timeframes are identified in each state statute. In addition, it is vital that the proper and precise documentation be maintained to support any charges of incompetence. Incompetency has not been used frequently to dismiss teachers. Studies in Illinois found only two of 95,500 teachers were terminated on grounds of incompetence. Other studies in West Virginia and California produced similar results.[63] Additional data will be required in future years to determine if these numbers may change as more states rely on student outcome data to determine incompetence

Insubordination

Insubordination is the willful disregard of or refusal to obey reasonable directives.[64] Teachers who refuse to obey reasonable and rational rules, regulations, policies, and contractual provisions may be released from their position. In addition, teachers are expected to maintain a cooperative environment with other teachers, parents, students, and school officials to promote the goals of the school. These provisions may not be trivial and may not infringe on the legal rights of an individual. Cases of insubordination are often found in the form of teacher absenteeism from the classroom. Other forms of insubordination are seen in teacher actions where the teacher is late or absent from school for short periods of time;[65] refuses to supervise halls when ordered to do so;[66] fails to produce lesson plans or teach specific lessons ordered by the school board;[67] is excessively absent, with adverse effect on student learning;[68] or strikes a student.[69] In most cases, the dismissal of a teacher for insubordination is the result of teacher actions that have not been corrected over a period of time.[70]

Dismissal for insubordination must be proven through the existence of a school rule or a superior's orders. In such a determination, consideration of several factors is important: the teacher's motive; whether harm occurred related to the violation; whether the rule or order was valid and reasonable from the beginning; and whether the rule or order was enforced based upon bias or discrimination.[71] In most cases, the dismissal is the result of an established pattern of behavior(s) that has occurred over a period of time in one or more setting.[72]

Immorality

Immorality has been interpreted as "a course of conduct that offends the morals of the community and is a bad example to youth whose ideals a teacher is supposed to foster and elevate."[73] In Louisiana, it is defined as any conviction of a felony offense affecting the public morals.[74] Standards for dismissal on the basis of immorality are vague.[75] The courts have generally interpreted the statutes narrowly, indicating that the school board typically requires proof of violation before dismissal proceedings.[76] Dismissal can occur if any teacher fails to meet the high standards of the profession. Sexual involvement with others is the most prevalent charge for immorality.[77] Obviously, a teacher involved with a student is looked upon by the courts with disdain. Sexual activity with other adults may also be suspect when there is a logical nexus to performance of a teacher's duties in school.[78] Some courts have sustained teacher dismissals on the grounds of immorality that involved: the commitment of a felony, smoking marijuana with a student,[79] acquiescing in the growing of and sale of illegal drugs,[80] illegally receiving welfare benefits,[81] soliciting students to vandalize another's property,[82] inappropriate uses of school technology,[83] and theft of school property.[84] While community standards do play a part in the determination, the main consideration is the nexus between the conduct and the teacher's ability to function effectively in the classroom.

Principals are often placed in a position of determining whether the school's personnel actions are immoral.[85] The State of California offers a formula to determine immoral conduct, measured by seven criteria:

1. The likelihood that the conduct may have adversely affected students or fellow teachers.
2. The degree of adversity anticipated.
3. The proximity or remoteness in time of the conduct.
4. The type of teaching certificate held by the employee involved.
5. Extenuating or aggravating circumstances, if any.
6. The likelihood of recurrence of the questioned conduct.
7. The extent to which disciplinary action may inflict an adverse impact or chilling effect upon the constitutional rights of the teacher or other school employee.[86]

Good cause

Most state tenure statutes require specific causes for dismissal of a tenured teacher. However, no statute can cover all possible causes for discharge. "Good cause" statutes are used to address this void and cover myriad situations.[87] Some of these situations may include and expand upon the identified causes for dismissal in statute, such as a decreased need for services in a particular teaching area, similar to a reduction in force. Other causes may be disloyalty, disobedience, financial liability, inefficiency, poor performance,[88] neglect of duty, conviction of a crime, fraud, realignment of school districts,[89] use of a racial epithet,[90] and posting derogatory remarks about students on Facebook.[91] These "good cause" provisions should not be construed as "blank checks" for principals to use in the dismissal of teachers.[92]

Principals must maintain objective criteria for evaluating all personnel. For example, the values of a community should not be used in a good cause dismissal; instead, the conduct should be measured against that of other teachers who are performing the same or similar duties.[93] Any dismissal, using the good cause standard, must be within the scope of the school's authority. Decisions must not be arbitrary and capricious, and all aspects of due process must be followed. It should be remembered that many of the examples of dismissal are not for instructional activities, but rather for incidents that occur before school, after school, or during non-instructional time.[94] The principal must be aware of his or her responsibility to all concerned in such situations.[95] Often the decision involves an analysis of whether the conduct causes a substantial disruption to the educational environment at school.

Some states also have nepotism laws that may be interpreted to include termination. These laws typically specify that a spouse or immediate family member cannot be the primary supervisor for another employee.[96] Often this means that when a spouse is promoted and becomes the supervisor of the other, one must be transferred, unless no other school is available.

Another area of concern that has arisen recently involves the legality and appropriateness of technology use, specifically social media.[97] Historically, society has held teachers to a higher level of ethical conduct, even during their off-duty times. Many state certification procedures indicate teachers must maintain appropriate professionalism and conduct themselves in a manner that is not detrimental to the teaching profession. A new debate over the application of these polices to the virtual world has captured the imagination of educators and the attention of the legal profession.[98] Consequently, social networking among and between educators and students has led to a multitude of responses from teacher associations, teacher preparation programs, school districts, and universities. With the rapid development and overwhelming use of social media, many school districts and some states have passed policies and laws designed to limit sexual misconduct between teachers and students that originate on social networking sites.[99] Many school districts restrict online communication between teachers and students to approved school district systems and prohibit online communication outside that system. As for teacher conduct on social media sites, it generally focuses on whether the communication causes a disruption at school or impacts the teacher's ability to effectively teach in the classroom. For example, a male teacher in San Diego placed an ad on Craig's List soliciting sex from men; some students saw it, and he was terminated.[100] In New York, a tenured fifth-grade teacher posted "I'm thinking the beach sounds like a wonderful idea for my 5th graders. I HATE THEIR GUTS" on Facebook the day after a student drowned during a school field trip. The court felt that termination was too harsh, based on the teacher's past positive record, but upheld a suspension.[101]

Teachers' ethical duty has not yet been defined for online environments.[102] Some educators have assumed the risk of posting personal information in public social networking sites.[103] Social networking technologies create new approaches to teaching and learning; however, they also present a number of ethical and legal dilemmas unlike others in education.[104] Unfortunately for many educators, the answer for many of these situations may be determined in a court of law, not the court of public opinion.[105] For example, in Missouri it is illegal for a teacher to have "exclusive online access" with current and former students who are minors.[106] The law was originally drafted after an investigation that "found eighty-seven Missouri teachers had lost their teaching licenses between 2001 and 2005 because of sexual misconduct, including many instances of exchanging explicit online messages with students."[107] Consequently, principals must remain vigilant in their efforts to protect the integrity of the educational process while permitting new technologies to evolve safely.[108]

Reduction-in-force

While some states may address reduction in staffing outside the good cause category, others designate reduction-in-force (RIF) as a special category of dismissal within the good cause portion of state teacher dismissal statutes. RIF is an action by a local board of education to reduce staff due to financial constraints of the district, or a reduced need for teachers due to population shifts, among other factors. If a school district claims financial hardship or a lack of need for teachers in a particular area, the board is responsible for detailed documentation and reasons for the RIF actions.

Many state statutes do not identify a specific procedure for RIF, but do provide indicators that must be used in creating the policy. If a district has a collective bargaining agreement, the RIF procedures are written into a school master contract with the collective bargaining unit. Often, a last in–first out process is used for reduction. Several mutations of this process occur in contract language and relate to the contract language of tenure at the local level; e.g., tenure at the department level or in an area certified to teach.[109] In Louisiana's new teacher education reform effort, the legislature changed the RIF process from last in–first out to "solely based upon demand, performance and effectiveness[110]

Both tenured and nontenured teachers may be subject to a RIF dismissal. Generally, nontenured teachers are not considered to be part of a reduction action[111] because they have no entitlement to a continuing contract. However, several courts have indicated that if the action to dismiss a teacher is due to a reduction-in-force, a nontenured teacher may have rights to a job.[112]

Often, principals are involved in the documentation of reasons for reduction-in-force, which places the principal in a difficult position. Policy shifts in states that have eliminated RIF policies will increase the difficulty for principals. Currently, there does not appear to be a pattern regarding the elimination of RIF policies by states. A search of RIF information tends to focus more on the policies of individual school districts rather than states overall. Therefore, it is imperative that principals clearly define the rationale for the reduction action and ensure that the reduction is based upon financial reasons, not a teacher performance issue.[113]

The Nontenured Teacher

The nontenured teacher is one who has engaged in a contract to teach in a school and may be pursuing a tenure contract through a probationary period. This period typically varies from one to three years, depending upon the state; however, some states are eliminating tenure or increasing the length of probation. The intent of the probationary period is to determine whether the nontenured teacher has the knowledge and skills a school is seeking for the purpose of continuing employment. In most states, tenure status is not transferable to another school district; usually, with such transfers, an additional probationary period of one year is required to attain tenure. Nontenured teachers are required to maintain all of the rules and regulations and are entitled to privileges of employment enjoyed by tenured teachers, except the continuing contract provisions. Schools are not under any obligation to reemploy a nontenured teacher at the end of the contract period.[114]

Most states require school districts to follow proper due process procedures in regard to a notice of intent to nonrenew the teacher's contract. The courts established that while nontenured teachers do not have the property right of tenure, they do have the right to employment for the period of their contract, and often to a hearing of some sort if they will not be offered a contract the following year. Unlike tenure procedures that define the causes for termination, not rehiring a teacher is much easier and may occur for almost any reason, other than an illegal reason such as discrimination.[115] Procedures for nontenured teachers are found in state statutes. The basic element of procedure is notice of why a contract is being terminated or not offered for the next year in a fair hearing—generally before the superintendent or designee, but less than a tenure hearing.[116]

In some states, boards of education are required to review performance of nontenured teachers to determine developmental needs of the nontenured teacher. A prescribed number of evaluations must occur. If poor performance is identified, the nontenured teacher is to be placed on a developmental plan where reasonable time must be provided for the teacher to improve. Interestingly, the courts have not always held schools accountable for this process. Failure to adhere to the state's procedures may result in automatic tenure for the nontenured teacher. However, in a Massachusetts case, the court determined that the state statute placed greater emphasis on school officials' rights to determine the teacher's performance than on the required number of evaluations.[117]

Many courts have taken the position that a nontenured teacher who is challenging his or her employment contract nonrenewal must demonstrate the denial of a property right. However, some courts have not adopted this position. Refusals by a school district to rehire a nontenured teacher, where the district does not make any charges that seriously damage the teacher's standing in the community or deny any opportunities for future employment, is not a liberty issue.[118]

Accountability in Teacher Dismissal

Recent federal mandates, such as NCLB and Race-to-the-Top, have also created possible avenues for teacher termination.[119] The accountability legislation of these mandates specifies that teachers can be removed for nonperformance, and that even entire schools can be closed or reconstituted. Again, these pieces of legislation are intended to address teacher quality and teacher accountability in terms of instructional performance and not moral or ethical considerations. Incompetence as a teacher is a difficult concept to prove, but this federal legislation specifies that teachers must be "highly qualified," meaning that they must be certified in the subject they teach.[120] These provisions are the first to hold principals accountable for placement and employment of teachers with appropriate credentials.[121] Whether the outcomes are beneficial or not will be proven over time, but there are new requirements for teacher quality.

New state regulations have increased the likelihood that teacher tenure will be tied to student performance.[122] For example, the Louisiana legislature just passed laws similar to Colorado that mandate teacher evaluation tied to student test scores for 50% of the total evaluation. Typical principal evaluation will account for the remaining 50%. The key to the Louisiana laws relates to the magnitude of the principal evaluation. In testing, principals reported spending more than fifteen hours on one teacher evaluation.[123] This creates an almost unmanageable situation for principals and assistant principals.

In May 2016, a New York Supreme Court judge ruled that the use of student test scores to evaluate a Long Island teacher was "indisputably arbitrary and capricious," although it was noted that the issue is moot since New York has placed a four-year moratorium on the use of state test scores in teacher evaluation.[124] While this has been noted as the first time a judge actually threw out test scores as part of the teacher evaluation process, it does not present a precedent. Other states, such as Florida, Tennessee, and New Mexico, are currently dealing with this issue in court cases.

The larger issue for many educators is that these regulations for teacher dismissal and evaluation could make filling vacancies extremely difficult. Certainly, poor teachers should be eliminated, but where are the new teachers to fill their positions?[125]

Recommendations for Practice

1. Principals must understand that in most cases of teacher dismissal, they are the ones who are providing the evidence for dismissal. Obtaining appropriate documentation and systematically observing teachers is critical.[126]

2. Teacher dismissal can have a negative impact upon a school. Principals, as instructional and school leaders, need to understand and use teacher performance appraisal as a means to improve the quality of education for all students.[127]

3. All federal, state, and school policies should be reviewed in light of new federal requirements found in NCLB and Race-to-the-Top.[128] Additionally, the Every Student Succeeds Act—signed into law Dec. 10, 2015, which rolls back much of the federal government's involvement in education policy as previously seen in No Child Left Behind—should be reviewed for the changes it makes on education policy, from testing and teacher quality to low-performing schools. The Every Student Succeeds Act takes full effect in the 2017-18 school year. It is likely that states will review their teacher evaluation procedures, as ESSA does not carry the same requirements as No Child Left Behind.

4. Principals need to stay abreast of case law governing the constitutional rights of teachers. Any acts that affect federal discrimination law may impact the decisions regarding tenure. This will become more prevalent with the use of student test scores. [129]

5. Principals must know federal, state, and local statutes pertaining to teacher qualifications, teacher dismissal, and their relationship to student and school performance. Changes in statute, policy, rules, and regulations appear imminent at the federal and state levels. Issues such as teacher evaluation, teacher dismissal, tenure, and reduction in force are changing.[130]

6. Principals and teachers need to be cognizant of their contract, written and implied, and its relationship to teacher dismissal. Most formal evaluations are conducted in the classroom to identify the instructional abilities of a teacher. Teacher dismissal occurs more often in the area of implied duties. [131]

7. Documentation of teacher performance is critical to the evaluation and dismissal of teachers. In all the cases reviewed, it is apparent that the principal must know what is going on in the classroom and have a record of teacher performance.[132]

8. Evaluation, improvement, and teacher development should be systematized to ensure a qualified, effective teaching staff. Principals and teachers must become competent in the use of student assessments to improve the curriculum and instruction of students. [133]

9. Current teacher certification and licensure statutes may be in conflict with NCLB requirements. This will require teachers, principals, and the school district to understand the law as they apply federal statutes to state and local requirements. Principals will need to stay fully abreast of the changes that occur at all levels and become involved in the development of new rulings.[134]

10. In all aspects of dismissal, principals must not engage in any unreasonable, arbitrary, or capricious actions.[135]

Summary

Teacher misconduct has gained increasing attention from teachers, administrators, and local school boards. Teachers are held to higher standards of conduct due to their extended interaction with students and the community. Some assert that the prevailing community standards should be the deciding factors for judging teacher behavior. However, most states have developed consistent standards for teachers. Increasingly, teachers have been dismissed for immorality and other definable behaviors by school boards who accept a responsibility to protect students and the teaching/learning atmosphere in the schools. Teachers and principals are also faced with the very real prospect of tenure being eliminated by state and federal legislation.

Endnotes

[1] HARRY GEHMAN GOOD & JAMES DAVID TELLER, A HISTORY OF AMERICAN EDUCATION. (1973).

[2] Michael Imber, *The Latest Chapter in Reform.* 190 AM. SCH. BD. J. 4, 62–63, 70 (2003).

[3] James H. VanSciver, *Teacher Dismissals*, 72 PHI DELTA KAPPAN 4, 318–19 (1990).

[4] David N. Figlio & Cecilia Elena Rouse. *Do Accountability and Voucher Threats Improve Low-Performing Schools?*, 89 J. OF PUB. ECON. 2–3, 381–394 (2006).

[5] Ron Sofo, *Beyond NCLB and AYP: One Superintendent's Experience of School District Reform*, 78 HARVARD EDUC. REV. 2, 391-411 (2008).

[6] RICHARD M. INGERSOLL, WHO CONTROLS TEACHERS' WORK: POWER AND ACCOUNTABILITY IN AMERICA'S SCHOOLS (2003).

[7] Suzanne R. Painter, *Principals' Perceptions of Barriers to Teacher Dismissal*, 14 J. OF PERSONNEL EVALUATION EDUC. 3, 253–64 (2000).

[8] Suzanne R. Painter, *Easing Dismissals and Non-renewals*, 57 SCH. ADMIN. 9, 40–43 (2000).

[9] Todd A. DeMitchell, *Competence, Documentation and Dismissal: A Legal Template*, 41 INT'L J. OF EDUC. REFORM, 88–95 (1995).

[10] Leslie S. Kaplan & William A. Owings, *Teacher Quality and Student Achievement: Recommendations for Principals*, 85 NASSP BULL., 628, 64-73 (2001).

[11] LEO H. BRADLEY, SCHOOL LAW FOR PUBLIC, PRIVATE, AND PAROCHIAL EDUCATORS (2005).

[12] Brian A. Jacob & Lars Lefgren, *Can Principals Identify Effective Teachers? Evidence on Subjective Performance Evaluation in Education*, 26 J. OF LAB. ECON. 1, 101-36 (2008).

[13] Geneva Gay, *The Rhetoric and Reality of NCLB*. 10 RACE, ETHNICITY AND EDUC., 279-293 (2007), doi: 10.1080/13613320701503256.

[14] Jim Hull, *Trends in Teacher Evaluation: How States Are Measuring Teacher Performance.* Center for Public Education (October 2013), http://www.centerforpubliceducation.org/Main-Menu/Evaluating-performance/Trends-in-Teacher-Evaluation-At-A-Glance/Trends-in-Teacher-Evaluation-Full-Report-PDF.pdf

[15] Stephen Sawchuk, *ESSA Loosens Reins on Teacher Evaluations, Qualifications* (January 6, 2016), http://www.edweek.org/ew/articles/2016/01/06/essa-loosens-reins-on-teacher-evaluations-qualifications.html

[16] Kimberly Scriven Berry & Carolyn D. Herrington, *States and Their Struggles with NCLB: Does the Obama Blueprint Get It Right?*, 86 PEABODY J. OF EDUC. 3, 272-290 (2011).

[17] La. Rev. Stat. 17:441-444 (2012)

[18] Paul Parkison, *Political Economy and the NCLB Regime: Accountability, Standards, and High-Stakes Testing.* 73 EDUC. FORUM 1, 44-57 (2009).

[19] MATTHEW G. SPRINGER, ET AL, TEACHER PAY FOR PERFORMANCE: EXPERIMENTAL EVIDENCE FROM THE PROJECT ON INCENTIVES IN TEACHING (2010).

[20] Christopher Jepsen, C. *Teacher Characteristics and Student Achievement: Evidence from Teacher Surveys.* 57 J. OF URBAN ECONOMICS 2, 302-19 (2005); Anthony Milanowski, *The relationship between teacher performance evaluation scores and student assessment: Evidence from Cincinnati,* 79 PEABODY J. OF EDUC. 4, 33-53 (2004).

[21] Matthew G. Springer, *The Influence of an NCLB Accountability Plan on the Distribution of Student Test Score Gains*, ECON. OF EDUC. REV. (2008), Doi:10.1016/j.econedurev.2007.06.004.

[22] Gerald W. Bracey, *Assessing NCLB*, 89 PHI DELTA KAPPAN 10, 781-782 (2008).

[23] Philip T. K. Daniel, Personnel *Evaluations in Education and the Law*, 69 SCH. BUS. AFFAIRS 7, 29–33 (2003).

[24] ARTHUR L. CORBIN, CORBIN ON CONTRACTS (1952).

[25] MICHAEL J. KAUFMAN & SHERELYN R. KAUFMAN, EDUCATION LAW, POLICY, AND PRACTICE: CASES AND MATERIALS (2005).

[26] Community Project for Students, Inc. v. Wilder, 298 S.E.2d 434 (N.C. Ct. App. 1982).

[27] El Camino Cmty. Coll. Dist. v. Superior Court, 219 Cal. Rptr. 236 (Cal. Ct. App. 1985); Wolf v. Cuyahoga Falls City Sch. Dist. Bd. of Educ., 556 N.E.2d 511 (Ohio, 1990).

[28] NATHAN L. ESSEX, SCHOOL LAW AND THE PUBLIC SCHOOLS: A PRACTICAL GUIDE FOR EDUCATIONAL LEADERS (2002).

[29] Reichert v. Draud, 701 F.2d 1168 (6th Cir. 1983).

[30] California Teachers Ass'n v. Cory, 202 Cal. Rptr. 611 (Cal. Ct. App. 1984).

[31] Cruciotti v. McNeel, 396 S.E. 2d 191 (W. Va 1990).

[32] Franklin v. Ala. State Tenure Comm'n, 482 So. 2d 1214 (Ala. Civ. App. 1985).

[33] Lawson v. Wayne Cmty. Sch. Dist., 233 N.W.2d 713 (Mich. Ct. App. 1975).

[34] Mich. Comp. Laws Ann. § 380.1232 (West 1988).

[35] Brendan P. Menuey, *Teacher' Perceptions of Professional Incompetence and Barriers to the Dismissal Process*, 18 J. OF PERSONNEL EVALUATION IN EDUC. 4, 309-325 (2007).

[36] Mo. Ann. Stat. § 168.108 (West, 1991), *supra* note 29 and accompanying text.

[37] Donald Boyd, Pam Grossman, Marsha Ing, Hamilton Lankford, Susanna Loeb & James Wyckoff. *The Influence of School Administrators on Teacher Retention Decisions*, 48 AM. EDUC. RES. J. 2, 303-333 (2011).

[38] Board of Educ. v. Jones, 823 S.W.2d 457 (Ky. 1992).

[39] BLACK'S LAW DICTIONARY 323 (6th ed. 1990).

[40] MICHAEL J. KAUFMAN & SHERELYN R. KAUFMAN, EDUCATION LAW, POLICY, AND PRACTICE: CASES AND MATERIALS (2005).

[41] Kuta v. Joint Dist. No. 50(J), 799 P.2d 379 (Colo. 1990).

[42] MICHAEL W. LAMORTE, SCHOOL LAW: CASES AND CONCEPTS (8th ed. 2005).

[43] Ind. Code Ann. § 20–6, 1–4–10(a)(3) (Mich. 1996).

[44] Sharif Shakrani, *Teacher Turnover: Costly Crisis, Solvable Problem*, Lansing, MI: Michigan State University, Education Policy Center (2008), http://www.eric.ed.gov/PDFS/ED502130.pdf

[45] N.D. Cent. Code § 15–47–28 (1993 & Supp. 1995); Tenn. Code Ann. § 49–5–508(b) (1996).

[46] S. Reeder, *The hidden cost of tenure*, SMALL NEWSPAPER GROUP (2005), http://thehiddencost-softenure.com/stor.etc/press=displaytid=295712

[47] N.D. Cent. Code § 15–47–28 (1993 & Supp. 1995). Tenn. Code Ann. § 49–5–508(b) (1996).

[48] Evans-Marshall v. Bd. of Educ. of the Tipp City Exempted Vill. Sch. Dist., 428 F.3d 223 (6th Cir. (2005).

[49] Donvito v. Bd. of Educ. N. Valley Reg'l High Sch., 5877 C 646 03 SB 1 04 (ST Bd. of Educ. 2005)

[50] Abrantes v. Bd. of Educ. of Norwood-Norfolk Cent. Sch. Dist., 630 N.Y.S.2d 220, 222 (N.Y. App. Div. 1995).

[51] Kransdorf v. Bd. of Educ. of Northport-E. Northport Union Free Sch. Dist., 613 N.E.2d 537 (N.Y. 1993).

[52] Douglas P. Wittemam, *Procedural Due Process Under the Kansas Teacher Due Process Act: Going Through the Motions Is Not Enough*, 29 WASHBURN L. J., 668 (1990).

[53] La. Rev. Stat. 17:442 (2012)

[54] Iowa Code Ann. § 279.19 (West 1996) [two years]; Colo. Rev. Stat. Ann. § 22–63–203.104 (West 1996) [three years]; Mo. Ann. Stat. § 168 (West 1995).

[55] Loftus v. Bd. of Educ. of Fairfield, 509 A.2d 500 (Conn. 1986); Dennery v. Bd. of Educ. of Passaic County Reg'l High Sch. Dist. No. 1, 622 A.2d 858 (N.J. 1993).

[56] La. Rev. Stat 17:442 (2012)

[57] BLACK'S LAW DICTIONARY 688 (5th Ed. 1985).

[58] Alabama State Tenure Comm'n v. Lee County Bd. of Educ., 595 So. 2d 479.

[59] Belcourt v. Fort Totten Pub. Sch. Dist., 454 N.W.2d 703.

[60] Clarke v. Shoreline Sch. Dist., 720 P.2d. 793 (Wash. 1986).

[61] McKenqie v. Webster Parish Sch. Bd., 609 So. 2d 1028 (La. Ct. App. 1992).

[62] Swanson v. Houston Indep. Sch. Dist., 800 S.W. 2d 630 (Tex. App. Houston 1990).

[63] Reeder, S., *supra* note 26.

[64] School Dist. No. 8, Pinal County v. Superior Court, 433 So.2d 28 (1967)

[65] Hargis v. LaFourche Parish Sch. Bd., 593 So. 2d 400 (La. Ct. App. 1991).

[66] Lockhart v. Bd. of Educ. Arapahoe County Sch. Dist., 735 P.2d 913 (Colo. Ct. App. 1986).

[67] *In re* Proposed Termination of James E. Johnson's Teaching Contract, 451 N.W.2d 343 (Minn. Ct. App. 1990).

[68] MacPherson v. Sch. Bd. of Monroe County, 505 So. 2d 682 (Fla. Dist. Ct. App. 1987).

[69] Ketchersid v Rhea County Bd. of Ed., E2004 01153 COA R3 CV (Tenn. Ct. App. 2005).

[70] Bellairs v. Beaverton Sch. Dist. FDA 04 01: A125893 (Or. Dist. Ct. App. 2006).

[71] 78 A.L.R. 3d 83–87.

[72] Horton v. Jefferson County - DuBois Area Voc'l Tech. Sch., 157 Pa. Commw. 424, 630 A.2d 481 (1993).

[73] Board of Educ. of Hopkins County v. Wood, 717 S.W.2d 837 (Ky. 1986).

[74] La. Rev. Stat. 17:442.

[75] Jason R. Fulmer, *Dismissing the "Immoral" Teacher for Conduct Outside the Workplace-Do Current Laws Protect the Interests of Both School Authorities and Teachers?*, 31 J. OF LAW AND EDUC. 3, 271-289 (2002).

[76] David Dagley, *Wow! Did You Hear What They Said? Trends in the Use of Immorality as a Cause of Dismissal for School Personnel*, Paper presented at the Educ. Law Association Winter Seminar (March 2001).

[77] V. D. Keating, *Pub. School Employee Termination for Sexual Misconduct*. 4 OHIO SCHOOL LAW J. 4, 65-68 (1992).

[78] Denise Skarbek, & Patricia A. Parrish, WHAT YOU DON'T KNOW WILL HURT YOU: SEXUAL ABUSE IN SCHOOLS (2009).

[79] Jefferson County Sch. Dist. No. 509-J v. Fair Dismissal Appeals Bd., 812 P.2d 1284 (Or. 1991).

[80] Stelzer v. State Bd. of Educ., 595 N.E.2d 489 (Ohio Ct. App. 1991).

[81] Scheiber v. New York City Bd. of Educ., 593 N.Y.S.2d 653 (App. Div. 1993).

[82] E School News. *Teacher's Website Is Grounds for Dismissal*. http://www.eschoolnews.com/news/showstory.cfm?articleID=4430.

[83] Cochran v. Bd. of Educ. of Mex. Sch. Dist., 815 S.W.2d 55 (Mo. Ct. App. 1991).

[84] Governing Bd. of ABC Unified Sch. Dist. v. Haar, 33 Cal. Rptr. 2d 744, 751 (Cal. Ct. App. 1994).

[85] V. D. Keating, *Pub. School Employee Termination for Sexual Misconduct*. 4 OHIO SCHOOL LAW J. 4, 65-68 (1992); C. C. Kent, *Protecting a District from Educator Sexual Misconduct*, 34 *Catalyst for Change* 2, 18-29 (2006).

[86] Ahmad v. The Bd. of Ed. of City of Chi., 03 CH 21482 (Ill. Ct. App. 2006)

[87] DENNIS R. DUNKLEE & ROBERT J. SHOOP, THE PRINCIPAL'S QUICK REFERENCE GUIDE TO SCHOOL LAW: REDUCING LIABILITY, LITIGATION, AND OTHER POTENTIAL LEGAL TANGLES (2002).

[88] La. Rev. Stat. 17:443 (2012).

[89] Michael Imber & Tyll van Geel, EDUC. LAW (3rd ed. 2004).

[90] Brown v. Chicago Bd. of Educ., No. 15.1857 (7th Cir. June 2, 1016).

[91] *In re* Tenure Hearing of Jennifer O'Brien, No. A-2452-11T4 (N.J. Super. Ct. App. Div. Jan. 11, 2013).

[92] MARTHA M. MCCARTHY, NELDA H. CAMBRON-MCCABE, & STEPHEN B. THOMAS, LEGAL RIGHTS OF TEACHERS AND STUDENTS (2004).

[93] Schulz v. Bd. of Educ. of Sch. Dist. of Freemont, 315 N.W.2d 633 (Neb. 1982).

[94] Clifford P. Hooker, *Terminating Teachers and Revoking Their Licensure for Conduct Beyond the Schoolhouse Gate*, 4 EDUC. LAW REPORTER 2, 285–99 (2004).

[95] John Matlock, *Solving the Problem of Problem Employees*, 14 *Executive Educator* 10, 39–40 (1992).

[96] Cybyske v. Indep. Sch. Dist. No. 196, 347 N.W.2d 356 (Minn. 1984); Degnan v. Bering Strait Sch. Dist. 753 P.2d 146 (Alaska 1988).

[97] Heather L. Carter, Teresa S. Foulger, & Ann Dutton Ewbank, *Have You Googled Your Teacher Lately? Teachers' Use of Social Networking Sites*, 89 PHI DELTA KAPPAN 9, 681-685 (2008).

[98] Alex Lehrer, (2011). *Keep the Poking to Yourself, Mrs. Robinson: The Missouri Facebook Statute and Its Implications for Teacher Free Speech Under the First Amendment*. Law School Student Scholarship (2011), http://erepository.law.shu.edu/student_scholarship/2

[99] Kathleen Conn, *Cyberbullying and Other Student Misuses of Technology Affecting K-12 Pub. Schools: Will Pub. School Administrators Be Held Responsible for the Consequence?*, 244 EDUC. LAW REPORTER 479 (2009).

[100] San Diego Unified School District v. Commission on Professional Competence, 124 Cal. Rptr. 3d 320 (Cal. App. Ct. 2011).

[101] Rubino v. City of New York, 950 N.Y.S.2d 494 (N.Y. Sup. 2012), *aff'd*, 106 A.D.3d 439, 965 N.Y.S.2d 47 (S. Ct. App. Div., 1st Dep't 2013).

[102] Christine Greenhow & Beth Robelia, *Informal Learning and Identity Formation in Online Social Networks*. 34 LEARNING, MEDIA AND TECHNOLOGY 2, 119–140 (2009).

[103] Amanda Lenhart & Mary Madden, *Teens, Privacy & Online Social Networks*, Pew Internet & Am. Life Project (2007); John Palfrey, Urs Gasser, Miriam Simun, & Rosalie Fay Barnes, *Youth, Creativity, and Copyright in the Digital Age*, 1 INT'L J. OF LEARNING AND MEDIA 2, 79-97 (2009).

[104] Heather L. Carter, Teresa S. Foulger, & Ann Dutton Ewbank, *Have You Googled Your Teacher Lately? Teachers' Use of Social Networking Sites*, 89 PHI DELTA KAPPAN 9, 681-685 (2008).

[105] Joseph P. Mazer, Richard E. Murphy, & Cheri Simonds, *The Effects of Teacher Self-Disclosure Via Facebook on Teacher Credibility.* 34 Learning, Media and Technology 2, 175–183 (2009).

[106] Katherine Bindley & Timothy Stenovek, *Missouri 'Facebook Law' Limits Teacher-Student Interactions Online, Draws Criticism and Praise,* HUFFINGTON POST (October 3, 2011), http://www.huffingtonpost.com/2011/08/03/missouri-facebook-law_n_916716.html

[107] Amy W. Estrada, (2011*). Saving Face from Facebook: Arriving at a Compromise Between Schools' Concerns with Teacher Social Networking and Teachers' First Amendment Rights,* 32 T. JEFFERSON L. REV., 283-286 (2011).

[108] Patricia Nidiffer, *Tinkering with Restrictions on Educ. Speech: Can Sch. Bd.s Restrict What Educators Say on Social Networking Sites?,* 36 UNIVERSITY OF DAYTON LAW REV., 115, 116 (2010); Brock Read, *A Myspace Photo Costs a Student a Teaching Certificate,* THE CHRONICLE OF HIGHER EDUC. (April 2007), http://chronicle.com/wiredcampus/article/2029/a-myspace-photo-costs-a-student-ateaching-certificate

[109] JULIE UNDERWOOD & WEBB, L. DEAN. (2006). SCHOOL LAW FOR TEACHERS: CONCEPTS AND APPLICATIONS (2006).

[110] La. Rev. Stat. 17:81.4 (2012).

[111] *See, e.g.,* Lezette v. Bd. of Educ., 319 N.E.2d 189 (N.Y. 1974); Hill v. Dayton Sch. Dist., 52 P.2d 1154 (Wash. 1975).

[112] Alexander v. Delano, 188 Cal. Rptr. 7095 (Ct. App 1983); Bonman v. Bd. of Educ. W. Clermont, 443 N.E.2d 176 (Ohio 1983); Carmody v. Bd. of Dirs., 453 A.2d 965 (Pa. 1982).

[113] HAUFMAN, M. J., & HAUFMAN, S. R. (2005). EDUC. LAW, POLICY, AND PRACTICE: CASES AND MATERIALS. New York: Aspen Publishers.

[114] Childer v. Indep. Sch. Dist. No. 1, 842 P.2d 355 (Okla. Ct. App. 1992).

[115] Board of Regents v. Roth, 408 U.S. 564 (1972).

[116] Stovall v. Huntsville City Bd. of Educ., 602 So. 2d 407 (Ala. Civ. App. 1992).

[117] Marotta v. Greater New Bedford Reg'l Vocational High Sch. Dist. Comm., 589 N.E.2d 334 (Mass. App. Ct. 1992).

[118] *Roth,* 408 U.S. at 573.

[119] Jesse Rothstein, *Teacher Quality in Educ.al Production: Tracking, Decay, and Student Achievement,* 125 QUARTERLY J. OF ECONOMICS 1, 175–214 (2010).

[120] Landon E. Beyer, *The Politics of Standardization: Teacher Educ. in the U.S.A.,* 28 J. OF EDUC. FOR TEACHING 3, 239–45 (2002).

[121] THOMAS C. DAWSON K. LLOYD BILLINGSLEY, UNSATISFACTORY PERFORMANCE: HOW CALIFORNIA'S K-12 EDUC. SYSTEM PROTECTS MEDIOCRITY AND HOW TEACHER QUALITY CAN BE IMPROVED (2000).

[122] Eric Hanushek & Steven Rivkin, *Using Value-Added Measures of Teacher Quality,* National Center for Analysis of Longitudinal Data in Educ.al Research, The Urban Institute (2010), www.urban.org/UploadedPDF/1001371 -teacher-quality.pdf.

[123] Steven Rivkin, Eric Hanushek, & John Kain, *Teachers, Schools, and Academic Achievement,* 73 ECONOMETRICA 2, 417-458 (2005); Jonah Rockoff, *The Impact of Individual Teachers on Student Achievement: Evidence from Panel Data,* 94 AM. ECONOMIC REV. 2, 247-252 (2004).

[124] Elizabeth Harris, *Court Vacates Long Island Teacher's Evaluation Tied to Test Scores.* NEW YORK TIMES (May 10, 2016), http://www.nytimes.com/2016/05/11/nyregion/court-vacates-long-island-teachers-evaluation-tied-to-student-test-scores.html?_r=0

[125] Kathleen M. Brown & Susan R. Wynn, *Finding, Supporting, and Keeping: The Role of Principal in Teacher Retention Issues.* 8 LEADERSHIP AND POLICY IN SCHOOLS, 37-63 (2009).

[126] Lars Lefgren & Brian A. Jacob, *When Principals Rate Teachers,* 6 EDUC. NEXT 2, 59-69 (Spring 2006).

[127] Todd A. DeMitchell, NEGLIGENCE (2007).

[128] Douglas Harris, *Value-Added Measures of Educ. Performance: Clearing Away the Smoke and Mirrors, Policy Brief 10-4,* Policy Analysis for California Educ. PACE (2008), www.stanford.edu/group/pace/PUB.ATIONS/PB/PACE_BRIEF_OCT_2010.pdf.

[129] Lars Lefgren & Brian A. Jacob, *When Principals Rate Teachers,* 6 EDUC. NEXT 2, 59-69 (Spring 2006); Leslie S. Kaplan & William A. Owings, *Teacher Quality and Student Achievement: Recommendations for Principals.* 85 NASSP BULL. 628, 64-73 (2001).

[130] NATHAN L. ESSEX, THE 200 MOST FREQUENTLY ASKED LEGAL QUESTIONS FOR EDUCATORS (2009).

[131] Nancy K. Freeman, *Professional Ethics: A Cornerstone of Teachers' Preservice Curriculum.* 22 ACTION IN TEACHER EDUC. 3, 12-18 (2000).

[132] Leslie S. Kaplan & William A. Owings, *Teacher Quality and Student Achievement: Recommendations for Principals.* 85 NASSP BULL. 628, 64-73 (2001).

[133] Sharif Shakrani, *Teacher Turnover: Costly Crisis, Solvable Problem*, Lansing, MI: Michigan State University, Educ. Policy Center (2008), http://www.eric.ed.gov/PDFS/ED502130.pdf

[134] Kathleen M. Brown & Susan R. Wynn, *Finding, Supporting, and Keeping: The Role of Principal in Teacher Retention Issues.* 8 LEADERSHIP AND POLICY IN SCHOOLS, 37-63 (2009), Doi:10.1080/15700760701817371

[135] Kern Alexander & M. David Alexander, M. D. AM. PUB. SCHOOL LAW (8th ed. 2011).

* The authors wish to acknowledge the contributions of Michael D. Richardson and Dennis VanBerkum, who aided in the development of this chapter in the previous edition of *The Principal's Legal Handbook*.

Key Words

accountability
adequate yearly progress
arbitrary and capricious
breach of contract
certification
classroom observation
collective bargaining
discrimination
due process
educational requirements
Elementary and Secondary Education Act (ESEA)
employment contract
evaluation systems
Every Student Succeeds Act (ESSA)
good cause
hearing
immorality
incompetency
insubordination
liberty rights
No Child Left Behind Act (NCLB)

nonrenewal
nontenured
online communication
performance reviews
probation
professional development
professionalism
property rights
Race-to-the-Top
reduction-in-force (RIF)
remediation
resignation
sexual misconduct
social media
standardized tests
state control of education
student achievement test scores
suspension
tenure
termination
value-added

Section III – Chapter 9

Collective Bargaining in Public Schools

Justin M. Bathon and Richard LaFosse

Introduction

For more than a half century, collective bargaining of teachers and other school personnel has been an integral part of public school employment in the United States. In 2015, approximately one-third of teachers were members of a collective bargaining unit.[1] Collective bargaining of these public school employees generally serves to strengthen the position of the employees against their employer, typically the school board. Given the unique nature of the relationship between public employees and their governmentally based employers, some states have individual state laws to govern this relationship when it comes to collectively negotiating employment contracts. Over the previous decade, though, states generally limited or even eliminated some of these laws granting collective bargaining rights to employees. While there are many potential benefits and detriments of collective bargaining in the public schools,[2] the process is better served when the individuals involved are clearly aware of the established legal framework within which they are operating.

This chapter outlines the legal framework within which most public school collective bargaining occurs. Teachers' unions engage in a variety of activities, many of which do not take place at the local level. Particularly in states that limit collective bargaining or where local unions are rare, much of the activity in the state focuses on lobbying state government, providing professional development, member access to legal support and insurance, and additional benefits such as student scholarships and family discounts to local attractions. This examination of collective bargaining provides an introduction to the specific relationship in the collective bargaining of the local teachers' contracts. It serves only as a broad introduction and not an exhaustive examination. Readers involved in legal issues related to collective bargaining in education should consult more detailed sources with specific state-related policies, or legal counsel.

First, this chapter examines the statutory and case law frameworks that either permit or deny collective bargaining of school employees in the United States. A brief historical perspective on the development of the right to bargain in the United States and the specific development of teachers' unions is also included. Additionally, this section includes some of the more recent history of public sector collective bargaining and the continuing policy debates in many states. Second, the chapter examines various issues related to the bargaining process. These legal aspects of the bargaining process include the definition of the bargaining unit, good faith bargaining and unfair labor practices, the acceptable subjects of collective bargaining, and related issues such as fair share provisions for nonunion members. Third, this chapter examines the procedures that are allowed or mandated when the collective bargaining process breaks down, including an examination of strikes. Fourth, since after an agreement is in place, most disputes cumulate in a grievance, this chapter examines the procedures surrounding those actions. Finally, recommendations with respect to the collective bargaining process are provided for administrators.

Legal Issues

The Right to Bargain

The right to bargain collectively has not always been guaranteed in the United States. Although unions have existed nearly since the creation of the country, they had few rights and little effect on the workplace until the 1930s.[3] During this time, important federal legislation was passed that set the framework for employees' collective bargaining today. While these federal acts were substantial steps toward the legitimacy of collective bargaining, such laws applied only to the private sector and did not address state or other governmental employees, including public school teachers. In 1960, Wisconsin—a state that still frequently finds itself at the center of such issues—was the first state to mandate bargaining by public employees.[4] These state laws, in combination with increasing teacher activism, such as a strike by teachers in New York City, led to a drastic increase in the unionization of teachers in the United States in the 1960s.[5]

Although the private sector legislation that emerged out of this contentious period of labor formation does not apply directly to public sector bargaining, many of the ideas and basic principles of these early acts still serve as the fundamental principles of all labor relations in the United States. Thus, familiarity with these statutes helps in understanding the basic requirements of collective bargaining in the public sector.

The first act Congress passed in relation to collective bargaining was the Norris-LaGuardia Act of 1932.[6] This act limited courts from using injunctions to stop collective actions by employees against employers and was an important first step toward the legitimization of collective bargaining. The second and more important act passed by Congress was the Wagner Act, in 1935.[7] Also known as the National Labor Relations Act (NLRA), this statute created the National Labor Relations Board, which safeguarded the basic rights of employees in their collective activities.[8] These new protections included a limitation on employer interference with union activities, limits on discrimination against unions in hiring, and a requirement that employers bargain in good faith. If employers violated any of these new union protections, the union could file an unfair labor practice claim against the employer with the National Labor Relations Board.[9] More than ten years later, the Taft-Hartley Act was passed as an attempt to balance the collective bargaining field by placing many of the same requirements on labor unions as were placed on employers.[10] The basic provisions established by these statutes still form not only the foundation for private sector collective bargaining, but also have been relied upon to varying degrees by public sector collective bargaining laws across the states.

One recent issue that has caused the issue of private versus public sector bargaining to come into question is the emergence of charter schools that utilize public money, but are run by private corporations. Teachers in charter schools across the U.S. have sought to collectively bargain, but whether private (largely federal law) or public (largely state law) sector laws apply has been challenged. In September 2016, the National Labor Relations Board issued two opinions finding two charter schools to be private, not public, even though usage of public funds was involved.[11] Thus, as additional school models evolve that rely on private operators, the line between public and private sector collective bargaining is likely to blur further.

While public sector collective bargaining is similar to private sector collective bargaining in many ways, there are some important differences. The most significant difference is that rather than a collectively bargained contract between two private individuals or corporations, in public sector bargaining one of the parties to the contract is the government itself. Governments have several powers that private companies do not have; one of these is the power to make many of the rules, including limiting the union's primary negotiating weapon: the strike.[12] In many cases, the governmental employer also retains more managerial rights than private companies. On the other hand, the public employer must work within a more structured time and budgetary framework. Concerning the ability of governmental employers to make rules limiting employee rights, an important ruling by the U.S. Supreme Court in 1967, in the case of *Keyishian v. Board of Regents of the University of the State of New York,* found that a public employer cannot force employees to give away their right to join a union.[13] Subsequent court cases have followed the *Keyishian* decision in protecting teachers' constitutional rights to join and participate in union activities. Even where a state legislature attempted to prohibit public employees from joining a union, it was found to be unconstitutional.[14] Thus, all public employees have, at a minimum, the right to join a union. However, while public employees may join unions, this does not mean that such unions have a right to be the recognized collective bargaining agent for the membership. Such a right has been legislatively recognized in thirty-five states,[15] and courts have found collective bargaining units recognizable in other states where legislation does not speak to the issue.[16] Five states, though—Georgia, North Carolina, South Carolina, Texas, and Virginia—have enacted legislation prohibiting collective contracts between public employers and employees. In other states, the courts have ruled that such bargaining cannot occur without enabling legislation from the state legislature.[17]

States have continued to consider the role of public sector collective bargaining in policymaking. Wisconsin has served as a test case of dramatically reducing the collective bargaining rights of teachers. In 2011, a conservative governor sought to greatly reduce governmental expenditures by taking away the collective bargaining rights of public employees, including teachers, on most issues outside of wages directly, thus saving the government significant dollars in healthcare and pensions.[18] Following mass protests and an election to recall the governor, the actions were challenged in court and made their way to the Wisconsin Supreme Court. In 2014, the court ruled that the limitations placed on public employee collective bargaining did not curtail public employee freedom of association, equal protection, or contractual rights in upholding the restrictions.[19] Other states have placed additional limitations on teachers' bargaining rights, as well. Idaho, Indiana, Michigan, and Tennessee all restricted the permissible subjects of collective bargaining for teachers.[20] Illinois, one of the few states that permits teacher strikes, required that three-fourths of all teachers must authorize a strike, a higher percentage than in the past.[21]

School administrators thus must be aware of the legal status of collective bargaining rights in their state before engaging in the collective bargaining process at all. This is especially important in this changing policy environment, as the complex legal nature of the collective bargaining bills hide potential benefits and pitfalls for schools in negotiating with teachers. For those states that prohibit or have not enabled collective bargaining for school employees, schools do not have to collectively bargain employee contracts. Instead, each school employee functions only with an individual employment contract, but still is influenced by union activities at the state legislative level. The remainder of this chapter will focus solely on the states that permit collective bargaining of public employees.[22]

Legal Issues in the Bargaining Process

In states that allow collective bargaining for teachers and other school employees, there are several similarities in terms of defining the bargaining unit, good faith negotiation and unfair labor practices, the permissible subjects of collective bargaining, and related issues. The next sections will use those broad categories to examine the collective bargaining rights and limitations in more detail. Remember, though, these provisions vary from state to state depending on the specific provisions contained in the different state collective bargaining laws. While most states are likely to have some or all of these elements, the specific rights for public employees will almost assuredly be unique to each state context.

Defining the Bargaining Unit

The definition of the bargaining unit is a crucial step in the collective bargaining process. First, local employees must form a union and certify that union with the state labor relations board. Once a union is certified as a representative of a particular bargaining unit, such units become the exclusive bargaining agent for the entire population of the defined bargaining unit, regardless of whether each individual employee is a member of the union. Thus, unions represent even nonunion employees within the bargaining unit. Second, state laws provide some clarity on who may be included in the bargaining unit. Typically, a bargaining unit must share some characteristics like similar working skills, wages, and conditions, as well as fit within a similar operative and administrative structure of the employer.[23] In schools, this typically translates into a distinct collective bargaining unit for teachers and a different unit for other staff such as custodial and central office staff.[24] For example, school bus drivers in New York are a distinct bargaining unit.[25] On the other hand, though, in 2014, Minnesota clarified that art therapists, music therapists, or audiologists were included under the definition of "teacher" for collective bargaining purposes,[26] and in the previous year permitted child care providers collective bargaining rights as their own unit.[27] In some cases, all nonadministrative employees of a public school can be within a single bargaining unit. When this happens, the unit is called a wall-to-wall bargaining unit. However, wall-to-wall bargaining units occur much less frequently than distinct units for professional employees and classified employees.

Administrative employees, such as principals and other management or senior officials, typically are not included in the bargaining unit. Specifically, exclusions to a bargaining unit have been made when employees are considered managerial, supervisory, or have access to confidential information regarding the employer's labor practices.[28] When principals or assistant principals have managerial and supervisory roles within the school, they are excluded from the teacher bargaining unit.[29] There has also been controversy surrounding other school personnel, such as department chairs,[30] superintendent secretaries,[31] networking engineers,[32] and technology assistants;[33] however, the central test remains whether such employees are managerial, supervisory, or have access to confidential information.

Good Faith and Unfair Labor Practices

Although there are multiple rights each party holds in the collective bargaining process, two specific rights are important for an understanding of public sector collective bargaining. First, there is a duty to bargain in good faith, which is necessary for parties to work together toward an agreement. If a party does not bargain in good faith or commits one of a multitude of other collective bargaining violations, they can be charged with committing an unfair labor practice, the primary legal mechanism used for remedying disputes in the bargaining process.

Once a bargaining unit is established and defined, it becomes the exclusive bargaining representative for the population of individuals contained within the definition of the bargaining unit. To ensure a productive bargaining process between the exclusive representation agent and the public sector employer, the law places a duty to bargain in good faith on both parties.[34] In public sector collective bargaining, the duty to bargain in good faith is not exactly akin to the private sector NLRA definition,[35] but it is similar. Because of the contentious nature of the good faith bargaining provision, some states have added further clarity to their public employee good faith bargaining requirement. For example, the following is the good faith bargaining requirement in California:

> Meet and confer in good faith means that a public agency, or such representatives as it may designate, and representatives of recognized employee organizations, shall have the mutual obligation personally to meet and confer promptly upon request by either party and continue for a reasonable period of time in order to exchange freely information, opinions, and proposals, and to endeavor to reach agreement on matters within the scope of representation prior to the adoption by the public agency of its final budget for the ensuing year. The process should include adequate time for the resolution of impasses where specific procedures for such resolution are contained in local rule, regulation, or ordinance, or when such procedures are utilized by mutual consent.[36]

Although good faith bargaining does not require the parties to reach an agreement, the failure to bargain in good faith results in an unfair labor practice. Unfair labor practices are the primary remedy for disputes arising around the formation of the collectively bargained agreement and cover not only failures to bargain in good faith, but the majority of all other illegal activities related to the formation of the union and the collectively bargained agreement. In the private sector, unfair labor practice charges are heard by the National Labor Relations Board.[37] However, in public sector collective bargaining, unfair labor disputes are heard by the state agency with authority for oversight of collective bargaining. If a dispute arises, a complaint typically is filed with the relevant state labor relations board. The board then investigates, and if it finds sufficient evidence of an unfair labor practice, it will file a complaint against the violating party. This complaint generally is first heard by an administrative law judge employed by the state labor relations board, with subsequent rights to appeal to the judicial system.[38]

A charge of an unfair labor practice may be filed with the relevant state agency by either the employer or the employee. For the most part, what constitutes an unfair labor practice is not well defined in statute. However, some legislation has attempted to provide greater definition as to what constitutes an unfair labor practice in regard to education. For example, Illinois law states that educational employers shall not interfere with employees in the exercise of their union rights, interfere with the formation of a union, discriminate against union members in hiring practices, refuse to bargain in good faith, or refuse to comply with a binding arbitration agreement, among others.[39]

In addition to statutory definitions of unfair labor practices, such as the ones mentioned above, courts frequently rule on charges of unfair labor practices. Courts have found that subcontracting bargaining unit work,[40] failing to promote to a nonunion position,[41] hiring a long-term substitute instead of a full-time position,[42] and refusing to provide information to the union[43] can be unfair labor practices, along with many other employer actions outside or counter to the collective bargaining agreement. While used less frequently, unfair labor practices against employee unions include intentionally coercing employees to join the union, refusing to bargain in good faith, and refusing to comply with a binding arbitration agreement, among others.[44]

Subjects of Collective Bargaining

One of the frequently contested aspects of collective bargaining in schools is what topics can be the subject of collectively bargained contracts. The relationship between employers' rights to manage their businesses and employees' rights to bargain elements of their employment has led to three different classifications for possible topics of collective bargaining: unlawful subjects of bargaining, mandatory subjects of bargaining, and permissive subjects of bargaining.

First, topics that are inherently managerial in nature cannot be bargained. These managerial topics are considered an essential part of the government's role in determining the policy and direction of schools and, as such, cannot be bargained away, even if the school board wished to bargain these items. Policy decisions that cannot be bargained include school curricular matters and school staffing needs.[45] Additionally, some courts have interpreted tenure decisions, the school calendar, dismissal procedures, and the choice of department heads and chairs as unlawful subjects of bargaining.[46] Further, even when a subject may be bargained, the implementation may not be subject to bargaining. Such was the case in Florida where a teaching-supplies reimbursement mechanism was in dispute. The teachers were reimbursed the same amount as was bargained, but the choice of repayment mechanism, debit cards instead of checks, was considered administrative in nature.[47]

Alternatively, some subjects must be bargained. State statutes that are modeled on the National Labor Relations Act use the general guideline that "wages, hours and other terms and conditions of employment" must be bargained in the formation of the collective bargaining agreement.[48] Clearly, then, subjects such as the salary of teachers and employees, their hourly responsibilities, and other fringe benefits must be bargained.[49] For instance, in 2016, Hawaii passed a law mandating the collective bargaining of teacher salary increases, rather than longevity or annual increases.[50] Other topics that have been found in some cases to be mandatory subjects of bargaining include reimbursement for education and professional development, holiday and overtime pay,[51] healthcare benefits,[52] vacation and sick leave, early retirement incentives, reduction-in-force plans, and teacher evaluation procedures.[53] Teacher evaluation procedures in particular have come under recent scrutiny with the growth of mandated value-added assessments and evaluation at the state policy level.[54] Illinois[55] and Washington, D.C.[56] have had cases in which both evaluation policies and bargained agreements were found to apply to the evaluation process.

Subjects of bargaining which are neither unlawful nor mandatory are considered permissive subjects; they may become elements of the collective bargaining agreement if both parties agree. Permissive subjects of bargaining have included mid-contract renegotiation, drug testing, and the implementation dates of layoffs.[57] For instance, in 2008, the Supreme Court of Montana found that teacher transfers were not a mandatory subject of bargaining and that the union only must show good faith on the issue if it chose to bargain on this topic.[58]

Some provisions of contracts frequently generate litigation to determine their status in the bargaining process. Among these especially contested subjects are class size, the school calendar, evaluations, and dismissals. While some may naturally consider class size a condition of employment and thus a mandatory subject of bargaining,[59] most courts have not found this to be the case, instead finding a managerial prerogative regarding class size because of the essential personnel and facilities issues underlying such decisions.[60] Similarly, the school calendar has been found to be both an unlawful subject of bargaining[61] and a mandatory subject of bargaining,[62] with a majority considering it either an unlawful or permissive subject.[63] For some subjects of bargaining, there is a distinction in the courts between bargaining the item itself and bargaining the impact of the subject. For instance, the impact of class size determinations has been found to be bargainable, even if the actual class size determination is solely a managerial decision.[64] At a school in Connecticut in 2010, for instance, special education teacher workloads were unilaterally increased after one special education teacher resigned. The school's unilateral actions were found to be improper, and the school was ordered to bargain on this issue.[65]

This type of interaction between the parties is similar for teacher evaluations. With some exceptions,[66] courts have found that the evaluation criteria of teachers are non-negotiable, while the procedures and practices administrators engage in when evaluating teachers may be permissive or mandatory subjects of bargaining.[67] Finally, teacher termination is a frequently contested subject of bargaining.[68] Teachers' unions want to have the maximum amount of control over the processes and timing of employment decisions, while school administrators contend that employment decisions are solely matters of educational policy and thus non-negotiable. In situations where dismissal decisions are predicated on financial concerns, commonly called reductions-in-force, courts have found that while the decision to eliminate positions was one solely for the board of education, the notice and timing of the job terminations could be negotiated.[69]

Also, unions attempt to negotiate provisions that aid them directly within the school context, such as direct payroll deductions for dues and access to school mailboxes and other communication outlets. Courts have generally found these provisions to be acceptable permissive subjects of bargaining because of their function of promoting labor peace and stability within the school.[70] States legislatures have also been active in setting limitations on unions, such as a recent law in Arkansas that permits teachers to join or leave the union at any time.[71]

Fair-Share Provisions and Right-to-Work Laws

In many states where public sector collective bargaining exists, unions are permitted to collect mandatory service fees from all individuals represented in the bargaining unit, even from nonmembers. These fees collected from nonmembers are commonly referred to as "fair share" or "agency shop" fees[72] and have grown increasingly controversial in recent years. Proponents argue that fair share fees help eliminate the "free rider" problem, in which individuals opt out of their union to avoid paying dues while still reaping the same benefits as dues-paying members.[73] Proponents further argue that granting a single collective bargaining unit the power to collect fair share fees promotes "labor peace," making it possible for employers to negotiate with a single unit rather than multiple competing unions.[74] Opponents, on the other hand, argue that collective bargaining is inherently political and that mandating payment to an inherently political organization is a violation of First Amendment freedom of speech and association protections.[75]

The Supreme Court has so far upheld the constitutionality of fair share provisions so long as the nonunion members' dues do not go to cover the political activities of the union[76] but instead "finance expenditures by the Union for the purposes of collective bargaining, contract administration, and grievance adjustment."[77] However, recent Supreme Court opinions have featured language demonstrating a potential willingness to break with precedent on this issue.[78] In what many speculated could be the end of fair share fees,[79] the Court reviewed *Friedrichs v. California Teachers Association,* in which petitioners brought a First Amendment challenge against the California Teachers Association's use of fair share fees. Due to the vacancy on the bench created by Justice Antonin Scalia's death, the Court decided *Friedrichs* in a 4-4 tie.[80] A tie on the Supreme Court has the effect of affirming the decision of the lower court (without setting new precedent), and, in this case, upheld the constitutionality of fair share agreements. Importantly, since the Supreme Court did not issue an opinion on the merits, the door has been left open for further challenges since Justice Neil Gorsuch was appointed to fill the vacancy. While fair share provisions remain constitutional, a growing number of states—now twenty-six, as well as the U.S. territory of Guam—have adopted "right to work" laws, prohibiting the collection of fair share fees.[81] The Supreme Court's review of *Friedrichs* has brought increased attention to fair share fees, and, as both state laws and U.S. constitutional law are currently evolving in this area, school leaders will want to closely follow any developments likely to occur in the coming years.

Implications of Non-Agreement in the Bargaining Process

When collective bargaining negotiations become stale and there is no longer any progress toward an agreement, the negotiations are said to have reached an impasse. At this stage, mediation, fact finding, and arbitration may be triggered. At least in the private sector, if none of the impasse procedures succeed in restarting negotiations toward an agreement, employees may begin the series of steps leading to a strike. However, in the public sector, many state legislatures have removed the unions' ability to strike, and numerous state courts have struck down or greatly limited striking rights where legislatures have remained silent. Often, schools can even get injunctions against unions when there is evidence of an attempt to induce a strike.[82]

Typically, the first step taken once parties have reached impasse is mediation. Mediation is a process where an outside, disinterested party is brought in to restart the bargaining process. Mediators will often make findings and suggest possible resolutions to parties, but will not make those findings or recommendations public. In fact finding, on the other hand, findings of the third-party mediator are made public, adding outside pressure to the collective bargaining process to encourage further negotiation toward resolution. Fact finding is required in some states and permissive in many more.[83] In both fact finding and mediation, the recommendations of the third party may be accepted or rejected by the parties. That is in contrast to arbitration—which is required in a few states[84] and permissive in many more—where the third party's decisions are binding. If all the required impasse procedures have been tried and there is still not an agreement, the parties may move toward a strike or a final offer, depending on what is permitted under state law.

The most intimidating implications of a failure to agree are strikes. As noted above, most states prohibit strikes by their public employees, including local school board employees and, if applicable, courts have generally found that strikes are not permissible as contrary to the public policy,[85] with some exceptions.[86] Because they are potentially harmful to the education of children, strikes usually are found to be legal in public school collective bargaining only when they are specifically provided for in state law. Teacher strikes are considered permissible in only about a dozen states,[87] and fewer than ten states legislatively grant a right for teachers to strike.[88] However, even in these states, there are often conditions that must be satisfied before a strike can legally occur. Such preconditions may include the expiration of the contract, filing an intent to strike document with the state labor relations board, and evidence that the strike will not pose a danger to the public health and safety.[89] When all expressed conditions have been satisfied in these states, teachers' unions can legally engage in a strike that may force the temporary closure of schools.

In the many states where strikes are not permitted, the union occasionally decides to engage in a strike illegally.[90] When this happens, there are a variety of penalties for the union and the teachers. Usually a school will immediately seek an injunction from the court to stop the union's activities.[91] The union and its leaders can be found in contempt of court if an injunction to stop the strike is violated, and eventually could be imprisoned if the violations continue. Also, unions may face fines and a loss of privileges previously acquired in the collective bargaining agreement. Teachers who join an illegal strike may face a loss of pay, required reimbursement to the board for costs of the strike, or even termination.[92] Keep in mind, however, that a strike can be more than a total work stoppage. Actions such as work slowdowns, sickouts, and refusing to perform duties under contract also can be considered strikes and can trigger penalties. However, when teachers continue to work but engage in informational picketing, this practice is usually upheld, unless the picketing creates an obstruction or disruption.[93]

Post-Agreement Grievances

After a contract has been agreed upon and it takes effect, disputes under the contract typically evolve into grievances. A grievance is generally defined as an allegation that there has been a violation of the contract on the part of the board.[94] Although courts have the ultimate authority to decide on grievances, arbitration has become the primary form of grievance resolution. Unless a statute expressly forbids schools from entering into arbitration agreements, or arbitration on a topic is preempted by state or federal law, courts have found the grievance arbitration clauses to be enforceable.[95] These grievance arbitration clauses largely remove the courts from the process of resolving disputes under the contract, because the arbitration is binding on both of the parties. Decisions will typically not be overturned, except if the arbitration award is not based on the contractual provisions or if the arbitration award concerns an illegal provision, such as taking inherent managerial rights from the school.[96] Because of this lack of oversight on the part of courts, arbiters have greater flexibility in crafting remedies to grievances.

One area related to grievance arbitration that has spurred litigation is the subjects that may be arbitrated. Typically, when crafting a grievance arbitration provision, the school will seek to make it as narrow as possible, including time limitations for filing, and the union will seek to make it as broad as possible.[97] Also contained in the collective bargaining agreement are a series of steps for processing a grievance once it is submitted by an employee to management. These steps typically provide management an opportunity to resolve the grievance to the satisfaction of the employee before the matter is sent to binding arbitration. As arbitration becomes an increasingly popular option in collective bargaining agreements, there has been an increase in litigation to determine the limits of this option. Also, the types of awards reached in arbitration have been challenged, such as in New York, where an award directed the board to stop assigning special education teachers to other districts.[98] On the other hand, a court in Indiana upheld an arbitration award that demanded the district issue a teacher a formal letter of apology.[99] The Pennsylvania Supreme Court referenced the "essence test" that examines whether the arbitration award derives from the essence of the collective bargaining agreement,[100] and this notion is one that school administrators might apply as well in interpreting arbitration awards.

Recommendations for Practice

1. Maintaining good working relations with teachers is the best recommendation not only for potentially avoiding disputes, but also for ensuring schools function at a high level. Good working relations should be the primary goal of all school leaders.

2. Schools and districts should be cognizant of a principal's position as middle-manager. Principals, positioned between school boards and school employees, should refrain from becoming involved too deeply in the process on either side of labor issues as matters are under discussion. Principals should also keep their own time constraints in mind when working in this area, as one can quickly get lost in the policy.

3. For any professional that becomes deeply involved in a bargaining process, it is also important to understand the distinctions between unlawful, mandatory, and permissive subjects of bargaining. Without that understanding, parties may inadvertently seek to include provisions in the contract that are unnecessary or illegal under the law. Parties must keep in mind the classification of topics of bargaining and have a plan concerning which permissive topics of bargaining the school is willing to address.

4. Perhaps most importantly, all parties should be open-minded regarding collective bargaining and should approach contract negotiations from a positive perspective. Because many state laws mandate such negotiation to occur once a union is recognized, approaching the bargaining without optimism can cause more harm to the school in the long run. Collective bargaining, in most cases, can be a helpful process for all parties by providing clarity and consistency in school-employee relations.

5. Finally, schools and districts should consider events as they unfold from the perspectives of both a student and a member of the community. Collective bargaining is a complex and highly misunderstood concept. School leaders, students, elected officials, and community members can easily become confused, overwhelmed, and frustrated by this process. At all times, schools and districts should keep their ethical responsibilities to students and communities, and make decisions accordingly.

Endnotes

1   U.S. Bureau of Labor Statistics, Union Members Survey, http://www.bls.gov/news.release/pdf/union2.pdf (2015).

2   *See* JAMES RAPP, EDUCATION LAW Ch. 7 § 7.01[4] (Matthew Bender & Co. 2016) (providing an extended list of benefit and detriments of collective bargaining in education).

3   STEPHEN B. THOMAS, NELDA H. CAMBRON-MCCABE & MARTHA MCCARTHY, PUBLIC SCHOOL LAW: TEACHERS' AND STUDENTS' RIGHTS 439 (6th. ed. 2009).

4   CHARLES J. RUSSO, REUTTER'S: THE LAW OF PUBLIC EDUCATION, 586 (5th ed. 2004).

5   Todd A. DeMitchell & Casey D. Cobb, *Teachers: Their Union and Their Profession. A Tangled Relationship.* 212 EDUC. L. REP. 1, 3 (2006).

6   29 U.S.C. §§ 101-115 (2007).

7   Pub. L. No. 74-198, 49 Stat. 449 (1935). *See also,* Theodore J. St. Antoine, *How the Wagner Act Came to Be: A Prospectus.* 96 MICH. L. REV. 2201 (1998).

8   29 U.S.C. § 153 (2007).

9   29 U.S.C. § 158 (2007).

10   Pub. L. No. 80-101, 61 Stat. 136 (1947).

11   *In re* Penn. Virtual Charter Sch., 364 NLRB No. 87, (2016) & Hyde Leadership Charter School – Brooklyn, 364 NLRB No. 88 (2016).

12   Martin H. Malin, *Public Employees Right to Strike: Law & Experience.* 26 U. Mich. J. L. Ref. 313, 317 (1993).

13   385 U.S. 589 (1967).

14   Atkins v. City of Charlotte, 296 F. Supp. 1068 (W.D.N.C. 1969).

15   Emily Workman, *State Collective Bargaining Policies for Teachers,* EDUCATION COMMISSION OF THE STATES (2011).

16   Board of Trs. of Univ. of Ky. v. Pub. Employees Council No. 51, 571 S.W.2d 616 (Ken. 1978).

17   Mila Sanes & John Schmitt, *Regulation of Public Sector Collective Bargaining in the States.* CENTER FOR ECONOMIC AND POLICY RESEARCH (2014).

18   For a point and counterpoint discussion of the events in Wisconsin and the implications for education, see Todd DeMitchell & Martha Parker-Magagna, *A 'Law Too Far?' The Wisconsin Budget Repair Act: Point,* 275 EDUC. L. REP. 1 (2012); Ralph D. Mawdsley, Charles J. Russo & James L. Mawdsley, *A 'Law Too Far?' The Wisconsin Budget Repair Act: Counterpoint.* 275 EDUC. L. REP. 16 (2012).

19   Madison Teachers Inc. v. Walker, 851 N.W.2d 337 (Wis. 2014).

20   Emily Workman, *State Collective Bargaining Policies for Teachers,* EDUCATION COMMISSION OF THE STATES (2011).

21   *Id.*

22   *Id.*

23   McCarthy, *supra* note 3, at 444. [Reference to McCarthy not in n. 2]

24   Russo, *supra* note 4, at 587.

25   *In re* Oxford Employee Support Pers., 836 N.Y.S.2d 355 (N.Y. App. Div. 2007).

26   Minn. Stat. § 179A.03 (2014).

27   Minn. Stat. § 179A.52 (2013).

28   Rapp, *supra* note 2, at § 7.02.

29   Chicago Principals Ass'n v. Educ. Labor Relations Bd., 543 N.E.2d 166 (1989); *But see* Wellesley Sch. Comm., 376 Mass. 112 (1978) (finding principals and assistant principals were not managerial); Chicago Teachers Union, IFT/AFT, AFL-CIO v. IELRB, 695 N.E.2d 1332 (1998) (assistant principals who had full-time teaching responsibilities were not managerial).

30   Parkway Sch. Dist. v. Local 902/MNEA, 807 S.W.2d 63 (Mo. 1991) (department heads can be members of bargaining unit because they are not confidential employees).

31   North Hills Sch. Dist. v. Pa. Labor Relations Bd., 762 A.2d 1153 (Pa. Commw. Ct. 2000) (secretary who participated in negotiations was a confidential employee and excluded from the bargaining unit); Barrington Sch. Comm. v. R.I. State Labor Relations Bd., 608 A.2d 1126 (R.I. 1992) (finding secretary to business manager excluded from the bargaining unit).

[32] Niles Twp. High Sch. Dist. 219 v. Ill. Educ. Labor Relations Bd., 900 N.E.2d 336 (Ill. App. Ct. 2008).

[33] Board of Educ. of Glenview Cmty. Consol. Sch. Dist. No. 34 v. Ill. Educ. Labor Relations Bd., 874 N.E.2d 158 (Ill. App. Ct. 2007).

[34] Rapp, *supra* note 2, at § 7.03.

[35] 29 U.S.C. § 158 (2007) ("For the purposes of this section, to bargain collectively is the performance of the mutual obligation of the employer and the representative of the employees to meet at reasonable times and confer in good faith with respect to wages, hours, and other terms and conditions of employment, or the negotiation of an agreement, or any question arising thereunder, and the execution of a written contract incorporating any agreement reached if requested by either party, but such obligation does not compel either party to agree to a proposal or require the making of a concession").

[36] CAL. GOVERNMENT CODE § 3505 (2007).

[37] 29 U.S.C. § 153 (2007).

[38] Rapp, *supra* note 2, at § 7.09.

[39] 115 ILL. COMP. STAT. 5/14(a) (2007).

[40] Vestal Employees Ass'n v. Pub. Employment Relations Bd. of the State of N.Y., 94 N.Y.2d 409 (2000).

[41] School Bd. of Martin Cnty. v. Martin Cnty. Educ. Ass'n, 613 So. 2d 521 (Fla. Dist. Ct. App. 1993).

[42] South Souix City Educ. Ass'n v. Dakota Cnty. Sch. Dist. No. 22-0011, 772 N.W.2d 564 (Neb. 2009).

[43] Chicago Sch. Reform Bd. of Trs. v. Ill. Educ. Labor Relations Bd., 734 N.E.2d 69 (App. Ct. 1st Dist. 2000).

[44] 115 ILL. COMP. STAT. 5/14(b) (2007).

[45] *See, e.g.,* In re Appeal of Matthew Kennedy,162 N.H. 109 (2011).

[46] Russo, *supra* note 4, at 587, 589;

[47] School Dist. v. Pub. Employees Relation Comm'n, 15 So. 3d 42 (Fla. Dist. Ct. App. 2009).

[48] 29 U.S.C. § 158(d) (2007).

[49] Adair v. Stockton Unified Sch. Dist., 77 Cal. Rptr. 3d 62 (Cal. Ct. App. 2008); Northwest Area Sch. Dist. v. Northwest Area Educ. Ass'n, 954 A.2d 111 (Pa. Commw. 2008).

[50] Haw. Rev. Stat.§ 302A-623 (2016).

[51] Waterloo Educ. Ass'n v. Iowa Pub. Employment Relations Bd., 740 N.W.2d 418 (Iowa 2007).

[52] Greater Nanticoke Area Educ. Ass'n v. Greater Nanticoke Area Sch. Dist., 938 A.2d 1177 (Pa. Commw. Ct. 2007).

[53] Russo, *supra* note 4, at 588; McCarthy, *supra* note 3, at 449;

[54] Regina Umpstead, Ann E. Blankenship, & Linda Weiss, The New State of Teacher Evaluation and Employment Laws: An Analysis of Legal Actions and Trends. 322 EDUC. LAW REP. 577, 591 (2015). *See also* MARK A. PAIGE, BUILDING A BETTER TEACHER: UNDERSTANDING VALUE ADDED MODELS IN THE LAW OF TEACHER EVALUATION (2016).

[55] Bd. of Educ. of Waukegan Cmty. Unit Sch. Dist. No. 60 v. Orbach, 991 N.E.2d 851, (Ill. Ct. App. 2013).

[56] Washington Teachers' Union, Local #6 v. D.C. Public Schs., 77 A.3d 441 (D.C. 2013).

[57] Russo, *supra* note 4, at 590.

[58] Bonner Sch. Dist. No. 14 v. Bonner Educ. Ass'n, 176 P.3d 262 (Mont. 2008).

[59] This was the finding of an Illinois Appellate Case, Decatur Bd. of Educ. v. Ill. Educ. Labor Relations Bd., 536 N.E.2d 743 (Ill. App. Ct. 1989).

[60] Kenai Peninsula Borough Sch. Dist. v. Kenai Peninsula Educ. Ass'n, 572 P.2d 416 (Alaska 1977); Tualatin Valley Bargaining Council v. Tigard Sch. Dist. 23J, 840 P.2d 657 (1992).

[61] City of Biddeford v. Biddeford Teachers Ass'n, 304 A.2d 387, 421 (Me. 1973).

[62] City of Beloit v. Employment Relations Comm'n, 242 N.W.2d 231 (Wis. 1976).

[63] West Cent. Educ. Ass'n v. W. Cent. Sch. Dist., 655 N.W.2d 916, 923 (S.D. 2002).

[64] *In re* West Irondequoit Teachers Ass'n, 315 N.E.2d 775 (N.Y. 1974).

[65] Board of Educ. of Region 16 v. St. Bd. of Labor Relations, 7 A.3d 371 (Conn. 2010).

[66] *See,* Aplington Cmty. Sch. Dist. v. Iowa Pub. Employment Relations Bd., 392 N.W.2d 495 (Iowa 1986), *superseded by statute,* 1998 Iowa Acts ch. 1215, § 41; ch. 1216, § 24.

[67] Board of Educ. U.S.D. No. 352, Goodland v. NEA-Goodland, 785 P.2d 993 (Kan. 1990).

[68] *See,* McCarthy, *supra* note 3, at 451-53.

[69] Central City Educ. Ass'n v. Ill. Educ. Labor Relations Bd., 599 N.E.2d 892 (Ill. 1992); Township of Old Bridge Bd. of Educ. v. Old Bridge Educ. Ass'n, 489 A.2d 159 (N.J. 1985).

[70] McCarthy, *supra* note 3, at 458.

[71] Ark. Code § 6-17-120 (2015).

[72] BRIAN A. BRAUN, ILLINOIS SCHOOL LAW SURVEY 253 (9th ed. 2006).

[73] *See* Stephanie Mencimer, *This Case Could Strike a "Mortal Blow" to Unions: Friedrichs v. California Teachers Association Could Dramatically Weaken Labor's Clout,* MOTHER JONES (Jan. 8, 2016), http://www.motherjones.com/politics/2016/01/friedrichs-california-teachers-union-supreme-court.

[74] *See id.*

[75] *See Supreme Court Denies Friedrichs Petition for Rehearing,* CENTER FOR INDIVIDUAL RIGHTS (June 28, 2016), https://www.cir-usa.org/cases/friedrichs-v-california-teachers-association-et-al/. The Center for Individual Rights is a self-described conservative public interest advocacy group which has provided the *Friedrichs* plaintiffs with legal representation at all stages of this lawsuit.

[76] Abood v. Detroit Bd. of Educ., 431 U.S. 209 (1977); *See also* Chicago Teacher's Union Local No. 1 v. Hudson, 475 U.S. 292 (1986); Lehnert v. Ferris Faculty Ass'n, 500 U.S. 507 (1991); Davenport v. Wash. Educ. Ass'n, 197 P.3d 686 (Wash. Ct. App. 2008).

[77] Abood v. Detroit Bd. of Educ., 431 U.S. 209, 225–26 (1977).

[78] *See, e.g.,* Harris v. Quinn, 134 S. Ct. 2618, 2621 (2014) ("The Abood Court also failed to appreciate the distinction between core union speech in the public sector and core union speech in the private sector, as well as the conceptual difficulty in public-sector cases of distinguishing union expenditures for collective bargaining from those designed for political purposes. . . . the Abood Court's critical 'labor peace' analysis rests on the unsupported empirical assumption that exclusive representation in the public sector depends on the right to collect an agency fee from nonmembers.").

[79] *See* Mike Antonucci, *Teachers Unions at Risk of Losing "Agency Fees": Friedrichs v. California Teachers Association Could Fundamentally Alter the Education Labor Landscape.*16 EDUCATIONNEXT, no. 1, 2016, at 23, *available at* http://educationnext.org/teachers-unions-risk-losing-agency-fees-friedrichs-california/.

[80] Friedrichs v. Cal. Teachers Ass'n, 136 S. Ct. 1083 (2016).

[81] The National Right to Work Legal Defense Foundation maintains a list of right-to-work states. *Right to Work States: Do You Work in a Right to Work State?* NATIONAL RIGHT TO WORK LEGAL DEFENSE FOUNDATION, INC., http://www.nrtw.org/rtws.htm.

[82] Commonwealth Employment Relations Bd. v. Boston Teachers Union, 908 N.E.2d 772 (Mass. App. Ct. 2009).

[83] McCarthy, *supra* note 3, at 461.

[84] *See* N.Y. CIV. SERV. LAW § 209 (2007); OR. REV. STAT. § 243.742 (2007).

[85] Norwalk Teachers' Ass'n v. Bd. of Educ., 83 A.2d 482 (Conn. 1951); Anchorage Educ. Ass'n v. Anchorage Sch. Dist., 648 P.2d 993 (Alaska 1982); Board of Educ. v. N.J. Educ. Ass'n, 247 A.2d 867 (N.J. 1968); Jefferson Cnty. Bd. of Educ. v. Jefferson Cnty. Educ. Ass'n, 393 S.E.2d 653 (W. Va. 1990).

[86] Cnty. Sanitation Dist. No. 2, Los Angeles Cnty. v. Los Angeles Cnty. Employees' Ass'n, 699 P.2d 835 (Cal. 1985); Davis v. Henry, 555 So. 2d 457 (La. 1990).

[87] MILLA SANES AND JOHN SCHMITT, REGULATION OF PUBLIC SECTOR COLLECTIVE BARGAINING IN THE STATES, CENTER FOR ECONOMIC AND POLICY RESEARCH, (March, 2014), *available at* http://cepr.net/documents/state-public-cb-2014-03.pdf.

[88] Workman, *supra* note 15.

[89] McCarthy, *supra* note 3, at 464.

[90] For instance, even though strikes are illegal in Michigan, the teachers in Detroit Public Schools have engaged in strikes in 1999 and 2006. Catherine Jun, *Detroit Teachers Strike, Pickets Begin as Union Rejects Pay Cut, Parents Worry about School Year*, THE DETROIT NEWS, Aug. 28, 2006.

[91] *See, e.g.*, Commonwealth Employment Relations Bd. v. Boston Teachers Union, 908 N.E.2d 772 (Mass. App. Ct. 2009).

[92] Russo, *supra* note 4, at 599–600.

[93] *Id.*

[94] Braun, *supra* note 72, at 257. [No citation to Braun at n. 62]

[95] United Teachers of Los Angeles v. Los Angeles Unified School Dist., 54 Cal. 4th 504 (Cal. 2012); Gazunis v. Foster, 929 A.2d 541 (Md. 2007).

[96] The U.S. Supreme Court explained the limited role of courts in reviewing arbitration decisions in the "Steelworkers Trilogy" cases of 1960: United Steelworkers of America v. American Mfg. Co., 363 U.S. 564 (U.S. 1960); United Steelworkers of America v. Warrior & Gulf Navigation Co., 363 U.S. 574 (U.S. 1960); United Steelworkers of America v. Enterprise Wheel & Car Corp., 363 U.S. 593 (U.S. 1960). *See also* Holmes v. Orleans Parish Sch. Bd., 698 So. 2d 429 (La. Ct. App. 1997).

[97] *See* Rapp, *supra* note 2, at § 7.04.

[98] Lawrence Teachers v. Lawrence Pub. Sch., 833 N.Y.S.2d 133 (N.Y. App. Div. 2007).

[99] Marion Cmty. Sch. Corp. v. Marion Teachers Ass'n, 873 N.E.2d 605 (Ind. Ct. App. 2007).

[100] *See, e.g.*, Phila. Hous. Auth. v. AFSCME, Dist. Council 33, Local 934, 617 Pa. 69 (Pa. 2012).

Key Words

agency shop

arbitration

bargaining unit

charter schools

collective bargaining

discrimination

evaluations

fair-share

good faith bargaining

grievance

healthcare

mandatory representation

mandatory subject

mediation

National Labor Relations Act (NLRA)

Norris-LaGuardia Act

pensions

permissive subject

picketing

public employees

public union

reduction-in-force

right to work laws

strike

Taft-Hartley Act

teachers union

unfair labor practices

unionization

unlawful subject

Wagner Act

Section III – Chapter 10

Teacher Certification

Tina Chang, Sean E. Maguire, and William E. Sparkman

Introduction

Teacher certification[1] traditionally has been viewed as a responsibility of the states, which have delegated authority to state boards of education to set standards for the certification or licensure of teachers and other professional educators. Despite this historical authority, the enactment of the No Child Left Behind Act of 2001 (NCLB) demonstrated the expanding role of the federal government in influencing teacher quality with the requirement that all core academic subject teachers be "highly qualified."[2] A notable shift in federal policy occurred with the enactment of the Every Student Succeeds Act (ESSA) in December 2015.[3] The ESSA served to reauthorize the Elementary and Secondary Education Act (ESEA) of 1965 and replaced NCLB of 2001. Among relevant changes in the new federal education law was the elimination of the "highly qualified" requirement and its replacement with "teachers who meet the applicable State certification and licensure requirements, including any requirements for certification obtained through alternative routes to certification…"[4] In addition to this important change, the new law also replaced "highly qualified" with "effective" in other sections of the ESEA.[5] These changes have added new wrinkles to teacher certification that will be discussed in more detail below.

At the time that politicians and policymakers were emphasizing teacher quality and standards-based education reforms, there was a corresponding push within many states for easing limitations on who may become a teacher. Greater access to educator preparation, including alternative and emergency certification programs, has emerged in response to teacher shortages. Similarly, calls to deregulate teacher certification, which is viewed by some as an inefficient mechanism restricting entry into the profession, have increased.

According to the U.S. Department of Education, there were 2,124 teacher preparation programs within the fifty states and other reporting jurisdictions[6] in 2011.[7] This included traditional teacher preparation programs (referred to as "alternative, IHE-based") housed in institutions of higher education (IHE) and alternative-route teacher preparation programs housed in or outside IHEs (referred to as "alternative, not IHE-based").[8] Traditional teacher preparation programs represented 69% of all reported programs; "alternative, IHE-based," 21%; and "alternative, not IHE-based," 10%.[9] Based on the relative percentages, there were about 658 alternative preparation programs, with 446 based in IHEs and 212 not affiliated with IHEs. All teacher preparation programs combined prepared 241,402 educators in 2009-10;[10] nearly 80% were prepared in traditional IHE programs. The remaining 20%, nearly 48,736 program completers, were prepared in alternative certification programs. It is likely that the number of teachers and other school personnel prepared in alternative certification programs will continue to increase.

As a result of the manifold demands arising from federal and state legislation, districts are entrusted with increased responsibility in the area of teacher certification. In particular, districts should be familiar with respective state laws and regulations related to educator certification given the proliferation of alternate-route laws and programs. License review, inspection, and verification can occur at all levels of a district. For example, in practice many principals now review the status of teacher certification in their buildings on an annual basis. Even where principals review teacher certification, many school district central offices also generally monitor the certification status of professional employees. This step is particularly apropos when a teacher is employed under a provisional endorsement or temporary certificate valid for only a year or two. Principals, who are closely involved in documentation of performance or questionable behavior, may be called to testify in hearings or other legal proceedings.

Although statutes and regulations governing teacher certification are state-specific, some general principles emerge from case law. Currently, there are three primary areas of concern in teacher certification: the basis of the state's interest in and authority for teacher certification, the relation of certification to employment, and the reasons and processes necessary to suspend or revoke a certificate. However, before discussing selected state court cases that illustrate these three key areas of concern, attention is given to some of the relevant changes in the ESSA that could impact the state certification landscape.

The Every Student Succeeds Act (ESSA) and Replacement of the "Highly Qualified" Standard

In an effort to improve K-12 students' educational experiences and hold schools accountable, NCLB of 2001 created the standard of a "highly qualified" teacher as one who has

> obtained full State certification as a teacher (including certification obtained through alternative routes to certification) or passed the State teacher licensing examination, and holds a license to teach in such State, except [when charter schools are involved] the terms means that the teacher meets the requirements set forth in the State's public charter school law...[11]

An additional, controversial section that expanded the above definition was added in the ensuing federal regulations. When these federal regulations were promulgated by the U.S. Department of Education in 2002, the phrase "highly qualified" also included a teacher *"participating* in an alternative certification route [who]...*demonstrates satisfactory progress* toward full certification as prescribed by the State..." (emphasis added).[12] This definition created a situation whereby teachers simply *participating* in an alternative route and making *satisfactory* progress toward certification could be considered "highly qualified." A California case out of the Ninth Circuit Court of Appeals exposed this apparent contradiction.[13] The appellants argued that the federal regulations were invalid because they permitted an alternative-route teacher who was still in the process of obtaining full state certification to be considered "highly qualified" as specified in the statutory language of NCLB. After its analysis of the language in both the statute and challenged regulation, the court ruled that the federal regulation was "invalid because it impermissibly expands the definition (of the federal statute) to include teachers who only "'demonstrate...satisfactory progress' toward full certification."[14]

The U.S. Congress addressed this issue as part of a continuing appropriations extensions act which became law in December 2010. Section 163 of the continuing resolution amended NCLB "to confirm that teachers in alternative route programs may continue to teach as full certified-highly qualified teachers under the provision of this regulation until 2012-13, subject to any provision that Congress may enact before then in a reauthorized (law)."[15] After the congressional action, the Ninth Circuit Court of Appeals supplemented its 2010 decision in the *Renee* case by concluding, among other things, that the passage of Section 163, and *so long as it is in effect* (emphasis added), rendered it consistent with NCLB.[16] Subsequent annual continuing appropriations acts of Congress continued to extend the NCLB definition of "highly qualified teacher" for an additional year.[17]

Although the "highly qualified" discrepancy was settled at that particular point, there still remained concern over the federal government overstepping its bounds and getting involved in what has traditionally been regarded as a state matter. When NCLB was replaced by the Every Student Succeeds Act (ESSA),[18] the phrase "highly qualified" was eliminated and changes were made to recognize the authority of the states in setting quality standards for its professional educators.

Specifically, the ESSA did the following with respect to the term "highly qualified":

1. Deleted the definition of "highly qualified" contained in paragraph 23 in Title IX (General Provisions) of NCLB.[19] However, the definition of "highly qualified teacher" contained in 34 C.F.R. § 200.56(a)(2)(ii) was made effective through the end of the 2016-2017 academic year by the Consolidated Appropriations Act, 2016, Pub. L. 114-113, §8(3), 129 Stat. 2245.

2. The term "highly qualified teachers" was replaced throughout the ESSA with: "teachers who meet the applicable State certification and

licensure requirements, including any requirements for certification obtained through alternative routes to certification, or, with regard to special education teachers, the qualifications described in section 612(a)(14)(C) of the Individuals with Disabilities Education Act."[20]

3. Repealed and replaced Title II of NCLB with new statutory language which continues grants to the states to assist in the preparation, training, and recruitment of high quality school personnel.[21] However, the term "highly qualified" is not included in the new Title II of ESSA. Instead, the new focus is on improving the quality and effectiveness of teachers, principals, and other school leaders. It also seeks to increase access to and the number of educators who are *effective* (emphasis added) in improving student academic outcomes, while leaving it up to the states to determine "effectiveness." The new law specifically prohibits the U.S. Secretary of Education from prescribing "indicators or specific measures of teacher, principal, or other school leader effectiveness or quality..."[22] The term "highly qualified paraprofessional" is not included in the new ESSA language contained in Title II.

4. Replaced the term "highly qualified" with "effective" in the Magnet Schools Assistance program.[23]

The ESSA eliminates the "highly qualified" designation, replacing it with "effective," and returns authority to the states to define teacher quality and measures of effectiveness. It reinforces the primacy of state certification requirements and specifically includes any certification requirements obtained through alternative routes to certification. This likely will continue to foster an increase in the number of alternative certification programs. States will have to develop measures of effectiveness for teachers, principals, and other school leaders regardless of whether they are certified through traditional or alternative-route programs.

While there is still significant federal involvement, the changes made by ESSA recognized the primacy of the state in determining the qualifications of educators. Authority over education, a constitutional right reserved for the states, has been restored; now states have the ability to once again determine what requirements a teacher must meet to be certified and deemed "effective" in their particular state. While it remains to be seen how federal incursion into what has long been a state responsibility will unfold, the landscape of professional certification for school personnel will not return to its more traditional roots in institutions of higher education. This is especially likely given the outcome of the 2016 presidential election and the appointment of a new U.S. Secretary of Education.

State Authority and Interest in Certification

The authority of the state to certify professional educators derives from its police power under the Tenth Amendment to the U.S. Constitution.[24] According to the U.S. Supreme Court, "[t]he traditional police power of the State is defined as the authority to provide for the public health, safety, and morals, and we have upheld such a basis for legislation."[25] This definition was reinforced in a New York teacher certification case in 2006, in which the Second Circuit Court of Appeals stated that "[t]here is little doubt that New York acts pursuant to its traditional police powers in performing a core state function—regulating the quality of public school teachers."[26]

Over the years, state courts have made numerous pronouncements about the purpose of teacher certification, its importance to the state, and its responsibility for education. For example, according to an Illinois judge, "[t]he predominant purpose in licensing a trade or profession is to prevent injury to the public by assuring that the occupation will be practiced with honesty and integrity and by excluding those who are incompetent or unworthy."[27] In 1982, the North Dakota Supreme Court stated, "we believe that teacher certification is an acceptable method of satisfying part of the constitutional mandate to the legislature to properly provide an education for its youth."[28] Finally, the Supreme Court of Michigan, in a long and contentious decision involving an alleged Establishment Clause violation by the state, ruled that teacher certification is a compelling state interest.[29] In reaching its conclusion, the court built its argument on the following logic:

> It is clear that Michigan's interest in education is long-standing and of the highest importance. ...The state's interest in education necessarily extends to an interest in teachers because a primary and vital ingredient to a good education is good teachers...Michigan has long recognized the importance of qualified teachers...Therefore, to the extent that certification of teachers furthers education, it can be considered a compelling state interest. Those certification requirements which involve gaining expertise in a particular substantive field, taking classes in a program of general or liberal education, student teaching, and taking a few basic courses in education, are clearly aimed at and closely related to the goal of producing competent teachers.[30]

As a practical matter, state legislatures typically delegate rule-making and regulatory authority for teacher certification to the state board of education. This authority to regulate teacher certification has been described by the Kansas Supreme Court as follows:

> The State Board of Education is statutorily the only agency authorized to set standards for teacher certification. Certification by the State Board of Education, rather than subjective qualifications set up by each local school board, determines

that a teacher is qualified to teach the subjects endorsed on the teaching certificate.[31]

The National Association of State Boards of Education (NASBE)[32] listed commonalities between state boards' responsibilities, which include, among other things: "[d]etermining qualifications for professional education personnel [and] [e]stablishing standards for accreditation of local school districts and preparation programs for teachers and administrators."[33] While there are slight variations, all state boards of education define what qualifications teachers need to meet in their specific states. ESSA may require teachers to meet state certification requirements, but details are left up to states to determine.

State courts have considered numerous cases in which plaintiffs have challenged their authority with respect to various certification requirements. State teacher performance requirements and related assessment instruments have generally been approved by various courts. A New York appellate court upheld a requirement that educators achieve passing scores on the National Teacher's Examination (NTE) in order to remain certified, as it was applied to several teachers who were terminated.[34] In an important en banc decision by a federal appeals court, a reading, writing, and mathematics examination required for entry into the teaching profession was upheld.[35] The court determined that the California Basic Education Skills Test (CBEST) satisfied a three-step test for job-relatedness.[36] The majority relied heavily on the fact that the CBEST was validated on three separate occasions and had been partially written and developed by the Educational Testing Service (ETS).[37] In Massachusetts, a regulation requiring math teachers in low-performing schools to pass an assessment prior to licensure renewal was upheld; Massachusetts' highest court stated that the rule was consistent with state school accountability measures.[38]

Legal challenges have mounted in several states by not only public, but private, sectarian schools operated by churches. Teacher certification and state authority over church-run schools are the most common issues brought before courts. These cases question whether such authority and interest are sufficient to allow the state to limit individual rights, such as the freedom of religion and expression. Plaintiffs working at religious schools in Iowa argued unsuccessfully that state certification requirements violated their freedom of expression, as well as the Free Exercise, Establishment, and Due Process clauses of the U.S. Constitution.[39] Judge Larson exposed the teachers' inconsistencies in fighting against certification:

> Plaintiffs believe that licensure wrongfully interferes with a teacher's calling by God to teach, yet they apparently do not object to the licensure of those in their church called by God to other occupations, such as doctor or lawyer, nor do they object to obtaining a driver's license for those serving in their bus ministry...[40]

The Court's conclusion was that Iowa's interest in requiring all teachers to be certified was sufficiently compelling to override the plaintiff's First Amendment claim that teachers in sectarian schools should not be subjected to such regulation.[41]

Although it is clear states have substantial control over K-12 public, and sometimes even private schools, it is important to note that federal laws and regulations take precedence and must be adhered to. As an example, actions related to certification must be neutral with respect to race, color, religion, sex, and national origin;[42] licensing requirements must be applied in a nondiscriminatory manner.[43] However, teachers can lawfully be mandated to show their allegiance toward the United States of America and their state, before obtaining a position at a school, by signing a loyalty oath.[44] Pledges such as "I solemnly swear or affirm that I will support the Constitution of the State of Colorado and of the United States of America and the laws of the state of Colorado and of the United States" have been upheld by the courts.[45]

Teacher Certification and Employment

A teaching certificate is a license, not a contract, and does not guarantee employment in a school district. The Seventh Circuit Court of Appeals established in a 2001 Illinois case that a teaching credential is a minimum requirement for job employment and that ultimately, the school board has the power to determine further qualifications.[46] A Kansas court reached the same conclusion, but under different circumstances, stating that "it is the judgment of the State Board of Education that matters when deciding who is fit to teach…not the courts."[47] Therefore, although schools and their employees must follow case law, courts generally defer to states when the qualifications of educators are questioned.

Although the possession of a teaching certificate does not guarantee employment in a school district, it is essential for an educator to be a competent party to an employment contract in order to be paid.[48] For example, an Illinois court found that a school board was no longer bound by an employment contract when a substitute teacher allowed her certification to expire.[49] When California allowed waivers for credentials, a probationary employee was found to have no statutory right to reemployment when she failed to make any progress toward meeting the qualifications needed for her bilingual teaching position.[50] A similar situation occurred in New York when an educator with a provisional license was suspended after not obtaining a permanent certificate, which was mandatory to retain his teacher status;[51] he was given one year to fulfill the necessary requirements and failed to do so.[52] The court held that the teacher was not entitled to back pay or rehiring.[53]

A question that is often troubling to educators is whether or not the state can change certification requirements. This point was highlighted in an older Indiana case involving the revocation of a teacher's certificate. In upholding the revocation, the judge wrote that "[a] license has none of the elements of a contract, and does not confer an absolute right, but only a personal privilege to be exercised under existing restrictions and such as may thereafter be reasonably imposed."[54] Connecticut's supreme court also noted that a statute requiring the exchange of permanent teaching certificates for five-year certificates that were renewable only upon completion of continuing education courses did not violate teachers' procedural or substantive due process rights.[55] The constitutionally protected right of educators to contract was not impaired by the changes made.[56] In another Connecticut case, the federal district court rejected an equal protection challenge to new state certification requirements mandating that certain teachers in the state's technical school system qualify for a new certificate in order to teach core mathematics courses.[57] Since the state had enacted the new, more rigorous requirements pursuant to the "highly qualified" standard under NCLB, the court determined the state department of education had a rational basis for imposing the newer, more rigorous standards required by federal law.[58] In each of the instances discussed above, it is easy to see why teachers did not prevail. Students, schools, and society evolve over time and it is reasonable, even necessary, for states to adapt and change requirements as needed.

An additional issue for currently certified teachers and administrators is whether a state can require them to take competency examinations to retain their credentials. As part of a state school reform package enacted in 1984, the Texas legislature did just that: requiring all school employees certified prior to 1986 to pass a reading and writing skills test as a condition of continued employment.[59] This law caused a great deal of consternation among teachers and resulted in several lawsuits against the state. The Texas Supreme Court ruled that the testing requirement was constitutional.[60] Justice Campbell explained that because "a teaching certificate is not a contract, the constitutional prohibition against impairment of contracts is not violated when the legislature imposes new conditions for the retention of the certificate."[61] State law also provided adequate due process protections for teachers who failed to pass the competency test.[62] Ultimately, the court rejected the contention that the law was fundamentally unfair by holding that the test had "a rational relationship to the legitimate state objective of maintaining competent teachers in the public schools."[63]

The issue of whether a teacher or administrator may be considered legally qualified for a particular position may depend upon specific statutory language governing the scope of one's certificate issued by the state. This has implications for situations whereby a teacher or administrator may have a temporary certificate with certain renewal conditions imposed by the state, or where an individual may lack a required endorsement to teach certain subjects not otherwise covered by a regular certificate. Several cases from Illinois illustrate these situations. A teacher sued her school district for breach of contract when she was dismissed because she was not certified to teach elementary school music. Even though the teacher had a state teaching certificate, she lacked an endorsement to teach music. When she failed to complete the required courses and tests for the music endorsement, she was dismissed by the school board. An Illinois court construed the state certification law to mean that "if a teacher's certificate does not contain an endorsement for a particular subject, then [the law] prohibits that teacher from teaching that subject."[64] Likewise, a potential applicant for a school music position was not minimally qualified to teach music because his certificate did not include a music endorsement as required by state law.[65] Finally, a court determined that a school principal, whose provisional certificate had been cancelled for failure to pass the required state tests within nine months of its issuance, no longer had a valid certificate.[66] Since he lacked a valid certificate, which state law required as "an essential condition of the contract," the school board was justified in transferring him to a noncertified position as a truant officer.[67]

Select Certification Court Cases

Wagenblast v. Crook County School District: An educator in Oregon was dismissed by a local school board when it was reported she held an invalid teaching certificate.[68] The teacher's basic teaching certificate had expired in September 1982, and she was sent a renewed certificate by the relevant state agency the same month. Later in the month, the agency notified her by U.S. mail that the renewed certificate had been declared invalid since the personal check she submitted as payment was not honored by her bank.[69] She was sent another letter the next month by the state agency advising her that her certificate was void, but the letter was returned as "unclaimed by addressee."[70] In 1984, the state agency informed her school district that she no longer held a valid certificate, and she was terminated by the school superintendent. She contested her dismissal in court, claiming that the board did not follow the necessary termination procedures. The Oregon Court of Appeals concluded that because she lacked a valid teacher's certificate, she was not "a teacher" within the meaning of the law; this occurred even though her certificate had not been revoked, but was not renewed by the state for failure to make the required payment.[71]

Nenana City School District v. Coghill: State law in Alaska required teachers to maintain current teacher certification.[72] A teacher working for the Nenana City School District had her license expire during the academic year, and it was not renewed until two months later; neither she nor the school district were aware of its expiration.[73] It was initially determined that the teacher lost her tenure status, but on appeal, the Alaska Supreme Court applied a statutory "substantial noncompliance standard" and overruled the decision of the hearing board.[74] Although the teacher's certification did lapse, it was of a short duration and "she easily and promptly obtained renewal."[75]

Board of Education of Taos Municipal Schools v. Singleton: In this New Mexico case, a teacher was dismissed for her lack of a valid certificate, despite her tenure status.[76] The proceedings were complicated; it took two years before the court of appeals reversed the adverse employment action and ordered compensation.[77] It was discovered that the New Mexico Department of Education had experienced administrative problems, which delayed the teacher's renewal certificate.[78] The court found that the lack of certification was related to these difficulties and ruled in favor of the teacher.[79]

Lucio v. School Board of Independent School District No. 625: While there is no doubt educators are responsible for keeping and maintaining valid certificates, districts and state agencies may also be at fault. In *Lucio*, a Minnesota principal allowed his license to expire, yet a school district still entered into a contract with him.[80] At the end of the year, the school board voted to not renew his contract and did not provide him with justification or the opportunity for a hearing.[81] The principal filed suit against the district and eventually prevailed.[82] While the central issue in this case involved due process, the licensure status of the principal was a key element in the court's determination of whether Lucio had standing to bring the legal action in the first place.

As a threshold matter, the court had to determine whether the principal had standing to sue, given that his license had expired for an extended period of time. The school board argued that Lucio was not a "teacher" since he did not hold a valid license for a fifteen-month period and since the district did not have a copy of his renewed certificate on file. The extant state law at the time included principals within the term "teacher." The court determined that the school district had a duty under state law to ascertain the licensure status of its teachers. According to the court, "[i]f the school district did not know that Lucio's license was renewed…it had a duty…to pursue the issue further."[83] Since the school district did not comply with state law and they entered into a contract with Lucio without first determining if he possessed a valid license, Lucio was free to pursue a due process claim in court. Judge Willis delivered the opinion of the Minnesota Court of Appeals, providing the following rationale for the court's decision:

> The school board entered into a contract with Lucio for the 1995-96 school year and then rehired him for the 1996-97 school year knowing that he was temporarily not licensed and that the school district did not have a copy of Lucio's license on file. The school board, therefore, did not comply with the requirement of Minn. Stat. § 123.35, subd. 5, that it employ only qualified teachers, and it is estopped from arguing that Lucio is not a qualified teacher…[84]

On the central claim of whether Lucio was entitled to due process before his nonrenewal, the court determined that the state tenure law "prescribes one period of probation for all teachers. It does not require any new probationary periods for new 'positions' that may be taken by the teacher, whether administrative or otherwise."[85] Therefore, Lucio had tenure as a principal and could not be discharged without "cause and after a hearing."[86]

The Revocation of a Teaching Certificate

States have the authority not only to certify teachers, but to revoke those certificates as well.[87] The suspension or revocation of a teaching certificate requires appropriate standards of due process as provided by law.[88] Reasons for suspension or revocation and requisite due process procedures are generally specified in state statutes. A common reason specified in state law justifying the suspension or revocation of an educator's certificate is immorality. For example, courts found that the following actions constituted immorality in revocation cases: "sending threatening and obscene letters to [a] supervisor,"[89] possessing dozens of marijuana plants,[90] perjury and extortion convictions,[91] indecent assault on children,[92] falsifying attendance records,[93] mail fraud,[94] and unsatisfactory evaluations.[95] Many states also provide that teachers' certificates may be suspended or canceled for abandoning existing contracts without good cause or their board of education's consent.[96] It is important to note, however, that "unprofessional conduct" that results in termination "must be conduct directly related to one's fitness to act in his or her professional capacity."[97]

Before an educator's license is revoked, all applicable standards of due process must be observed.[98] This includes providing proper notice and a hearing.[99] In New York City, two terminated teachers filed suit against their boards of education arguing that an absence of pre-revocation license hearings violated their due process rights.[100] The federal district court that initially heard the case denied the board's motion to dismiss the plaintiffs' due process claims on the grounds that they had a right to "offer evidence to support [their] claims," regardless of whether or not they would "ultimately prevail."[101] However, when the case came back for trial, the court concluded that the teachers "received all of the process to which they were entitled" and the city department of education "acted within its statutory authority" in revoking the licenses.[102]

Two more cases, one from South Carolina and the other from New Jersey, both dealt with due process, specifically with regard to teacher certification examinations. In South Carolina, a teaching certificate was deemed void when the Educational Testing Service (ETS) notified the state board to "cancel" a teacher's test scores.[103] ETS provided no explanation for why the test scores were cancelled. The South Carolina Supreme Court reversed the decision of a trial court, which had affirmed the state board's cancellation of the teacher's certificate. It remanded the matter because the state board did not afford the teacher an "opportunity to contest the allegations against her."[104] The state supreme court ruled that the regulation under which her certificate was cancelled was unconstitutional because it did not provide for notice and a hearing.[105] The court found that the procedures provided by ETS and the state board did not comport with the required due process since the teacher was not afforded the opportunity to confront her accusers or contest the allegations against her, in this case the validity of her test scores. However, a New Jersey court ruled that due process did not require a testing service to prove actual wrongdoing by a teacher suspected of cheating.[106] The Superior Court of New Jersey concluded that test scores could be cancelled "upon an adequate showing of substantial question as to their validity, without any necessity for a showing of actual cheating or other misconduct."[107]

It is vital to understand when examining court cases that once a teacher is certified by the state, he or she is considered competent party to a subsequent employment contract. The state bears the burden of proof in all revocation cases. The Fourth District Court of Appeals in Florida made this clear, noting that the prosecutor in a revocation case must prove a strong point, the record must substantiate the findings, and the hearing board must review contents of investigative files and actually accept such files into evidence.[108] A California court of appeals expanded on the importance of this and discussed hearsay evidence, stating that "[i]t is well settled that a board commits an abuse of discretion when it revokes a license to conduct a legitimate business without competent evidence establishing just cause of revocation, and that hearsay evidence alone is insufficient to support the revocation of such a license."[109] In contrast, the Supreme Court of Oregon rejected the position that hearsay evidence alone, even if inadmissible in a civil or criminal trial, is not capable of being "substantial evidence."[110] Although the rules of evidence in administrative proceedings are generally relaxed, they are not so much so that due process or fundamental rights are disregarded.[111]

Due to the increased importance of student academic assessments, many states have passed statutes and regulations ensuring the integrity of the testing process; teachers who violate these procedures may be subject to termination or suspension.[112] A teacher in Georgia had his license revoked for "improperly coaching his students" on standardized tests.[113] Another teacher's certificate was suspended for six months after she altered student responses on standardized examinations.[114] Even though interfering with students' scores is inexcusable, teacher involvement in criminal matters is another problem entirely, requiring higher standards of due process.

Eyewitness testimony describing indecent exposure provided sufficient evidence for the revocation of a Texas teacher's license, despite the fact that the charges were dismissed and arrest records expunged.[115] A similar situation occurred in Indiana when a trial testimony describing rape was deemed to be sufficient evidence of "immorality and misconduct," which resulted in revocation even though the rape conviction was subsequently reversed.[116] Statements made by a New York teacher charged with sexual misconduct were considered inadmissible at the criminal trial; however, they were found to be relevant in determining his moral fitness to teach.[117]

The Supreme Court of Utah ruled that certain testimony based on evidence contained in an expunged criminal record, which was the basis for the state board's decision to revoke a teacher's certificate, was prohibited by state law.[118] A teacher was arrested and charged with two counts of marijuana distribution and one count of agreeing to distribute. These charges were later dismissed and the teacher's record was sealed and expunged by a state district court. The teacher was subsequently terminated by the local school board. Later, the state board of education held a hearing to revoke his certificate. During the hearing, two witnesses testified using evidence from the teacher's expunged court record. Based on this testimony, the teacher's certificate was revoked by the state. The teacher filed a lawsuit arguing, among other things, that the board's use of the evidence contained in his expunged records violated a court's expungement order. Ultimately, the state supreme court agreed with the teacher's legal argument.[119] After analyzing the state law on the expungement of court records and considering the role of the two witnesses (the arresting officer and a paid informant), the court concluded that the evidence used in the hearing was prohibited.[120] The court did note, however, that employers are not prohibited from making "independent" inquiries into the background of applicants or employees.[121]

The final concern that is frequently brought before the courts involves the issue of authority to revoke licenses. In Rhode Island, the state Supreme Court ruled that the Board of Regents exceeded its authority when it canceled certificates prior to the stated expiration dates.[122] The Appellate Court of Illinois addressed a similar issue, ultimately ruling that the state superintendent lacked authority to revoke a license after the teacher certification board voted against it.[123] Finally, a court in Florida stated that the Education Practices Commission was not authorized to permanently revoke a teaching certificate when the administrative complaint sought only revocation with a possibility of reinstatement.[124]

Recommendations for Practice

It is clear that any person seeking state teacher certification has the responsibility to see that all requirements are met, appropriate paperwork is completed, and required payments are made to the cognizant state agency. It is also that person's responsibility to ensure that his or her certificate is current and that appropriate action is taken to renew the certificate upon its expiration. Below are notes for districts to keep in mind:

1. District personnel should work in concert while carefully monitoring the certification status of their staff, ensuring that certificates are current and in order. This may require consultation between and among principals, as well as district-wide personnel.

2. Districts may find the processes related to initial assignment of teachers or related to their reassignment growing more complex because of fiscal problems or changing state curriculum regulations. Whether teachers may be assigned to teach outside of their area of certification is a question to be determined by the individual state. Districts should be aware that states differ in their interpretation of this issue.

3. School principals may be called upon to provide documentation in a certificate revocation case. Such documentation must provide substantial evidence of the alleged wrongdoing.

Endnotes

1 In some states, a teaching certificate may be referred to as a license. For example, in Nevada, state statute refers to "Licensing of Education Personnel." See, NRS 391.031. In this chapter, we will use the term teacher certification, but the legal principles discussed are relevant to teaching licenses.

2 Pub. L. 107-110, 115 Stat. 1425. The No Child Left Behind Act of 2001 (NCLB) reauthorized the historic Elementary and Secondary Education Act (ESEA), which has provided the basic framework for federal K-12 education law with a commitment to equal opportunity for all students since its enactment in 1965.

3 Every Student Succeeds Act, Pub. L. 114-95, 129 Stat. 1802. Codified at 20 U.S.C. § 6301.

4 *Id.*

5 *Id.*

6 This included the District of Columbia, Guam Puerto Rico, Virgin Islands, American Samoa, Micronesia, Marshall Islands, Northern Mariana Islands, and Palau. For the 2011 Title II report required, however, Guam, Marshall Island, and Micronesia did not submit reports.

7 Preparing and Credentialing the Nation's Teachers – The Secretary's Ninth Report on teacher Quality (2013). Washington, D.C.: U.S. Department of Education, Office of Postsecondary Education. P. xiv. https://title2.ed.gov/Public/TitleIIReport13.pdf

8 *Id.*

9 *Id.*

10 *Id.*, p. xv.

11 *See* note 2 at 115 Stat. 1425, 1959.

12 34 C.F.R. § 200.56(a)(2)(ii).

13 Renee v. Duncan, 623 F.3d 787 (9th Cir. 2010).

14 *Id.* at 800.

15 Pub. L. 11-322, 124 Stat. 3518, 3521.

16 Renee v. Duncan, 686 F.3d 1002, 1004 (9th Cir. 2012).

17 See Pub. L. 112-175, § 145, 126 Stat. 132; Pub. L. 113-46, Div. A. § 144, 127 Stat. 565; Pub. L. 114-53, Div. B, § 140, 129 Stat. 510; Pub. L. 114-113 § 8(3), 129 Stat. 2245.

18 Every Student Succeeds Act, *supra* note 3.

19 Pub. L. 114-95, Title VIII – General Provisions, 129 Stat. 1802, 2089.

20 Pub. L. 114-95, 129 Stat. 1802, 2160.

21 Pub. L. 114-95, 129 Stat. 1802, 1914.

22 Pub. L. 114-95(e)(1)(B)(iii)(X), 129 Stat. 1802, 1843.

23 Pub. L. 114-95, 129 Stat. 1802, 2014.

24 U.S. CONST. amend. X.

25 Barnes v. Glen Theatre, Inc., 501 U.S. 560, 569 (1991).

26 Gulino v. New York State Education Dept., 460 F.3d 361, 376 (2d. Cir. 2006).

27 Trigg v. Sanders, 162 Ill. App. 3d 719, 727, 515 N.E.2d 1367, 1373 (Ill. App. Ct. 1987).

28 North Dakota v. Rivinius, 328 N.W.2d 220, 229 (N.D. 1982).

29 Sheridan Road Baptist Church v. Michigan Dept. of Educ., 426 Mich. 462, 396 N.W.2d 373 (Mich. 1986).

30 *Id.* at 480-483, 380-381.

31 Bauer v. Bd. of Educ., U.S.D. No. 452, 244 Kan. 6, 16 (Kan. 1988).

32 National Association of State Boards of Education. (2016). *State boards of education.* Retrieved from http://www.nasbe.org/about-us/state-boards-of-education/

33 *Id.*

34 Feldman v. Bd. of Educ. of City Sch. Dist. of N.Y., 686 N.Y.S.2d 842 (N.Y. App. Div. 1999).

35 Ass'n of Mexican-American Educators v. California, 231 F.3d 572, 578 (9th Cir. 200), *en banc.*

36 *Id.* at 577.

37 *Id.* at 584, 588.

38 Massachusetts Fed'n of Teachers v. Bd. of Educ., 767 N.E.2d 549 (Mass. 2002).

39 Fellowship Baptist Church v. Benton, 815 F.2d 485, 492 (8th Cir. Iowa 1987).

40 *Id.* at 493.

41 *Id.* at 500.

42 U.S. Equal Employment Opportunity Commission (EEOC). (n.d.). *Title vii of the civil rights act of 1964.* Retrieved from https://www.eeoc.gov/laws/statutes/titlevii.cfm.

43 Hosford v. Sch. Comm. of Sandwich, 659 N.E.2d 1178 (Mass. 1996).

44 Hosack v. Smiley, 276 F. Supp. 876 (D. Colo. 1967), *aff'd per curiam,* 390 U.S. 744 (1968); *See also* Gough v. State, 667 A.2d 1057 (N.J. Super Ct. App. Div. 1995).

45 *Id.* at 878.

46 Epelbaum v. Chicago Bd. of Educ., 19 Fed. App'x. 384, 385 (7th Cir. 2001).

47 Wright v. Kansas State Bd. of Educ, 268 P.3d 1231 (Kan. Ct. App. 2012).

48 Bradford Cent. Sch. Dist. v. Ambach, 451 N.Y.S.2d 654, 656 (N.Y. 1982).

49 Lewis-Connelly v. Bd. of Educ. of Deerfield Pub. Schs., Dist. 109, 660 N.E.2d 283, 287 (Ill. App. Ct. 1996).

50 Royster v. Cushman, 261 Cal. Rptr. 458, 469-70 (Cal. Ct. App. 1989).

51 Smith v. Andrews, 504 N.Y.S.2d 286, 311 (N.Y. App. Div. 1986).

52 *Id.* at 312.

53 *Id.* at 313.

54 Stone v. Fritts, 82 N.E. 792, 794 (Ind. 1907).

55 Conn. Educ. Ass'n v. Tirozzi, 554 A.2d 1065 (Conn. 1989).

56 *Id.* at 1073.

57 Buell v. Hughes, 596 F.Supp.2d 380, 381-82 (D.Conn. 2009).

58 *Id.* at 388.

59 Tex. Educ. Code Ann. § 13.047 (West 1986). Note § § 13.045 to 13.050 were repealed by Acts 1995, 74th Leg. Ch. 260, § 58(1), eff. May 30, 1995.

60 State v. Project-Principle, Inc., 724 S.W.2d 387, 390 (Tex. 1987).

61 *Ibid.*

62 *Id.* at 391.

63 *Ibid.*

64 Lewis-Connelly v. Bd. of Educ. of Deerfield Pub. Schools, Dist. 109, 277 Ill. App. 3d 554, 559, 660 N.E. 2d 283, 286 (Ill. App. Ct. 1996).

65 Bd. of Educ. of City of Chicago v. Cady, 369 Ill. App. 3d 486, 860 N.E. 2d 526 (Ill. App. Ct. 2006), *cert. denied by* Cady v. Northeastern Ill. Univ., 552 U.S. 1148 (2008).

66 Jackson v. Bd. of Educ. of Rockford Public Schools, 2012 U.S. Dist. LEXIS 133614 (N.D. Ill. 2012).

67 *Id.* at 5.

68 Wagenblast v. Cook County Sch. Dist., 707 P.2d 69 (Or. Ct. App. 1985).

69 *Id.* at 71.

70 *Id.*

71 *Id.* at 73.

72 Nenana City Sch. Dist. v. Coghill, 898 P.2d 929, 930 (Alaska 1995).

73 *Ibid.*

74 *Id.* at 934.

75 *Ibid.*

76 Bd. of Educ. of Taos Mun. Schools v. Singleton, 712 P.2d 1384, 1386-87 (N.M. Ct. App. 1985).

77 *Id.* at 730.

78 *Id.* at 726-27.

79 *Id.* at 729.

[80] Lucio v. Sch. Bd. of Indep. Sch. Dist. No. 625, 574 N.W. 2d 737 (Minn. Ct. App. 1998).

[81] *Id.* at 739

[82] *Id.*at 743.

[83] *Id.* at 740.

[84] *Id.* at 743.

[85] *Id.* at 741.

[86] *Id.* at 742.

[87] NEV. REV. STAT, § 391.330, which states:
The State Board may suspend or revoke the license of any teacher, administrator or other licensed employee, after notice and an opportunity for hearing have been provided pursuant to [state law] for: 1. Immoral or unprofessional conduct. 2. Evident unfitness for service. 3. Physical or mental incapacity which renders the teacher, administrator or other licensed employee unfit for service. 4. Conviction of a felony or crime involving moral turpitude. 5. Conviction of a sex offense…in which a pupil enrolled in a school of a county school district was the victim. 6. Knowingly advocating the overthrow of the Federal Government or of the State of Nevada by force, violence or unlawful means. 7. Persistent defiance of or refusal to obey the regulations of the State Board, the Commission or the Superintendent of Public Instruction, defining and governing the duties of teachers, administrators and other licensed employees. 8. Breaches in the security or confidentiality of the questions and answers of [certain] examinations that are administered pursuant to [state law]. 9. Intentional failure to observe and carry out the requirements of a plan to ensure the security of examinations and assessments adopted pursuant to [state law]. 10. An intentional violation of [state laws prohibiting adverse intervention and physical and mechanical restraints]. 11. Knowingly and willfully failing to comply with the provisions of [state law requiring staff members to report to principals incidences of bullying and cyber-bullying].

[88] Greenwald v. Cmty. Sch. Bd. No. 27, 329 N.Y.S.2d 203, 242 (N.Y. App. Div.1972).

[89] Richardson v. N.C. Dept. of Public Instruction Licensure Section, 681 S.E.2d 479, 484 (N.C. Ct. App. 2009).

[90] Adams v. State, Prof'l Practices Council, 406 So.2d 1170, 1172 (Fla. Dist. Ct. App. 1981).

[91] Homer v. Pennsylvania Dep't of Educ., 458 A.2d 1059 (Pa. Commw. Ct. 1983).

[92] Couch v. Turlington, 465 So. 2d 557, 558 (Fla. Dist. Ct. App. 1985).

[93] Balentine v. Ark. State Bd. of Educ., 684 S.W.2d 246, 247 (Ark. 1985).

[94] Startzel v. Pennsylvania Dep't of Educ., 562 A.2d 1005, 1006-07 (Pa. Commw. Ct. 1989).

[95] Eiche v. La. Bd. of Elementary and Secondary Educ., 582 So. 2d 186, 188 (La. 1991).

[96] *See, e.g.,* NEV. REV. STAT. § 391.350 ("Any teacher or other licensed employee employed by any board for a specified time who willfully refuses or fails to fulfill his or her employment obligations [after accepting employment] or to comply with the provisions of his or her contract after it has been signed without first obtaining the written consent of the board may be found guilty of unprofessional conduct. The board shall not unreasonably withhold its consent…..") *See also* NEV. REV. STAT. § 391.330 (which lists "unprofessional" conduct as a ground for suspension or revocation of a license to teach).

[97] Boss v. Fillmore County Sch. Dist. No. 19, 559 N.W.2d 448 at Headnote 7 (Neb. 1997). *See* Hoffman v. State Bd. of Educ., 763 N.E.2d 210 (Ohio Ct. App. 2001).

[98] Brayton v. Monson Pub. Sch., 950 F. Supp. 33 (D. Mass. 1997).

[99] *Id.* at 37.

[100] Behrend v. Klein, 2006 U.S. Dist. LEXIS 68652 at *22 (E.D.N.Y. 2006).

[101] *Id.* at 20.

[102] Behrend v. Klein, 2010 U.S. Dist. LEXIS 15364 at *30 (E.D.N.Y. 2010).

[103] Brown v. South Carolina St. Bd. of Educ., 301 S.C. 326, 391 S.E.2d 866 (S.C. 1990).

[104] *Id.* at 329.

[105] The state regulation in question provided that "If any testing company invalidates a test score, the State Board of Education shall accept that determination and, if a teaching certificate has been issued based upon the invalid score, shall automatically invalidate that certificate effective the date of receipt of notification of the score invalidity by the Office of Teacher Education and Certification." *See Brown*, note 99 at 328.

[106] Scott v. Educ. Testing Serv., 252 N.J. Super. 610, 600 A.2d 500, 504 (N.J. Super. Ct. App. Div. 1991).

[107] *Id.* at 618.

[108] Fields v. Turlington, 481 So. 2d 960, 962 (Fla. Dist. Ct. App. 1986).

[109] Carl S. v. Comm'n for Teacher Preparation and Licensing, 126 Cal. App. 3d 365, 369 (Cal. Ct. App. 1981).

[110] Reguero v. Teacher Standards and Practices Comm'n, 312 Ore. 402, 417, 822 P.2d 1171, 1180-81 (Or. 1991).

[111] Matter of Renewal of Teaching Certificate of Thompson, 893 P.2d 301, 309 (Mont. 1995).

[112] NEV. REV. STATS. § 391.750 2(a)(b).

[113] Professional Standards Comm'n v. Smith, 257 Ga. App. 418, 420 (Ga. Ct. App. 2002).

[114] Professional Standards Comm'n v. Denham, 252 Ga. App. 785, 785-86 (Ga. Ct. App. 2001).

[115] Gomez v. Texas Educ. Agency, Educator Certification and Standards Div., 354 S.W.3d 905, 915-17 (Tex. App., 2011).

[116] Ulrich v. State, 555 N.E.2d 172, 173-74 (Ind. Ct. App. 1990).

[117] Moro v. Mills, 70 A.D.3d 1269, 1270-71 (N.Y. App. Div., 2010).

[118] Ambus v. Utah Bd. of Educ., 800 P.2d 811, 813 (Utah 1990).

[119] *Id.* at 812.

[120] *Id.* at 813.

[121] *Id.* at 813-14.

[122] Reback v. Rhode Island Bd. of Regents for Elementary and Secondary Educ., 560 A.2d 357, 358-59 (R.I. 1989).

[123] Hunt v. Sanders, 554 N.E.2d 285 (Ill. App. Ct. 1990).

[124] Williams v. Turlington, 498 So.2d 468 (Fla. Dist. Ct. App. 1986).

Key Words

alternative certification programs

certification

competency examination/skills test

continuing education

documentation

due process

Due Process Clause

Elementary and Secondary Education Act (ESEA)

endorsement

Establishment Clause

Every Student Succeeds Act (ESSA)

expiration

First Amendmen

Free Exercise Clause

highly qualified versus effective

institutions of higher education (IHE)-based teacher preparation programs

license

licensure status

loyalty oath

National Association of State Boards of Education (NASBE)

National Teacher's Examination (NTE)

No Child Left Behind Act (NCLB)

nondiscrimination

private sectarian schools

revocation

standards-based education reform

tenure status

Section III – Chapter 11

Student Injury

Suzanne E. Eckes and Jesulon Gibbs-Brown

Introduction

Torts are civil wrongs stemming from the unreasonable conduct of one individual resulting in another individual's personal injury, property damage, and/or reputational harm. Such liability stemming from student injury generally occurs in one of two ways. Either parents, on behalf of the injured student, bring a tort claim against the school district under state tort law, and/or parents pursue relief under federal and state civil rights acts. This chapter solely examines the former, tort law, and how it is applied in school law cases.

Schools and districts are expected to minimize potential tort liability for student injuries through the effective implementation and enforcement of policies and procedures. For example, school districts have implemented student discipline policies and anti-bullying policies as an attempt to prevent student injury, and are expected to oversee the proper implementation and enforcement of such policies. Therefore, schools and districts must remain aware of how their many responsibilities directly influence potential liability stemming from student injuries.

There are three overarching categories of torts: negligence, intentional torts, and defamation. Negligence occurs when the conduct of school personnel unintentionally fails to meet a reasonable standard of care. In contrast to negligence, liability in intentional tort cases is imposed due to an individual's conscious decision to cause the particular harm.[1] Intentional torts include assault and battery, false imprisonment, and intentional infliction of emotional distress. Also considered a tort is defamation, which involves an injury to one's reputation, generally through libel and/or slander. Most tort actions are heard in state court. Generally, punitive damages are not available in tort cases, and a plaintiff must affirmatively prove actual compensatory damages. Each of the aforementioned tort categories is explained in this chapter.

Legal Issues

Elements Needed to Establish Negligence

Four elements must be proven to prevail in a negligence claim: (1) the plaintiff must demonstrate that the school owes a particular duty to the injured student(s); (2) the duty must be breached by the failure to exercise an appropriate standard of care; (3) the negligent conduct must be the proximate cause of the injury; and (4) an actual injury must occur.[2] In order for liability to be imputed to school officials, school personnel must have knowledge or notice of the particular dangerous practice or activity with respect to which the injury occurred.[3]

Duty of Care

School boards have a duty to reasonably supervise students through their employees, such as principals, teachers, or others acting within the scope of their employment. To this end, courts generally begin their negligence analysis with a determination of whether a duty was owed and, if so, the extent of the duty. Courts have consistently held that school personnel are not required to anticipate all acts that occur in schools nor every mindless behavior resulting in an injury.[4] In turn, courts have adopted the common law standard for determining reasonableness.[5] This objective standard requires that school officials provide the same level of care as can be expected of competent professionals of similar education and background faced with parallel circumstances. Some factors that may be taken into consideration when determining such a standard include the age, training, education, and experience of the school officials, as well as the students.[6] Consistent with this reasoning is that when students are adequately supervised, school personnel protect them from reasonably foreseeable dangers.

In a case on point, a school district's duty to supervise students did not extend to activities occurring out of the teacher's sight and under a student's desk, particularly when no previous problems had occurred.[7] However, after a female student was sexually assaulted under her desk by a fellow male student, the school district then had a duty to supervise the interactions between the students, specifically ensuring that the two students were not enrolled in the same classes. The court reasoned that the school district's duty of care was heightened, given its knowledge of the prior sexual conduct.

A duty to supervise also extends to extracurricular activities and field trips sponsored by the school. One court did not find a school district liable when a young student was injured on a hayride during a school field trip.[8] Although the student's parents alleged that the district did not provide adequate supervision on the trip, the court found that the district met its duty in supervising the students because there were plenty of adults present.[9] However, in another case, the court questioned the school district's level of supervision on a school-sponsored field trip.[10] The student was injured when she fell off a rope while participating in an obstacle course on the field trip. Reversing the trial court's opinion, an appellate court found that issues of fact precluded summary judgment in favor of the school board. The appellate court held that the student did not assume the risk involved in this obstacle course and that questions of fact remained about whether there was proper supervision of the event.[11]

School officials may also have a duty before or after school. For example, once school officials know, or should know, that students are present before or after school, they must take the necessary steps to supervise the students.[12] In one case, a court explained that the duty of care owed to a student working on his science project in the school lab after school is the same as that owed to him during the school day.[13] In this incident, two students suffered severe burns when one of the students accidentally started a fire in the science lab after school. The teacher left the students unattended for twenty minutes while she walked down the street to the local deli. The school district argued that it did not owe the students a duty of care because the fire did not start while the student was actually working on his project. Nevertheless, the court held that the teacher was responsible for monitoring the students in the lab because she allowed them to use the facilities to work on an academic project. Similarly, courts have extended the duty to supervise athletic practices and events before and/or after school and to ensure that the student athletes are practicing in safe conditions.[14] However, the requisite level of supervision may decrease during these non-school hours if school officials are not aware that students are on school property.

Further, a school district has a duty to protect students walking to and from school in certain situations. To illustrate, when a student walking home from school was struck by a truck as she crossed a street, the school district was liable because of the negligence of the crossing guard, the district's failure to provide adequate safety precautions, and the district's failure to provide instructions for the students.[15] However, in another case, a court did not find that a school district owed a duty to supervise students after they left school premises.[16] In this case, a male student was sexually assaulted by another male student after getting off the school bus to go home with his assailant. The court ruled that the duty of care is applicable only when students are within the custody of the school board.[17] Often, a duty to protect arises with school buses. For example, a school district was found to have breached its duty when it failed to provide a bus stop on the student's side of the highway. A regulation adopted by the state board of education required that students who live on four-lane highways needed to be picked up and discharged on the side of the road where they live. According to the court, this regulation created a duty of care.[18]

Finally, the amount of duty one must provide often depends on the age of the student. Some states have recognized that a different set of criteria are used when considering the tortious acts of minors. When determining the negligence of a minor defendant, courts often consider the following: minors under the age of 7 are conclusively presumed incapable of negligence; minors over the age of 14 are presumptively capable of negligence; minors between the ages of 7 and 14 are presumed incapable of negligence; however, such presumption is rebuttable and grows weaker as students approach age 14.[19]

Breach of Duty

A breach of duty occurs when school officials omit or fail to exercise reasonable judgment under the circumstances to satisfy their job responsibilities and the risk of danger was within the realm of protection expected under the duty of care. A total lack of supervision or ineffective supervision may constitute a breached duty.[20] To illustrate, a school board and one of its teachers were found liable after a student broke his arm during recess. The court also found that the teacher breached her duty to intervene on the playground when she was specifically informed by the injured student that the other students were bothering him. The teacher failed to respond, and the boy was injured by the same group he complained about earlier. The student was awarded $125,000 in general damages.[21] In another case, a court determined that a school district breached its duty to supervise when a student stabbed another student immediately upon both students returning to school after being suspended for three previous altercations.[22] The court ruled that the increasing intensity of the interactions between the students and animosity between them was such that the principal and teachers could have anticipated another altercation when the students returned to school.[23] The principal admitted that the students had not been offered counseling, per common school practice for students with violent tendencies, and teachers were not outside their classrooms where the stabbing occurred, as was required of them.

In contrast, a school board was not held liable for student injuries resulting from an altercation when school officials could not have foreseen the possibility of the encounter between the two students.[24] Even though school teachers were informed about the taunting and teasing of a student due to her facial hair, the court did not equate this knowledge with the foreseeability of the subsequent altercation between the student's cousin and her harasser.[25] In addition, teachers were appropriately monitoring the cafeteria when the altercation arose. Therefore, school officials did not breach their duty to supervise the students.

The different outcomes in the two aforementioned cases illustrate how courts analyze the facts of claims of negligence by way of the actions and inactions of school personnel based upon established school policies and practices. When a school board is faced with a negligence claim based on a student's injury, the principal of the school where the injury occurred is usually called upon to speak on behalf of the school culture and how he or she established and enforced policies and procedures that are the bases for the action against the school district. Before negligence liability is attributed to a school board, courts engage in an assessment of the surrounding circumstances to determine what school officials knew or should have known, and if any degree of supervision could have prevented the injury. If it cannot be proven that school officials were on notice of the potential for harm, courts will not determine that a breached duty resulted in a student's injury.

Causation

There must be a causal connection between school officials' breached duty and the resulting injury, based upon the foreseeability of the harm. Cause-in-fact and proximate cause are two types of causation. When examining cause-in-fact, the court might employ the "but for" test to determine whether the school official's conduct was the cause-in-fact of the student's injury.[26] With the cause-in-fact analysis, the student plaintiff would need to demonstrate that "but for" the school official's act or failure to act, there would not have been an injury. With proximate cause, courts would analyze whether the school official's action is close enough to the chain of events that caused the harm. In other words, there must be a causal connection between the alleged misconduct and the resulting injury. When making a determination regarding proximate cause, courts might ask whether the incident was foreseeable. The proximate cause examination is intended to address the "logic, fairness, policy, and practicality" of holding the defendant liable for the plaintiff's injuries.[27] Specifically, the proximate cause determination prevents a court from imposing liability on a defendant where the connection between the defendant's negligence and the plaintiff's harm is too "remote" or tenuous.[28]

To illustrate, when a 7-year-old was injured after going down a slide on her knees, there was no district liability because there was no causal connection. This student had been repeatedly told to not slide on her knees. The court also found that the supervision ratio of two teachers for forty students was adequate. Specifically, the accident could not have been avoided with more intense supervision, which negated the plaintiff's claim that the lack of supervision was the proximate cause of the injury.[29] In a similar case, the court held that any lack of supervision of a student was not the proximate cause of injuries that a seventh-grade student sustained when tripping during a gym obstacle course. The court observed that district provided adequate supervision.[30] Likewise, when a student injured himself by walking backward into a pole, it was a spontaneous event that could not have been anticipated by school officials. The court also found that any lack of supervision was not the proximate cause of the student's injury.[31]

In another case; however, the court ruled that the district may have been the proximate cause of an injury that occurred when a 5-year-old was molested by a school's computer technician in the cafeteria during breakfast.[32] Even though the technician was the actual cause of the student's injury, the court decided that this did not negate the school board's liability as the proximate cause of the injury.[33] The teachers assigned to cafeteria duty could not confirm that they were in the cafeteria that morning or what they did to ensure that the students were safe. Thus, the inadequate supervision could foreseeably result in a variety of injuries, including molestation.

Injury

Even if the above three elements are met, there must also be evidence of an actual injury to prevail on a negligence claim. For example, if a student falls off a swing during recess because the swing was broken, the student must have an actual injury in order to bring a negligence claim. A scraped knee, for example, would probably not suffice. Also, as will be discussed, plaintiffs can recover for emotional injuries.

Defenses to Negligence

School districts defend themselves from actions based on negligence using four principal defenses: the doctrines of immunity, assumption of risk, contributory negligence, and comparative negligence.[34]

Immunity

A school district might contend that it is immune from liability. Specifically, the district might argue that the state (which includes the public school district) is immune from tort liability because the state legislature has enacted laws that shield the government from liability. Thus, unless liability is permitted by a constitutional provision or state statute, a school district could avoid liability. Under several state laws, a school district would not be liable for acts committed within the scope of the board's discretionary duty.[35] It is important to note that immunity statutes vary widely among states. One court accepted the immunity defense when a student sustained injuries after a mini-trampoline accident at school.[36] The court relied on a state code that insulated school districts from liability when a defendant did not act in a "willful or wanton" manner.[37] In this case, the court found that school officials acted reasonably and that the state's immunity law therefore protected the school district from liability. Likewise, immunity protected a teacher supervising the physical education class from a negligence action brought by an injured student. The court reasoned that if school teachers performing everyday functions were hauled into court for similar conduct, fewer individuals will aspire to be teachers.[38] The court stated more specifically that those who have embarked on a career in education will be reluctant to act, and the orderly administration of the school systems (and, by extension, an important arm of the government) will suffer, all to the detriment of our youth and the public at large.[39]

However, in another case, a school district and various employees sought immunity from a middle school student claiming negligence, negligent infliction of emotional distress, and assault. The student allegedly had been bullied, and he argued that the school employees had failed to punish the bullies or to assist him. The defendants motioned for summary judgment, citing immunity under state law, but the court denied the motion. Affirming the trial court's decision, the appellate court held that the student could prove facts that might entitle him to relief.[40]

Many states have repudiated sovereign immunity; thus, school districts tend to focus on the remaining three defenses.[41] While some school districts still use immunity, courts are moving toward requiring school districts to be responsible for their actions.[42]

Contributory Negligence

School districts use the defense of contributory negligence when the student contributed to his or her own injuries. Contributory negligence is a strict rule because a plaintiff who is one percent negligent can be prohibited from recovery. The plaintiff's contributory negligence bars recovery against a defendant whose negligent conduct would otherwise make him liable to the plaintiff for the harm sustained by him. In other words, when the defendant has violated his duty, has been negligent, and would otherwise be liable, the plaintiff is denied recovery because his or her own conduct, in conjunction with the defendant's, disentitles him or her to maintain the action. Under this defense, both parties are at fault, and the defense is one of the plaintiff's disability rather than the defendant's innocence.[43]

In one case, a student brought an action against a teacher and the school district for injuries stemming from an explosion after another student took potassium chlorate from an unattended chemical storage room without the teacher's knowledge or consent.[44] The court held that the 15-year-old student and the student who took the chemical knew that the chemical formula was powerful, dangerous, and risky. Given their knowledge of the danger involved, the court concluded that the students were contributorily negligent in this situation.[45] In another case, a man fell off a set of bleachers and was injured during a high school basketball game. The man filed a negligence action against the school district because there was no back rail on the bleachers. The school district argued that the man was contributorily negligent. The court agreed, reasoning that the man could see that the bleachers had no back rail and he therefore contributed to his own injuries.[46]

No contributory negligence was found in a case involving a student who choked and died in the school cafeteria while eating his lunch. The school district argued that the student was contributorily negligent because he had been laughing at the lunch table. The court found no evidence that the student's actions contributed to his own injuries.[47]

Assumption of Risk

Assumption of risk occurs when school officials argue that the student knew of the risk involved, yet still participated in the activity. While assumption of risk is somewhat related to contributory negligence, the two doctrines are not synonymous. In contrast to contributory negligence, assumption of risk means that the plaintiff, in advance, has given his or her express consent to relieve the defendant of responsibility for injuries common to the activity.[48] Similar to contributory negligence, a plaintiff who voluntarily assumes a risk of harm rising from the negligent or reckless conduct of the defendant cannot recover for such harm.

Specifically, to satisfy the assumption of risk defense, the evidence must show that the victim had general knowledge of a possible danger or harm and understood the specific risk confronting him or her. For example, when a student sued for injuries he sustained while playing hockey in gym class, the court found that the student had assumed the risk of his injury, reasoning that participants in sports assume all commonly appreciated risks that are inherent in the sport.[49] Likewise, a court ruled that an injured cheerleader had assumed the risk during practice,[50] and another student had assumed the risk that a baseball could injure him during practice.[51] There was also no school district liability when a student assumed a risk during a pickup game of football on a Saturday on the school's field. The court noted that the hole the student fell in was open and obvious.[52] However, in another case, when a student sued the board of education after he was struck by a bat while playing catcher in a softball game at a school district summer camp, the court found that there was an issue of fact regarding whether the player assumed the risk of playing the role of catcher without any protective gear. The court suggested that the student's age and experience and the defendant's failure to warn of risks were relevant considerations in their decision.[53] Finally, assumption of risk did not bar a negligent supervision claim that arose out of a break dancing injury in an unsupervised classroom.[54]

Comparative Negligence

The comparative negligence defense divides the damages between the parties who are at fault. Under comparative negligence, there is a reduction of damages to be recovered by the negligent plaintiff in proportion to his or her fault. There are generally two basic ways for determining comparative fault (e.g., pure comparative or modified comparative), and these approaches vary by state.[55] "Pure" comparative fault is used to apportion the costs of an accident based on the relative fault of both the plaintiff and the defendant. In so doing, it reduces the amount of damages the plaintiff can recover based on the plaintiff's percentage of fault. For example, an elementary school student was injured when she fell at school. The parent alleged that the school district was negligent because the teacher did not provide proper supervision in the bathroom and because the slippery floor was unreasonably dangerous. The court found that the school board was 75% liable and the student was 25% liable in this case. In another case, a school district was found 80% liable for injuries sustained by an eighth-grade student who cut herself while dissecting a plant with a scalpel. The court observed that the teacher knew that other students had been injured in the past during this activity, and more should have been done to prevent it.

The most common legislative approach for apportioning fault is the modi-fied, or "50 percent" system, under which a plaintiff's contributory negligence does not bar recovery as long as it remains below a specified proportion of the total fault. Specifically, if the plaintiff's own negligence surpasses the percentage bar, the plaintiff is prohibited from recovering any damages. There are two varieties of the 50 percent comparative negligence approach. Under the "equal fault bar" approach, a plaintiff cannot recover anything if his fault is equal to or greater than that of the defendant. Under the "greater fault bar" system, the plaintiff is prevented from all recovery only if his or her fault exceeds the defendant's; he or she is therefore allowed to recover if his or her negligence is equal to or less than that of the defendant.

The rise of comparative negligence has forced the courts and commentators to reconsider the role of assumption of risk and contributory negligence. In several states, general statutes applicable to all negligence actions have annulled the contributory negligence rule and have created the doctrine of comparative negligence. Bearing this in mind, it is important for educators to be aware of the legal trend in their respective state.

Intentional Torts

An intentional tort requires a deliberate act toward another individual. As mentioned, liability is imposed without fault in intentional tort cases. For school districts, the most common types of intentional torts include assault, battery, false imprisonment, and intentional infliction of mental or emotional distress.

Assault and Battery

Assault occurs when someone is placed in apprehension of immediate harm. Generally, an assault must contain not only threatening words but also an offer of physical violence. In order to be successful in an assault claim, the plaintiff must feel reasonable apprehension. An example would be a student threatening another student with a toy knife. If the student being threatened believed the knife was real and was fearful, the student with the knife could be liable for assault. In contrast, battery is an actual physical attack. In the example just cited, the student with the toy knife would actually need to physically strike the other student for the injured student to have a battery claim.

In the past, students have made battery claims against school personnel. In one case, a student was unsuccessful when she accused the assistant principal of assault and battery when he physically restrained the student for failing to present her hall pass.[56] The court reasoned that the assistant principal was reasonably carrying out his duties.[57] In other cases, students have also claimed that corporal punishment constitutes battery, but courts have generally not agreed with this claim unless the educator acted with malice.[58]

False Imprisonment

False imprisonment may be claimed when students are unjustifiably restrained against their will. While the student must be aware of the restraint, the student does not need to demonstrate specific damages. Generally, school authorities could be liable for false imprisonment if the student is confined within certain fixed boundaries, a school official's action directly or indirectly results in such a confinement of the student, and the student is conscious of the confinement or is harmed by it.[59] For example, there was enough evidence for a successful false imprisonment claim when a teacher chained a student to a tree while the rest of the students in the class were painting feed troughs in the vicinity.[60] The teacher chained the student to the tree in order to prevent him from leaving the class early.[61] In contrast, a parent's false imprisonment claim among other claims was unsuccessful in a case involving school officials strapping a student with special needs to a chair in the classroom. The court did not find school officials' actions to be willful and wanton.[62]

In another case, a school district was found liable for having an elementary student arrested without producing evidence necessary to substantiate the arrest.[63] A call was made to the local police station about the 11-year-old student being out of control. However, when the dispatched officers arrived, the student was quietly sitting on a bench outside. The officers did not believe the student posed a physical threat to anyone, and they never received information about what transpired prior to their arrival to justify the arrest. The court held the school district and the city, on behalf of the police officers, liable for falsely detaining the student.[64] The court did not believe the police officers satisfied the test for probable cause, and school officials did not meet their lesser burden of demonstrating reasonable suspicion, particularly since they admitted to not following their established policy for disruptive behavior.[65]

Intentional Infliction of Mental or Emotional Distress

Intentional infliction of emotional distress is available to individuals who have suffered from severe mental anguish. In order to prevail on such a claim, the plaintiff must prove that the extreme and outrageous conduct occurred intentionally or recklessly and caused severe mental or emotional distress. Although this standard is a tough threshold to cross, a few plaintiffs have prevailed on a claim of intentional infliction of emotional distress.[66] In the case discussed at the end of the previous section, in addition to holding the school district liable for false imprisonment, the court also ruled in favor of the student for intentional infliction of mental and emotional distress.[67] Even though the student was already under doctor's care for emotional issues, the court agreed that his issues multiplied to include depression, distrust, food deprivation, lack of sleep or too much sleep, withdrawal, and a dislike of school. The court considered these behaviors to be a result of the outrageous treatment the student experienced when he was handcuffed and transported to the police station.[68]

In another case, a parent filed tort claims against the district for his mental and emotional anguish after school officials wrongfully released a student to an unauthorized person, resulting in the kidnapping of the student.[69] The school supposedly received a call indicating that the student would be picked up for a doctor's appointment, but the student's father was not contacted for permission. The person who came to the school was not an authorized contact for the student. The student was believed to have been kidnapped by his mother and taken to Mexico. The court dismissed the father's intentional infliction of emotional distress claim because he failed to establish that school officials were reckless at the time of the misconduct.

Claims for intentional infliction of mental or emotional distress are prevalent in the area of special education. Even though satisfying the requirements for a showing of such distress is not predicated on individual sensitivities, students with special needs have been the subject of the growing count of rulings in favor of students with injuries for mental or emotional distress. In one case, a special education teacher repeatedly engaged in physical, emotional, and verbal abuse of a mentally retarded and severely autistic student.[70] During one incident, the teacher jerked the student out of his desk, flipped him down on the desk, bent his arms behind him, and leaned down on the student as she pushed his head into the desk. On other occasions, the teacher would hit the student hard enough to leave fingerprints. The court reasoned that the evidence presented could satisfy the student's claim for intentional infliction of emotional distress, in addition to the criminal charges of which the teacher was found guilty.[71]

Defamation

Defamation is an injury to one's reputation. It involves the intentional or negligent unprivileged communication of a false statement by an individual to a third party. When considering whether defamation has occurred, courts consider whether the targeted person is a public or private individual.[72] While private individuals need to prove only that the statement was false, public individuals (i.e., public officials or public figures) must also demonstrate that the statement was made with malice or reckless disregard for the truth. Definitions of who constitutes a public official or public figure vary by state.[73] Written defamation is known as libel, while spoken defamation is known as slander.

In one case, a parent claimed that her son was defamed when school teachers engaged in conversations with students about her son being a computer hacker and also for comments made directly to her son.[74] The court denied the claim of defamation based on the fact that it could not be proven that the statements were made to third parties. In another case, a court determined that the professional recommendations included in a special education student's individualized education program (IEP) did not amount to defamation.[75] The statements were stated as opinions and not facts or false statements, as required for defamation. Therefore, the parents' dislike for the characterization of their son's special needs and the accompanying recommendations for his education did not constitute defamation.

Recommendations for Practice

1. Student handbooks should include all policies and expectations regarding appropriate behavior.
2. Rules and expectations of students should be reviewed with all students, staff, and parents.
3. School personnel must establish a school culture that does not trivialize bullying and harassment.
4. School personnel should routinely inspect facilities to reduce potential hazards, such as faulty equipment, dangerous surfaces, or protruding objects in and around the school building.
5. School personnel should be trained on the elements of negligence, along with various policies and procedures to ensure that students are adequately supervised.
6. If an item is in disrepair on the playground or in the school, appropriate school personnel should be notified immediately, and the problem should be rectified.
7. Parents should be informed of any major change in the school climate that is potentially hazardous. The school should discuss how it will remedy the problem.
8. When physical restraints are necessary, school authorities need to document the circumstances detailing why such actions were necessary.
9. School personnel should establish supervision responsibilities for events and extracurricular activities, including athletic events, and consider known or foreseeable dangers, such as physical altercations.
10. Prior to off-campus, school-sponsored trips, school personnel should be reminded of their duty of care and that permission slips do not negate negligent supervision.
11. Educators should receive professional development on their state-specific tort claims act and how it is applied to the school setting.

Endnotes

[1] MARTHA M. MCCARTHY, ET AL., PUBLIC SCHOOL LAW: TEACHERS' AND STUDENTS' RIGHTS 102 (7th ed. 2014).

[2] SUZANNE E. ECKES & JANET R. DECKER, TORT LAW AND PUBLIC SCHOOLS, in THE YEARBOOK OF EDUCATION LAW, 143-162 (Charles J. Russo ed., 2010).

[3] See e.g., Johnson v. Ken-Ton Union Free Sch. Dist. 850 N.Y.S.2d 813 (App. Div. 2008) (finding teacher had notice of a particular dangerous situation). See also, Shannea M. v. City of New York, 886 N.Y.S.2d 483 (App. Div. 2008) (finding teacher had no notice of a particular dangerous situation).

⁴ *See, e.g.,* Musachio v. Smithtown Cent. Sch. Dist., 892 N.Y.S.2d 123 (App. Div. 2009) (finding that school officials could not have anticipated the injury in this case because school officials had no knowledge of the puddle of water on the floor).

⁵ *See* CHARLES J. RUSSO, REUTTER'S, THE LAW OF PUBLIC EDUCATION (7th ed. 2009).

⁶ *See id.*

⁷ Hood v. Ouachita Parish Sch. Bd., 41 So. 3d 1253 (La. Ct. App. 2010).

⁸ David v. City of New York, 835 N.Y.S.2d 377 (N.Y. App. Div. 2007).

⁹ *See id.*

¹⁰ Garman v. E. Rochester Sch. Dist., 850 N.Y.S.2d 306 (N.Y. App. Div. 2007).

¹¹ *See id.*

¹² *See* RUSSO, *supra* note 5 at 414–15.

¹³ Nash v. Port Washington Union Free Sch. Dist., 922 N.Y.S.2d 408 (N.Y. App. Div. 2010).

¹⁴ Stirgus v. St. John the Baptist Parish Sch. Bd., 71 So. 3d 976 (La. App. 2011).

¹⁵ Robin C. Miller, Annotation, *Tort Liability of Public Schools and Institutions of Higher Learning for Injury to Student Walking To Or From School,* 72 A.L.R. 5th 469 (2004).

¹⁶ BL v. Caddo Parish Sch. Bd., 73 So. 3d 458 (La. App. 2011).

¹⁷ *Id.*

¹⁸ Davis v. Board of Educ. for Prince George's County, 112 A.3d 1034 (Md. App. 2015).

¹⁹ Berman v. Phila. Bd. of Educ., 456 A.2d 545 (Pa. 1983). *See also,* Clay City Consol. Sch. Corp. v. Timberman, 918 N.E.2d 292, 300 (Ind. 2009).

²⁰ A.C. v. Pomona Unified Sch. Dist., 2010 Cal. App. Unpub. LEXIS 3596 (Cal. Ct. App. 2010).

²¹ *See* Brammer v. Bossier Parish Sch. Bd., 183 So.3d 606 (La.App. 2015).

²² Walley v. Onondage Cent. Sch. Dist., 917 N.Y.S.2d 461 (N.Y. App. Div. 2011).

²³ *See id.*

²⁴ Glenn v. Grant Parish Sch. Bd., 49 So. 3d 1049 (La. Ct. App. 2010).

²⁵ *See id. See also,* Dixon v. William Floyd Union Free Sch. Dist., 25 N.Y.S.3d 363 (N.Y.App. Div. 2016) (school district established that it did not have actual or constructive knowledge of dangerous conduct).

²⁶ David G. Owen, *The Five Elements of Negligence,* 35 HOFSTRA. L. REV. 1680 (2007).

²⁷ *Id.* at 1681.

²⁸ *Id.* at 1682.

²⁹ Simonides v. Eastchester Union Free Sch. Dist., 31 N.Y.S.3d 210 (N.Y. App. Div. 2016).

³⁰ Santos v. City of New York, 30 N.Y.S.3d 258 (N.Y. App. Div. 2016).

³¹ Jorge C. v. City of New York, 8 N.Y.S.3d 307 (N.Y. App. Div. 2015).

³² *A.C.,* 2010 Cal. App. Unpub. LEXIS at 3596.

³³ *See id.*

³⁴ It should be noted that in addition to the defenses to negligence discussed below, the Paul D. Coverdell Teacher Protection Act of 2001 ("Coverdell Act") is a federal law that states that school officials are immune to lawsuits if a student is injured while an employee is attempting "to control, discipline, expel, or suspend a student or maintain order or control in the classroom or school." *See* 20 U.S.C. §§ 6731 – 6738, 2002.

³⁵ Suzanne Eckes, Janet Decker & Emily Richardson. *Trends in Court Opinions Involving Negligence in K-12 Schools: Considerations for Teachers and Administrators,* 275 EDUC. L. REP.505 (2012).

³⁶ Murray v. Chi. Youth Ctr., 864 N.E.2d 176 (Ill. 2007).

³⁷ *See id.*

³⁸ Lentz v. Morris, 372 S.E.2d 608 (Va. 1988).

³⁹ *See id.*

⁴⁰ Wencho v. Lakewood Sch. Dist., 895 N.E.2d 193 (Ohio Ct. App. 2008).

⁴¹ PAUL THURSTON & DONNA METZLER, STUDENT INJURY, in PRINCIPAL'S LEGAL HANDBOOK 213, 219 (William E. Camp et al. eds., 2000).

⁴² SUSAN D. LOONEY, EDUCATION AND THE LEGAL SYSTEM, in TORTS AND SCHOOL LIABILITY 23, 44 (2004).

⁴³ PROSSER AND KEATON, ON THE LAW OF TORTS 131 at 481 (W. Page Keeton ed. 5th ed. 1984).

[44] Hutchison v. Toews, 476 P.2d 811 (Or. Ct. App. 1970).

[45] *See id.*

[46] Funston v. Sch. Town of Munster, 849 N.E.2d 595 (Ind. 2006).

[47] LaPorte Cmty. Sch. Corp. v. Rosales, 936 N.E.2d 281 (Ind. Ct. App. 2010).

[48] *See* PROSSER & KEETON, *supra* note 44 at 481.

[49] Mayer v. Gulmi, 883 N.Y.S.2d 579 (N.Y. App. Div. 2009).

[50] Jurgensen v. Webster Cent. Sch. Dist., 5 N.Y.S.3d 663 (N.Y.App. Div. 2015)

[51] Woo v. United Nations Intern. Sch., 27 N.Y.S.3d 18 (N.Y.App. Div. 2016).

[52] Tinto v. Yonkers Bd. of Educ., 32 N.Y.S.3d 176 (N.Y.App. Div. 2016).

[53] Merino *ex rel.* Encarnacion v. Bd. of Educ. of the City of New York, 873 N.Y.S.2d 65 (App. Div. 2009).

[54] Jimenez v. Roseville City Sch. Dist., 202 Cal.Rptr.3d 536 (Cal.App, 2016).

[55] *See* Matthiesen, Wickert & Lehrer, *Contributory Negligence/Comparative Fault Laws in all 50 States,* Dec. 15, 2015, *available at* https://www.mwl-law.com/wp-content/uploads/2013/03/contributory-negligence-comparative-fault-laws-in-all-50-states.pdf.

[56] *Ex parte* Turner, 840 So. 2d 132 (Ala. 2002).

[57] *See id.*

[58] Hinson v. Holt, 776 So. 2d 804 (Ala. Civ. App. 1998).

[59] *See* MCCARTHY, *supra* note 1, at 489–90.

[60] Banks v. Fritsch, 39 S.W.3d 474 (Ky. Ct. App. 2001).

[61] *See id.*

[62] A.B. v. Adams-Arapahoe 28J Sch. Dist., 831 F.Supp.2d 1226 (D. Colo. 2011). *But see*, Schafer v. Hicksville Free Sch. Dist., 2011 U.S. Dist. LEXIS 35435 (E.D.N.Y. 2011) (denying school district's motion for summary judgment in a case involving a student with special needs who was confined to a time-out room).

[63] C.B. v. Sonora Sch. Dist. 2011 U.S. Dist. LEXIS 112902 (E.D. Cal. 2011).

[64] *See id.*

[65] *See id.*

[66] *See e.g.,* Nims v. Harrison, 768 So. 2d 1198 (Fla. Dist. Ct. App. 2000).

[67] *C.B.*, 2011 U.S. Dist. LEXIS at 112902.

[68] *See id.*

[69] Ramirez v. Escondido Unified Sch. Dist., 2016 U.S. App. LEXIS 6941 (9th Cir. 2016).

[70] M.S. v. Seminole County Sch. Bd., 636 F. Supp. 2d 1317 (M.D. Fla. 2009).

[71] *See id.*

[72] *See* MCCARTHY, *supra* note 1, at 492.

[73] *See id.*

[74] Harris v. Pontotoc County Sch. Dist., 635 F.3d 685 (5th Cir. 2011).

[75] Luo v. Baldwin Free Sch. Dist., 2011 U.S. Dist. LEXIS 26835 (E.D. N.Y. 2011), *aff'd* 2013 U.S. App. LEXIS 25487 (2d Cir. 2013).

Key Words

arrest

assault

assumption of risk

athletics

battery

breach of duty

bullying

"but-for" test

causation

cheerleader

comparative negligence

compensatory damages

contributory negligence

defamation

duty of care

emotional distress

extracurricular events

facilities

false imprisonment

field trip

foreseeable

harassment

immunity

intentional torts

physical restraints

police officer

proximate cause

reasonableness

sexual assault

special needs

student injury

supervision

tort liability

Section IV – Applying the Law to Practice

Sample Cases for Class Exercises

Mark A. Paige and Adam Ross Nelson

In the pages that follow, you will find cases that address various themes that are discussed in this book. The hypotheticals are based on actual cases and the citations are included. It is our recommendation that readers use the hypotheticals as a springboard for class exercises or professional development activities first, and then review the original cases to see how a court treated the facts.

This text provides an essential reference for many areas of law that may be implicated to the given hypotheticals. For example, in working with the *Small v. Springfield District* hypothetical, readers will likely make extensive reference to Bathon's chapter outlining collective bargaining, Mense and Lane's chapter on teacher dismissal, and others. Those working with *Lewiston v. Jamestown City School* will reference Rumel's chapter on anti-discrimination and anti-retaliation. If readers had yet to reference Alexander and Sughrue's chapter on sexual harassment, the *Simpson v. Unified Wiscesota District* hypothetical will provide that opportunity. The *Simpson* hypothetical also provides facts and circumstances that would call readers to reference Sharp and Oltman's chapter on academic freedom. The preceding list is not exhaustive; there may be additional legal issues that you find as you read the cases.

Specific Recommendations

• **Issue spot** – Spotting legal issues is an step toward using legal knowledge and skills as what this book's introduction described as a "lever of opportunity." The ability to spot legal issues (i.e., finding and articulating the relevance of a specific legal framework) is an important skill for all those within the range of this book's intended audience.

In the classroom, once readers or learners spot an issue or a potential issue, they can propose measures that would reduce risk and ensure appropriate outcomes. Likewise in practice, once educators learn to spot potential issues, those levers of opportunity will become more accessible.

When assigning students to spot an issue, provide a clear framework that calls for the identification of relevant statutes, cases, or regulations (relevant

193

law). After identifying the relevant law, engage students in the process of identifying facts that will be relevant in the subsequent legal analysis.

• **Writing activities** – These hypotheticals offer several writing activity starting points which could take several forms, including:

Write a memorandum assessing the case as an attorney. Both lawyers and nonlawyers alike are asked to draft written case assessments. Case assessments often identify relevant law, describe party strengths or weaknesses, identify what additional information may be needed before proceeding further, while also providing other case-specific analyses.

Write an advocacy piece. Lawyers, of course, are advocates. The hypotheticals provide an opportunity for students to advocate for a position. With this exercise, students can weave facts with law. Writing in favor of a position can be useful in preparing for hearings, trials, or policy debates. Writing for a position can also be useful in researching the opposition. Advanced students can be asked to establish or propose new legal theory.

Write as an opinion from the court (or decision maker). Students can take the position of a judge (or another decision maker) and issue a written opinion. For example, students or learners could imagine and write the decision that returned the teacher to work following the grievance of the district's nonrenewal in *Small v. Springfield District.*

Conducting or planning an internal investigation. Many organizations must investigate themselves from time-to-time. These hypotheticals also provide fictional settings in which students may plan and potentially role-play internal investigations. The hypothetical *Simpson v. Unified Wiscesota District* was, in part, written for the purpose of providing background for a mock investigation activity. Instructors might ask students to draft interview questions for potential witnesses. Consider asking students to conduct practice interviews using each other as witnesses. With its rich cast of characters, *Lewis v. Jamestown* provides extensive opportunities for planning or conducting mock investigative interviews.

Planning for meetings with staff and drafting memoranda to the file. As Frels, Horton, and McBride explain the importance of documentation in Chapter 8, these hypotheticals can provide context for asking students to plan mock meetings with staff and then drafting memoranda to the file following those meetings. The events and circumstances as outlined in *Williams v. Janesville High School* conclude at a spot which is ripe for the principal (or others) to conduct a meeting with Williams. At that meeting, school officials may wish to gather information about the incidents and/or express a clear set of expectations for Williams moving forward. Instructors could ask students or learners to plan, role-play, and then document that meeting.

Discussing or developing best practices, practicing assessment or audit. As an attorney, professor, or school administrator, assess how the school district treated a particular situation and ask the following question: What, if any, actions could the school district have taken to reduce the risk or even prevented the litigation that occurred? Another common audit scenario is to confirm that existing regulations comply with other superseding laws. Instructors could instruct students or learners to review the "Relevant Statutes in the State of 'Statesville'" from *Small v. Springfield District*, with the goal of checking conflicts of law. Where there may be conflicts with updated or revised federal statutes, students could propose revisions.

Compare and contrast. Retrieve the cases that form the basis for these hypotheticals. Students can compare treatment of the case with the court's treatment. Some questions to ask (among others) are: Did the court seem to adequately address all the issues? Did the court's result match the student or learner's result? What factual or legal differences could account for the different results? After reading the court's treatment, what other positions might be more compelling or persuasive?

Case 1
Applying Law to Practice: Employee Evaluation, Dismissal and Tenure
Williams v. Janesville School[1]

Teacher Gary Williams began working at Janesville High School in 2010, when the school committee hired him as a special education teacher. A few years later, he was assigned to teach social studies and history. Before the events leading to his dismissal, Williams already had established a disciplinary history at the school for using profanity in front of students and other teachers.[1] The school was also aware that Williams suffered from various mental health issues. During the 2014–2015 school year, he received an accommodation in his school schedule because of a diagnosis of attention deficit hyperactivity disorder. In 2015, Williams took a leave of absence to recover from depression, and, in early 2017, evidence was presented in connection with a profanity-related suspension that he suffered from anxiety.

Throughout his career, Williams had a stellar teaching record. Numerous students had attributed their success in college to Williams's innovative approach to education. Several attended Ivy League institutions, like Princeton and Harvard. Parents in the community frequently pressured administrators to have their students placed in his classes, because of this reputation.

Against this backdrop, the events leading up to Williams's dismissal are as follows. In May 2017, the school department of Janesville planned to hold

---

[1] The case is based on events from *School Comm. of Chicopee v. Chicopee Educ. Ass'n*, 80 Mass. App. Ct. 357 (2011).

an Armed Services Career Day on May 21, 2017, mandating attendance by all high school students and teachers. Fueled by his negative feelings about U.S. involvement in multiple wars and international armed conflicts, and based on his belief that the event would send an inappropriate message to young and impressionable students, Williams decided to organize a protest of it. To that end, he, his son, and some friends made protest signs and pamphlets to hand out during the event. When he arrived at school on May 21, however, Williams noticed that the school building had been vandalized with antiwar comments. Knowing he would be a suspect, Williams called off the protest and informed the school's principal, Roland R. Benedict, Jr., that he did not commit the vandalism, but that he knew who probably did. After his conversation with Benedict, Williams again changed his mind about the protest and, seeing that his students had already gone to the event, took his protest signs and protested from the event's perimeter. At some point thereafter, Benedict noticed the protest and told Williams to return to class. Williams did so, but shortly thereafter he suddenly felt anxious and went home sick.

That night, Williams called in sick for the following day. He also got in touch with his son's friend, Barry Scott, the person he believed had committed the vandalism. Williams convinced Scott to turn himself in, and, in a show of support, accompanied Scott to court the next day. While there, Williams continued his protest outside the courthouse and told a reporter that "a little defacement of a public building is a lot less than the crimes being committed at Janesville High School by trying to seduce these young children to join the military."

On May 23, Williams reported to school as usual. As the day progressed, however, he began to engage in odd behavior. While monitoring a test, he posted a sign stating: "Rogue Teacher Beware." Later, when he noticed that his classroom computer was missing, he wrote his department chairperson a note stating that he believed a crime had been committed, that the police should be notified, and that "I believe an incredible 'moral' crime is about to be [committed] by the administration of [Janesville High School]. (Know I forgive you and will pray for you all!)"

A short time later, during the school lunch break, Williams apparently felt compelled to continue the protest. Benedict later found him walking outside, barefoot, with his pant legs partially rolled up, wearing an olive green military coat and hat, bearing a protest sign, and beating a bongo drum. When Benedict informed Williams that it was time for him to return to teach his class, Williams insisted, "I'm not Gary Williams, I'm Sergeant Pepper." At that point, Benedict observed that Williams did, indeed, appear to be dressed as a member of Sergeant Pepper's Lonely Hearts Club Band, as portrayed on the Beatles' classic album cover. Despite several further warnings that his refusal would constitute insubordination and result in disciplinary action, Williams continued in what he described as his "guerilla theater" efforts and headed toward the center of Janesville. He was placed on administrative leave later the same day, and in June 2017, his employment was terminated for insubordinate conduct, improper use of a sick day, and his prior disciplinary record.

Following the May 23 incident, Williams sought professional help and was diagnosed with bipolar II disorder. His treating psychiatrist, Dr. Bennett Tish, reported to the school committee by letter, dated June 18, 2017, that prior to their initial June 5 appointment, Williams was "hypomanic." In deposition testimony, Dr. Tish further opined that antidepressant medication Williams had been taking for years to treat depression "was wrong and may have been responsible for ... Williams's behavior on May 22nd and May 23rd." Williams was prescribed mood-stabilizing medication to treat his disorder, and he has since reported feeling better than he has in years.

Applicable State Law in *Statesville*
Section 3-41

> A teacher with professional teacher status, pursuant to section forty-one, shall not be dismissed except for inefficiency, incompetency, incapacity, conduct unbecoming a teacher, insubordination or failure on the part of the teacher to satisfy teacher performance standards or other just cause.
>
> In determining whether the district has proven grounds for dismissal consistent with this section, the arbitrator shall consider the best interests of the pupils in the district and the need for elevation of performance standards.

Case 2
Applying the Law to Practice: Federal Anti-Discrimination Law
Lewis v. Jamestown City School District
(in the city of "New State" in the United States)[2]

Teacher Shirley Lewis (herein Plaintiff) is an African American female who is currently 69 years old. In 2003, Plaintiff was hired as a teacher's aide at the Jamestown City School District's Middle School (herein District or District's schools). Plaintiff testified that in 2009 or 2010, she obtained a New State State "Truant License," which is also referred to as a "School Attendance Teacher" License. Plaintiff does not possess other professional licenses or certifications.

During Plaintiff's tenure as a teacher's aide, David Johnstone ("Johnstone") served as the Principal of the Middle School. Johnstone was terminated on August 31, 2010. Plaintiff testified that Johnstone was terminated after a teacher and guidance counselor complained that he sexually harassed them.

---

[2] This case is based on *Jones-Khan v. Westbury Bd. of Educ.*, U.S. Dist. LEXIS 62897 (E.D.N.Y. April 25, 2017).

Plaintiff alleged that she believed Johnstone was innocent and supported him by requesting that teachers provide "character letters" to Johnstone's attorney.

Plaintiff testified that sometime after she received her Truant License, she spoke with the District's then-human resources manager about an available permanent substitute teacher position at the Middle School. Plaintiff was selected for the position by former Middle School Principal Dennis Hanson ("Hanson"). Plaintiff testified that she started as a permanent substitute in about 2010 or 2011.

In 2010, Plaintiff was formally evaluated by Hanson; Felicia Crossen ("Crossen"), who is African American and serves as Assistant Principal at the Middle School; and Cassandra Kimball. Crossen testified that they performed a formal performance evaluation to ensure that Plaintiff "understood that [administration] wanted her to work on certain things, specifically, her language use in the classroom with students."

In 2011, the District hired David Harrington ("Harrington"), a white male in his 40s, as the principal of the Middle School. Plaintiff alleged that Harrington made the working environment "uncomfortable" for faculty members who openly supported Johnstone, and Harrington made her "uncomfortable" by ignoring her in the hallways. Harrington testified that he was hired by the District after Johnstone's termination, he did not know why Johnstone was no longer employed by the District, and he was unaware that teachers prepared "character letters" for Johnstone. Crossen testified that she and Harrington did not discuss the circumstances surrounding Johnstone's termination.

In 2013, students complained to Harrington about Plaintiff and reported that Plaintiff "called them stupid and dumb and stated that Hispanic kids always give [her] trouble in the classroom." Plaintiff denied calling the students "stupid and dumb," but stated that she asked two Hispanic students "[w]hy don't you do like the other Hispanic kids and sit down and obey."[3] At Plaintiff's request, Harrington tasked then-Dean Kenya Rallis ("Rallis"), who is African American, with re-interviewing the students. Rallis confirmed that Plaintiff made inappropriate comments about Hispanic students. Harrington prepared a memorandum memorializing his meeting with Plaintiff and Rallis's findings; this memorandum states that Harrington advised Plaintiff that the District would likely pursue disciplinary action against her if her behavior recurred. Plaintiff testified that during this meeting, Harrington stated: "I dealt with your kind of people."

Eudes Rossman ("Rossman"), who Plaintiff alleges is Hispanic, was appointed Assistant Superintendent for Curriculum, Instruction, and Person-

---

[3]   At her deposition, Plaintiff testified as follows:

Then [Harrington] said to me the student said I said something about the Hispanic kids always give me trouble in the classroom. No. I said the Hispanic kids always give me trouble in the classroom. And I referred back to him, and I didn't say the Hispanic kids give me trouble. I said, I have all these Hispanic kids in the classroom, and you two students, kids, always give me problems. Why? I said, [w]hy don't you sit down like the other students? . . .I said, [w]hy don't you do like the other Hispanic kids and sit down and obey?

nel, in or about 2012. Previously, Rossman served as the District's Director of Second Language Acquisition and Adult Learning Center for ten years. Rossman was not the Assistant Superintendent when Plaintiff was hired as a permanent substitute teacher.

Rossman "routinely checks the certifications of District staff to ensure that the District is in compliance with state requirements." During an "audit[ ]" in March 2013, Rossman discovered that Plaintiff did not possess the appropriate certification for her position. Rossman scheduled a meeting with Plaintiff for March 8, 2013. Prior to the meeting, Rossman sent Plaintiff a letter in which he advised Plaintiff that she did not possess the appropriate certification, and he provided her with an opportunity to proffer "evidence of other teaching certification and or enrollment in an accredited graduate program, at the rate of not less than six semester hours per year."

During their meeting, Rossman showed Plaintiff the relevant New State regulations regarding the certification requirements for her position and told her that she was not qualified for her position. Plaintiff asked Rossman why this issue was not raised sooner, and Rossman told her that the District made an error. Rossman testified that he advised Plaintiff that she would be eligible for the permanent substitute position if she enrolled in an education program geared toward certification. Plaintiff was not enrolled in any classes at the time of her termination, and had not enrolled in classes since 2012.

Plaintiff advised Rossman that she had conflicts with Harrington. Rossman testified that he told Plaintiff that Harrington had nothing to do with her termination and indicated that Plaintiff could pursue the District's per diem substitute teacher list. Rossman testified that he did not provide Harrington with advance notice of Plaintiff's termination.

Rossman sent Plaintiff a letter confirming her termination, which included instructions regarding applying for the per diem substitute teacher list. Plaintiff refused to apply for the per diem list. Plaintiff testified that she tried to call into the per diem substitute list phone number but her assigned code number was not accepted. Plaintiff did not try do anything else to get on the per diem list after that attempt.

Presently, the District's Middle School employs two permanent substitute teachers: Marie Pignatelli, an African American who is 54 years old, and Joseph Cabale, who is Hispanic and 34 years old. At the time of her application, Ms. Pignatelli was certified to teach English to Speakers of Other Languages and French. At the time of his application, Mr. Cabale was certified to teach Students with Disabilities and Childhood Education.

Case 3
Applying the Law to Practice: Labor Relations
Small v. Springfield District (in the City of Statesville)[4]

Small was a music teacher in the Springfield middle and high schools for approximately ten years and a member of a bargaining unit represented by the union. The school district and the union were parties to a collective bargaining agreement (CBA), which contained a grievance procedure providing for, among other things, binding arbitration. Springfield is located in the city of Statesville.

Citing lack of student participation, the school district attempted to not renew Small's employment for the 2018-2019 school year. Small filed a grievance and was successful on the grounds that the school district had failed to provide timely notice of nonrenewal. He returned to work for the year of 2018-2019 as a music and band teacher. On March 26, 2019, the school district again notified Small that he was not being renewed due to declining enrollment for the next year, 2019-2020.

Prior to Small's nonrenewal, the school district had two music teachers: Small, who was in charge of the band program, and a second teacher who headed the choral program. This second teacher continues to be employed by the district. The history of the school's band program had been marked by steadily declining enrollment. In 2006, nearly seventy students participated in the band program. During the 2017-2018 school year, forty students participated. During the 2018-2019 school year, only twenty students participated in the band. Of these, five received credit, and fifteen participated on a "drop-in" basis, receiving no credit. Due to difficulties in rescheduling the band class after the petitioner's earlier nonrenewal was overturned, the union and the school district had agreed that the class would be held after the end of the normal school day. For the 2019-2020 school year, only fourteen students indicated interest in participating in band.

Prior to the start of the 2019-2020 school year, the school district eliminated the Springfield band program and entered into an agreement with Brattleboro High School, whereby interested Springfield students could receive credit for participation in Brattleboro's music offerings; these included band and choral programs, music theory electives, after-school jazz band and madrigal groups, and music festival ensembles. The school district had previously entered into a similar arrangement for students to take vocational training courses at Brattleboro because of declining participation at Springfield. In addition, Springfield students could participate in the Springfield community band program, though not for credit. The school district also offered online music classes through the Virtual High School program.

---

[4]   The case is based on *In re Kennedy,* 162 N.H. 109 (2011).

Relevant Statutes in the State of Statesville

Section 91-A: Definitions

I. "Board" means the public employee labor relations board created by
RSA 273-A:2.

II. "Board of the public employer" means the executive body of the public
employer, such as the city council, board of selectmen, the school board or
the county commissioners.
  (a) For purposes of this chapter:
    (1) The board of the public employer for executive branch state
        employees means the governor and council.
    (2) The board of the public employer for the judiciary means the
        chief justice of the supreme court with the advice and consent of
        the judicial branch administrative council appointed pursuant to
        supreme court rule 54.
  (b) In certain political subdivisions of the state the board of the public
      employer may also be the legislative body.

III. "Budget submission date" means the date by which, under law or
practice, the public employer's proposed budget is to be submitted to the
legislative or other similar body of the government, or to the city council
in the case of a city, for final action. In the case of a town, school district or
supervisory union it means February 1 of each year, except in the case of a
city school district or city school administrative unit which has a separate
budget submission date applied to it by the city.

IV. "Cost item" means any benefit acquired through collective bargaining
whose implementation requires an appropriation by the legislative body of
the public employer with which negotiations are being conducted.

V. "Grievance" means an alleged violation, misinterpretation or misappli-
cation with respect to one or more public employees, of any provision of an
agreement reached under this chapter.

VI. "Impasse" means the failure of the 2 parties, having exhausted all their
arguments, to achieve agreement in the course of good faith bargaining,
resulting in a deadlock in negotiations.

VII. "Legislative body" means that governmental body having the power
to appropriate public money. The legislative body of the state community
college system and university system shall be the board of trustees.

VIII. "Professional employee" means any employee engaged in work predominantly intellectual and varied in character, involving the consistent exercise of discretion and judgment, and requiring knowledge in a discipline customarily acquired in a formal program of advanced study.

IX. "Public employee" means any person employed by a public employer except:
   (a) Persons elected by popular vote;
   (b) Persons appointed to office by the chief executive or legislative body of the public employer;
   (c) Persons whose duties imply a confidential relationship to the public employer; or
   (d) Persons in a probationary or temporary status, or employed season ally, irregularly or on call. For the purposes of this chapter, how ever, no employee shall be determined to be in a probationary status who shall have been employed for more than 12 months or who has an individual contract with his employer, nor shall any employee be determined to be in a temporary status solely by reason of the source of funding of the position in which he is employed.

X. "Public employer" means the state and any political subdivision thereof, the judicial branch of the state, any quasi-public corporation, council, commission, agency or authority, the state community college system, and the state university system.

XI. "Terms and conditions of employment" means wages, hours and other conditions of employment other than managerial policy within the exclusive prerogative of the public employer, or confided exclusively to the public employer by statute or regulations adopted pursuant to statute. The phrase "managerial policy within the exclusive prerogative of the public employer" shall be construed to include but shall not be limited to the functions, programs and methods of the public employer, including the use of technology, the public employer's organizational structure, and the selection, direction and number of its personnel, so as to continue public control of governmental functions.

XII. [Repealed.]

Section 91-F: Unfair Labor Practices

I. It shall be a prohibited practice for any public employer:
   (a) To restrain, coerce or otherwise interfere with its employees in the exercise of the rights conferred by this chapter;
   (b) To dominate or to interfere in the formation or administration of any employee organization;

(c) To discriminate in the hiring or tenure, or the terms and conditions of employment of its employees for the purpose of encouraging or discouraging membership in any employee organization;

(d) To discharge or otherwise discriminate against any employee be cause he has filed a complaint, affidavit or petition, or given information or testimony under this chapter;

(e) To refuse to negotiate in good faith with the exclusive representative of a bargaining unit, including the failure to submit to the legislative body any cost item agreed upon in negotiations;

(f) To invoke a lockout or engage in impermissible subcontracting;

(g) To fail to comply with this chapter or any rule adopted under this chapter;

(h) To breach a collective bargaining agreement;

(i) To make any law or regulation, or to adopt any rule relative to the terms and conditions of employment that would invalidate any portion of an agreement entered into by the public employer making or adopting such law, regulation or rule.

II. It shall be a prohibited practice for the exclusive representative of any public employee:

(a) To restrain, coerce or otherwise interfere with public employees in the exercise of their rights under this chapter;

(b) To restrain, coerce or otherwise interfere with public employers in their selection of agents to represent them in collective bargaining negotiations or the settlement of grievances;

(c) To cause or attempt to cause a public employer to discriminate against an employee in violation of RSA 273-A:5, I(c), or to discriminate against any public employee whose membership in an employee organization has been denied or terminated for reasons other than failure to pay membership dues;

(d) To refuse to negotiate in good faith with the public employer;

(e) To engage in a strike or other form of job action;

(f) To breach a collective bargaining agreement.

(g) To fail to comply with this chapter or any rule adopted hereunder.

Case 4
Applying the Law to Practice: Investigating Alleged Discrimination
Simpson v. Unified Wiscesota District[5]

Unified Wiscesota District (Wiscesota) is a district located in a state subject to the 7th U.S. Circuit Court. The district maintains a small staff—

---

[5]   Based on *Simpson v. Beaver Dam Cmty. Hosps., Inc.*, 780 F.3d 784 (2015).

usually less than one full-time equivalent employee—whose responsibility it is to conduct internal complaints of discrimination. Simpson is a teacher who worked for Wiscesota and who has filed a complaint of discrimination with the district. Forrester has recently been hired by Wiscesota as an internal investigator with responsibilities for investigating complaints alleging discrimination in the district. Below is a summary of the complaint that had been drafted by Forrester's predecessor:

Background

This document provides an overview of information gathered regarding a pending complaint of discrimination from Ms. Simpson, who was formerly a teacher here at Wiscesota. She taught for one semester in our new program designed to provide specialized instruction for students interested in business and engineering at college. Simpson has complained that her department and her supervisor have discriminated against her on the basis of her gender. Simpson is female.

Summary of Information from *Simpson*

Ms. Simpson was recruited to Wiscesota's specialized business and engineering program. Simpson explained that her decision to take the position at Wiscesota was influenced by Wiscesota's deputy superintendent Kimberly Miller.

The offer of employment, which Simpson accepted, included a generous salary, a large budget for classroom equipment, support for professional development, plus standard health and other benefits. The offer also included promises of specialized instructional spaces and an office. However, support for professional development was contingent upon submission of a set of lesson plans specific to the new business and engineering curriculum.

Simpson began her position with Wiscesota and settled into her office during August (Simpson also explained that the office ended up being a cubicle shared with two other instructors). Simpson spoke with Superintendent Miller about the cubicle arrangement. Miller indicated that an adjustment might be possible, but that such a request would need to be requested through Joel Mason (chair of the business education department who oversaw the business and engineering program).

Simpson explains she was under the impression that she would be reimbursed for conference-related expenses. She understood that such expenses would be included in the offer's professional development provisions. Simpson reports that other instructors were attending conferences and that fellow instructors (all men in the business and engineering department) indicated they anticipated reimbursement as well. Her fellow instructors reportedly cautioned Simpson that, in their experience, getting timely reimbursement required persistence and an effort to "stick up for yourself." Simpson attended a conference in late September. At that conference, Simpson chaired a panel presentation consisting of self-identified LGBT men and women working in business and engineering. The title of the panel discussion was "Out For Business." In early October, Simpson visiting the district budget office to submit documentation for her conference-related expenses and to inquire about the process for obtaining reimbursement for the conference.

Simpson explains she expressed frustration when the budget staff explained they would be unable to provide reimbursement because Simpson had not followed proper procedures. Additionally, the budget staff explained, since Simpson had not yet submitted paperwork related to her licensing, the office would be further limited in their ability to provide reimbursement. Finally, the budget office reports that Mason would not sign off on the reimbursement. Mason's explanation, according to the budget office, was incomplete lesson plans. Simpson reports explaining that she believed everything was in order since she was already on payroll, teaching, and receiving other benefits. Simpson also indicates she thought it was unfair that other instructors (who are men) were receiving reimbursement, but that she was not.

By the middle of October, Mason contacted Simpson to explain that a final version of the new lesson plans would be due no later than November 1st. Simpson reports her lesson plans were nearly complete, but that she had one remaining instructional unit to finalize entitled "Women In Business & Engineering: Are the Mansplainers Ready?" As inspiration for her lesson plans, Simpson reports having relied on similar work conducted by her graduate school's faculty advisors.

Upon receipt of the lesson plans, Mason replied by email asking Simpson to explain how the unit regarding 'mansplaining' related to the study of business or the science of engineering. Simpson provided her response, which is as follows:

> Mr. Mason, thanks so much for the question about my lesson plans. Yes, I would consider lessons about prejudice and discrimination germane to the study of business and the science of engineering. My plans make extensive use of, and reference to scholarly (and trade) publication on the topic. I've identified a set of lesson plans that were recently implemented by other teachers in a district similar to ours. I'd be happy to get you a copy of those (actually, I'll make sure to drop it off at your classroom next time I'm by that way.) Sincerely, M.S.

Mason then thanked Simpson for the submission and explained he would provide comments soon. Finally, Mason asked Simpson if she had any thoughts or feedback about the first semester at Wiscesota. Simpson responded to Mason with information about the conference from September and her disappointment regarding the funding. Simpson also wrote about her disappointment regarding the cubicle assignments. Additionally, Simpson says she expressed frustration over the added stress of the lesson plans, which she believed none of her fellow instructors were required to complete. Following Simpson's response, Dr. Miller responded, thanking her for the comments and also indicating the importance of always putting best foot forward, striving to fit in, and being on her best behavior.

Just before Thanksgiving, due to an unexpected family illness, Simpson's principal left the district and Mason became the acting principal. On the day after Thanksgiving holiday, Simpson indicates that Mason invited Simpson to his classroom for a conversation. According to Simpson, Mason indicated that he had extensive comments for Simpson's lesson plans that included opinions that many of the topics were inappropriate for high school students. Mason told Simpson her plans too often deviated from the core topics. Simpson reported being upset that Mason specifically said he did not want Simpson discussing women's issues in business or engineering classes. Simpson says Mason thinks business and engineering are not fields in which to discuss women's issues. Simpson described how Mason explained that he was concerned there would be insufficient time for Simpson to revise and submit acceptable lesson plans. Mason also explained that the budget staff said there was a problem with Simpson's license. According to Simpson, Mason explained that Wiscesota had discussed her semester and that the sentiment was that she did not "fit in." Mason specifically explained that the new joint business and engineering program, and the field in general, was "a difficult club to join." Mason wanted to offer Simpson the opportunity leave Wiscesota at the end of the semester, because if Simpson did not finish the lesson plans and if her license did not clear up, Wiscesota would be forced to let her go. If this occurred, especially due to her licensing problems, it would be very difficult for Simpson to find a position in another district. Mason encouraged Simpson to seek opportunities that would be a "better fit" for her.

After that conversation, Simpson wrote to Mason:

> *To whom it may concern,*
>
> *I have decided to leave Wiscesota. At this time, it is my best interest to pursue other opportunities. I wish you well.*
>
> *Best Regards,*
>
> *Ms. Simpson*

By email, Mason responded:

> *Ms. Simpson,*
>
> *We accept your decision. We also wish you well in finding an opportunity that is a better fit for a teacher with your instructional and pedogogical interests .*
>
> *Best Regards,*
>
> *Mr. Mason*

Supplemental Information

Simpson also intimated that she consulted an attorney, who encouraged her to emphasize a series of comments that she asserts was discriminatory intent on the part of Mason, or others, in the district. Examples are that she did not "fit in," that the department and field were difficult "clubs," and also Mason's email, which used the phrase "better fit."

Another frequent refrain from Simpson is that she felt others perceived her as a bully. She complained that others (male instructors) in the district were praised and rewarded when they showed initiative, leadership, and an effort to advocate for themselves. However, when she did the same, she was told to "mind her own business" and got coached on "best behaviors." Simpson also indicated that she believes her academic freedom was violated because her range of instructional and pedagogical discretion had been infringed. She believes that disallowing, discouraging, and possibly suppressing her lesson plans was motivated by gender-based animus and bias.

Key Words Index

Section I – Introduction and the U.S. Legal System

appellate court
binding precedent
certiorari
circuit court of appeals
Civil Rights Act of 1964
common law
constitution
court of last resort
district court
Education for All Handicapped
  Children Act
Elementary and Secondary
  Education Act of 1965
en banc
enumerated powers
Every Student Succeeds Act (ESSA)

federal court system
implied powers
Individuals with Disabilities
  Education Act (IDEA)
judicial decision
legal citations
legal resources
No Child Left Behind Act (NCLB)
persuasive precedent
regulation
source of law
statute
supreme court
Tenth Amendment
trial court
U.S. Department of Education

Section II – Federal Law

academic freedom
censorship
communication
complaints
criticism
curricular choices
dismissal
disruptive to educational
  environment/process
expression
First Amendment
freedom of speech
gay
instructional materials/methods
insubordination
matters of public concern
MySpace
nonrenewal

obscene
official responsibilities
online
Pickering balancing test
political speech
private citizen
private versus public speech
protected conduct
protected speech
public employees
public schools
religious materials
retaliation
sexually explicit
social media
termination
vulgar

Section III – State and Local Laws

constitutional
adverse employment action
anecdotal records
arbitrary and capricious
collective bargaining
correctable
defamation claims
deficiencies
discrimination
documentation
due process
evaluation criteria
Every Student Succeeds Act (ESSA)
feedback
free speech
growth plan

hearing
insubordination
intentional misconduct
liberty interest
litigation
needs assessment
No Child Left Behind
nonrenewal
observation
performance criteria
policies
procedure
professional growth
property right
remediation
retaliation

adverse employment action
assessment document
close-out memorandum
conclusory statement
conference
contract status
directives
discipline
documentation system
e-mail communication
electronic personnel record
   system
evaluation
fair treatment
file memorandum/memorandum
   to the file

First Amendment
growth plan
hearing
memoranda
procedural due process
remediation
reprimand
social media
specific incident memorandum
summary memorandum
termination
third-party complaint
visitation memorandum
webpage
write-up

accountability
adequate yearly progress
arbitrary and capricious
breach of contract
certification
classroom observation
collective bargaining
discrimination
due process
educational requirements
Elementary and Secondary Education
  Act (ESEA)
employment contract
evaluation systems
Every Student Succeeds Act (ESSA)
good cause
hearing
immorality
incompetency
insubordination
liberty rights
No Child Left Behind Act (NCLB)

nonrenewal
nontenured
online communication
performance reviews
probation
professional development
professionalism
property rights
Race-to-the-Top
reduction-in-force (RIF)
remediation
resignation
sexual misconduct
social media
standardized tests
state control of education
student achievement test scores
suspension
tenure
termination
value-added

agency shop
arbitration
bargaining unit
charter schools
collective bargaining
discrimination
evaluations
fair-share
good faith bargaining
grievance
healthcare
mandatory representation
mandatory subject
mediation
National Labor Relations Act (NLRA)

Norris-LaGuardia Act
pensions
permissive subject
picketing
public employees
public union
reduction-in-force
right to work laws
strike
Taft-Hartley Act
teachers union
unfair labor practices
unionization
unlawful subject
Wagner Act

www.ingramcontent.com/pod-product-compliance
Lightning Source LLC
Chambersburg PA
CBHW060257220326
41598CB00027B/4145